Study Skills Connected

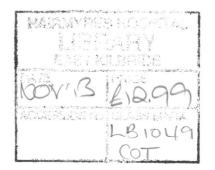

Palgrave Study Skills

Other titles in this series by Stella Cottrell

Critical Thinking Skills (2nd edn)
The Exam Skills Handbook (2d edn)
The Palgrave Student Planner
Skills for Success (2nd edn)
Study Skills Connected
The Study Skills Handbook (3rd edn)
Teaching Study Skills and Supporting Learning
You2Uni

Business Degree Success
Career Skills
Cite Them Right (8th edn)
Critical Thinking Skills (2nd edn)
e-Learning Skills (2nd edn)
The Exam Skills Handbook (2nd edn)
Great Ways to Learn Anatomy and Physiology
How to Begin Studying English Literature (3rd edn)
How to Manage Your Distance and Open Learning
    Course
How to Manage Your Postgraduate Course
How to Study Foreign Languages
How to Study Linguistics (2nd edn)
How to Use Your Reading in Your Essays
How to Write Better Essays (2nd edn)
How to Write Your Undergraduate Dissertation
Improve Your Grammar
Information Skills

The International Student Handbook
IT Skills for Successful Study
The Mature Student's Guide to Writing (3rd edn)
The Mature Student's Handbook
Practical Criticism
Presentation Skills for Students (2nd edn)
The Principles of Writing in Psychology
Professional writing (2nd edn)
Researching Online
Skills for Success (2nd edn)
The Student's Guide to Writing (3rd edn)
Study Skills for International Postgraduates
The Study Skills Handbook (3rd edn)
Study Skills for Speakers of English as a Second
    Language
Studying History (3rd edn)
Studying Law (3rd edn)
Studying Modern Drama (2nd edn)
Studying Psychology (2nd edn)
The Undergraduate Research Handbook
The Work-Based Learning Student Handbook
Work Placements – A Survival Guide for Students
Write it Right (2nd edn)
Writing for Engineers (3rd edn)
Writing for Law
Writing for Nursing and Midwifery Students
    (2nd edn)

Pocket Study Skills

14 Days to Exam Success
Blogs, Wikis, Podcasts and More
Brilliant Writing Tips for Students
Completing Your PhD
Doing Research
Getting Critical
Planning Your Essay
Planning Your PhD
Reading and Making Notes

Referencing and Understanding Plagiarism
Reflective Writing
Report Writing
Science Study Skills
Studying with Dyslexia
Success in Groupwork
Time Management
Writing for University

Palgrave Research Skills

Authoring a PhD
The Foundations of Research (2nd edn)
The Good Supervisor (2nd edn)
The Postgraduate Research Handbook (2nd edn)
Structuring Your Research Thesis

For a complete listing of all our titles in this area please visit www.palgrave.com/studyskills

Study Skills Connected

Using Technology to Support Your Studies

Stella Cottrell and Neil Morris

First published 2012 by
PALGRAVE MACMILLAN

Palgrave Macmillan in the UK is an imprint of Macmillan Publishers Limited, registered in England, company number 785998, of Houndmills, Basingstoke, Hampshire RG21 6XS.

Palgrave Macmillan in the US is a division of St Martin's Press LLC, 175 Fifth Avenue, New York, NY 10010.

Palgrave Macmillan is the global academic imprint of the above companies and has companies and representatives throughout the world.
Palgrave® and Macmillan® are registered trademarks in the United States, the United Kingdom, Europe and other countries.

ISBN: 978-1-137-01945-5

This book is printed on paper suitable for recycling and made from fully managed and sustained forest sources. Logging, pulping and manufacturing processes are expected to conform to the environmental regulations of the country of origin.

A catalogue record for this book is available from the British Library.
A catalog record for this book is available from the Library of Congress.

10 9 8 7 6 5 4 3 2 1
21 20 19 18 17 16 15 14 13 12

Printed in China

Contents

Acknowledgements   viii
Abbreviations   ix

Introduction   x
Who is the book for?   xi
What is this book about?   xii
Chapter outlines   xiii
The approach taken by the book   xiv
How to use the book   xv

1 Studying with new technologies   1
Introduction   1
Self-evaluation: identify your priorities   2
Using new technologies at college or uni   4
Being part of an online learning community   5
Basic netiquette   6
Netiquette: managing your tone   7
Netiquette in academic and work contexts   8
Self-evaluation: netiquette   9
Your netiquette and ground rules   10
Your online presence   11
Protect yourself and others   12
Taking care of your privacy and security   13
Respect for others' online material   15
Plagiarism and cheating   16
Using new technologies as a student   17
What equipment do I need?   19
Identifying resource requirements   20
Developing the right academic skills   21
Identifying your academic skills needs   22
Basic IT skills   23
Summary   24

2 Virtual learning environments   25
Introduction   25
What is a virtual learning environment (VLE)?   26
How are VLEs used to support learning?   27
Using the VLE: interaction and discussion   29
Using the VLE: resources and assessment   30
Using the VLE: collaboration and links   31
Using the VLE: course information and
    administration   32
Case study: a student's use of the VLE   33
Online assessment practice   34
Making effective use of online feedback   35
Using discussion boards for study   36
Using discussion boards for assignments   37
Case study: discussion board thread   38
Summary   40

**3 Managing online information
     for academic study**   41
Introduction   41
Self-evaluation: what would be useful to me?   42
Stages in managing information for study   43
Finding suitable material for your assignments   44
Locations for finding academic material online   45
Using the Internet for academic purposes   46
Narrowing or extending your online search   47
The impact of your search strategy   48
Developing your search strategy   49
Bibliographic databases   50
Digital repositories   51
Saving, retrieving, sharing and using
    information   52
Using Google tools for study   53
Online tools for study: group presentations   54
Online tools for study: written group report   55

Case study: conducting literature
  searches for projects 56
Evaluating material on YouTube for study 57
Using YouTube for study 58
Making YouTube videos for assignments 59
Summary 60

4 Podcasts **61**

Introduction 61
What are podcasts? 62
Finding and subscribing to podcasts 63
Evaluating quality for academic purposes 64
Selecting podcasts for academic use 65
Podcasts made specially for your course 66
Organisational skills for using podcasts 67
Making notes when using podcasts 68
Applying critical thinking to podcasts 69
Referencing podcasts in your work 70
Using podcasts for exam preparation and recall 71
How helpful are podcasts? 72
Good podcast design 73
Producing your own podcasts 74
Summary 76

5 Blogs **77**

Introduction 77
What is a blog? 78
What students say about blogs 79
Reasons for creating a blog 80
Creating a blog 82
Blog design: what works? 84
Good blog design 85
Writing blogs for an audience 86
Sharing and publicising your blog 87
Comments in blogs 88
Constructive commenting 89
Creating blogs for academic assignments 90
Using blogs for academic reflection 91
Blogs to support project development 92
Blogs to support professional development 93
Checklist: creating blogs for academic study 94
Case study: blog to support a student project 95
Case study: work placement blog 96
Using other people's blogs for academic study 97
Applying critical thinking to blogs 98
Thinking critically for academic blogs 99
Summary 100

6 Wikis **101**

Introduction 101
What is a wiki? 102
Wikipedia: the five principles or 'pillars' 103
Searching on Wikipedia 104
Understanding the Wikipedia layout 105
Finding good quality material on Wikipedia 106
Using Wikipedia as a source of information 107
The accuracy of Wikipedia for student work 108
Student assignment: edit a live wiki page 109
Editing the content of a live wiki page 110
How to edit a wiki page 111
Creating a wiki page or article 112
Collaborative writing assignments using wikis 113
Checklist for writing and editing wikis 117
How useful are wikis for students? 118
Student reflections on using wikis in their
  studies 119
Summary 120

7 Social media **121**

Introduction 121
Social networks and social networking sites 122
Features of key social networking sites 123
Understanding Facebook 124
Using Facebook to support academic study 125
Using Facebook for peer support 126
Making Facebook work for group projects 127
Facebook: wider considerations for study 128
Micro-blogging and Twitter 129
Getting started with Twitter 130
Using Twitter for academic purposes 131
Students' use of Twitter: Sarah 132
Students' use of Twitter: Imran 133
LinkedIn: build your professional community 134
LinkedIn: features of interest to students 135
LinkedIn: for entrepreneurial students 136
Case study: a student's use of social
  networking tools 137
Referencing social networking sites 138
Summary 140

**8 Classroom and
    communication technologies** **141**

Introduction 141
Exploring the terrain 142
Student voting handsets 143

Making use of voting handset opportunities 144
Lecture capture 145
Lecture capture: chat 146
Preparing to use collaborative learning tools 147
Using collaborative learning tools in class 148
Case study: collaborative tutorial 149
Video conferencing tools 150
Using video conferencing as a student 151
Case study: video conferencing for research project interviews 152
Case study: video conferencing for support on placement 153
Mobile devices 154
Mobile devices: tablets and e-readers 155
Using mobile devices for study 156
Apps to support your studies 157
Apps for study: Android and BlackBerry 158
Mobile devices in practical study settings 159
Summary 160

9 Drawing it together 161
Case study: combining the technologies (1) 162
Case study: combining the technologies (2) 163
Case study: combining the technologies (3) 164
Using technology to resolve study difficulties 165
Self-evaluation: how well do I use the technologies available to me? 166
Self-evaluation: achievements to date and future priorities 167
Technologies not covered in this book 171
Closing comments 172

Glossary 173
Useful resources 177
References and further reading 180
Feedback on activities 181
Index 183

A companion website is available at www.studyskillsconnected.com and provides:

- videos showing how to use technologies such as Google Scholar and social media for your studies
- interactive self-evaluations to help you identify how you could use technology more effectively for your academic work

Acknowledgements

We would like to give our thanks to those who have contributed to the development and production of this book. First of all, we would like to thank all of the staff and students we have interacted with over the years who have inspired the contents. We have received invaluable input from readers of the early manuscripts, for which we are extremely grateful. These have helped us to refine our thinking and shape the content of the book. Thanks are due to the 'extended team', the staff at Palgrave Macmillan: Suzannah Burywood, the commissioning editor, Caroline Richards (copy-editor), Mark Cooper (digital editor), Tina Graham (production controller); Jim Weaver (designer/ typesetter) and all the staff who work behind the scenes to support production, marketing and distribution.

The author and publishers wish to thank the following for permission to reproduce copyright material:

Dear Panda for the CourseNotes logo from www.coursenotesapp.com
Dropbox for logo from www.dropbox.com
Evernote Corp. for logo from www.evernote.com
Google Docs for logo from docs.google.com
Luminant Software Inc for the Audionote logo from Luminantsoftware.com
Mekentosj B.V for Papers logo from www.mekentosj.com
Mendeley Ltd for logo from www.mendeley.com
Omaxmedia for the MaxJournal logo from www.omaxmedia.com
Referey for logo from www.referey.web44.net
Spring2 Partners Inc. for the SPRINGPAD logo from www.springpadit.com
    SPRINGPAD is a registered trademark of Spring2 Partner, Inc. Used with permission.
Urmoblife for the Life Mate logo from Urmoblife.com
Vimukti Technologies Pvt Ltd for the StudentBuddy logo from www.vimukti.com

Every effort has been made to trace rights holders, but if any have been inadvertently overlooked the publishers would be pleased to make the necessary arrangements at the first opportunity.

Above all, we are indebted to our partners and families who provided support in a thousand ways over many months and without whom there would be no book.

Abbreviations

app	application
blog	web log
CV	curriculum vitae, the British term for résumé
FAQs	frequently asked questions
HEI	higher education institution
IT	information technology
LMS	learning management system
MCQ	multiple choice question
NQF	National Qualifications Framework
PC	personal computer
PDF	portable document format
PhD	Doctor of Philosophy; a postgraduate research-based qualification
PIN	personal identification number
pod	playable on demand
RSS	Really Simple Syndication
SMS	short message service
TED	technology, education and design
URL	uniform resource locator
VLE	virtual learning environment
VoIP	voice over Internet protocol

Introduction

Why use technologies for academic study?

Most of us are familiar in our everyday lives with a wide range of electronically based technologies – whether personal computers, tablet devices, mobile or cell phones, smartphones, MP3 and MP4 players, e-readers, the Internet and many more. They provide practical ways of bringing together different aspects of our lives, from finding out what we need to know, to organising and planning events and communicating with other people.

Such tools and resources are also used, increasingly, within higher education (HE), as an integral part of programme delivery. They may be used to supplement, enhance or replace class-based delivery. It is not unusual for students to be asked to make use of at least the Internet and certain educational technologies such as virtual learning environments (VLEs), and a range of others.

Many students enjoy, as part of their social life and general lifestyle, frequent use of mobile devices, apps, texting, instant messaging, blogs and social networking. However, relatively few have given much consideration to how they might harness those technologies that they like best, and are often expert at using, in order to enhance their studies.

This book aims to help students to make more effective use of technologies to improve their study. You might wish to use the book for one or more of the following reasons.

Reasons to use the book

- **To feel more confident** You are required to use some of these technologies and want to feel more knowledgeable about how to use them for academic study.
- **To make better use of opportunities** Your lecturers provide opportunities to use technologies or encourage their use, but you aren't sure how to get the most of what is available.
- **Curiosity** You want to understand the potential for using and combining technologies for supporting your studies.
- **Problem solving** You are experiencing gaps or difficulties with some aspect of your study – whether in communications, finding information, studying from a distance, feeling isolated or in other areas – and want to see if there are technologies that can help.
- **Making better use of your own technologies** You have a mobile device and want to get more out of this.
- **Enjoyment** You enjoy using the technologies in other contexts and want to use them more in your academic studies.

Be selective

It is unlikely that you want, or need, to use all of the technologies covered in the book. Select those that interest you and that are most relevant to studying on your programme.

Navigating the book

An outline of each chapter is provided below in order to help you to navigate your way around the book, finding what you need as and when you need it.

Who is the book for?

You can benefit from this book if you are:

- a student in higher education already; *or*
- about to take a programme at university or college and already feel familiar with some of the technologies; *or*
- taking work-based training at an equivalent level to university learning. Although the book is aimed primarily at students in higher education, you may find it helpful if you want or need to use technologies to undertake your training.

This book is for those who want to ...

(Tick ✓ those items that apply.)

... learn more effectively and be better students by harnessing the advantages offered by online resources, mobile devices and other technologies.

☐ That's me

... be able to study effectively when studying:
- online
- for distance learning
- on e-learning courses
- during independent study sessions.

☐ That's me

... draw on expertise they already have in using new technologies in work or social life, applying it effectively for academic purposes.

☐ That's me

... be able to respond effectively when asked by their lecturers or workplace trainers to use online learning as part of their programme of study.

☐ That's me

Assumed levels of expertise

This book isn't for absolute beginners in higher education or for those new to using technology. It assumes the following broad levels of expertise.

IT skills: It will help if you are already comfortable using some technology such as a personal computer, and know such things as how to word-process, print a document and use the Internet, at least for everyday or work-related purposes.

Academic skills: It will help if you already have a strong foundation in the study skills outlined in Chapter 1, pages 21–22.

Do students need such a book?

Although most students now use Internet-based resources and 'smart' technologies in everyday life, in practice many do not use these effectively, if at all, in their academic study.

Students are highly individual in:
- which technologies they use, and for which purposes;
- how much background knowledge they have;
- their comfort levels in applying these flexibly for diverse purposes;
- their awareness and expertise in using these for academic study.

Many students use technologies in their personal life without having thought about their potential from an academic perspective. This book opens up the potential of harnessing tools that you might already enjoy, as well as new ones, to support and enhance your study.

What is this book about?

The purpose of this book

This book is designed to assist you to:

- **enjoy study more, through using new technologies** that can make this more interesting, effective and practical;
- **know how to apply new technologies for academic study,** adapting your everyday use to suit the academic context;
- **develop good study skills, habits and time management** when using new technologies as part of your study and for academic assignments;
- **make sense of the demands made of you as a student** if lecturers require you to use new technologies as part of your study;
- **feel confident** in using the technologies for study and in working online;
- **develop critical and reflective perspectives** when using technology for academic purposes, as appropriate for higher-level study;
- **gain better marks in student assignments** that require the use of new technologies.

My own purpose in using this book?

Below is a list of ways this book can help you. To focus your use of the book, identify those purposes that you feel are relevant to you.

I want to:

- [ ] become familiar with ways technology is used to support and enhance learning within higher education;
- [ ] manage effectively the time I spend in independent study, especially when using electronic resources;
- [ ] apply technologies to study in order to make it more enjoyable, useful or effective;
- [ ] apply academic conventions appropriately when using different kinds of technology;
- [ ] consider ways that technologies I might use in other contexts, such as for social networking, can be used to enhance my study;
- [ ] do better in assignments that require, or would benefit from, the use of new technologies;
- [ ] consider my 'audience' from an academic viewpoint when using new technologies.

Where first?

This book is intended for use in different ways by different audiences.

To help you decide where to start first, use one or more of the following approaches:

- Use the 'Priorities' resource on pp. 2–3 to identify where you want to start.
- Read the chapter outlines below and decide from there.
- Consider the three approaches charted on p. xv, 'How to use the book'. Choose the approach that best suits you.

Chapter outlines

Studying with new technologies

Chapter 1 offers a general background for using new technologies within academic study so that you can feel more confident of the culture, responsibilities and safeguards associated with working online and as part of an academic community. It includes a self-evaluation tool to help you to identify your own priorities and navigate the rest of the book.

Virtual learning environments

Chapter 2 introduces virtual learning environments (VLE), also known as learning management systems (LMS). The chapter looks at some of the diverse ways that VLEs are used to provide learning resources, enable student discussion and collaboration, and support assessment and feedback.

Managing online information

Chapter 3 provides a grounding in searching for, identifying and storing good quality sources of information for academic assignments. It provides details of resources available to assist you in using automated searches, finding information when you need it, sharing information with other students and producing references for your assignments.

Podcasts

Chapter 4 introduces study skills and approaches that can help to you to use podcasts as a student. It also looks at how you can create and use your own podcasts to assist revision, memory, and other aspects of your study.

Blogs

Chapter 5 provides guidance on how to create, design and publicise your own blog. It looks at methods you could use to attract a readership for your blog to develop its profile. In particular, it offers guidance on applying study skills when using blogs for academic study. It also addresses issues such as blog 'netiquette', privacy, confidentiality and constructive commenting.

Wikis

The use of wikis, especially Wikipedia, tends to receive a mixed response in higher education. Chapter 6 looks at when and how it is appropriate to use wikis as a source of information for academic study, and when not. It looks at the study skills involved in writing wiki pages as part of an academic assignment.

Social media

Chapter 7 looks at ways that you can harness the use of your social networking tools to enhance your learning as well as student life. It covers such themes as building networks as part of a learning community, and the study skills involved when using social media for academic work. It identifies ways that you could combine multiple networking tools to support your study and professional development.

Classroom and communication technologies

Chapter 8 identifies some of the technologies used for class-based and distance learning, from voting handsets and lecture capture with chat through to video conferencing and collaborative working with other students. It provides examples of ways you can take part in class in more interactive and dynamic ways, use communication tools for group work or in student projects, and mobile devices and apps to access and coordinate your use of technologies.

The closing section of the book offers some examples of how students draw on and combine the technologies in individual ways. These illustrate how the diverse technologies can be integrated into your day-to-day life as a student.

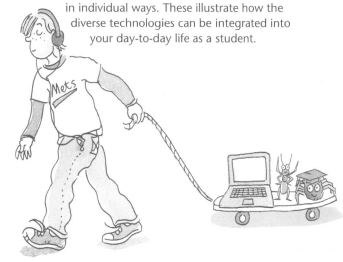

The approach taken by the book

Academic focus

The academic world has its own conventions. The ways that new technologies are used in everyday life, such as for social networking with friends or telling someone about an interesting website, are not always appropriate within an academic context. This book aims to help students make use of new technologies to enhance their studies whilst also meeting academic requirements.

Study skills

Although this book can be used as a stand-alone text, it assumes a certain level of familiarity with the academic skills, strategies and thinking appropriate to a higher level of study. Chapter 1 looks briefly at the kinds of study skills that you would need in order to be an effective student in general. A more in-depth and rounded understanding of the academic skills needed in higher education would be provided by a specialist study skills text. For this, the reader is referred to:

Cottrell, S. (2008) *The Study Skills Handbook* 3rd edn.
Cottrell, S. (2012) *The Exams Skills Handbook*, 2nd edn.
North American readers should look out for:
Cottrell, S. (2012) *The Study Skills Handbook*, 1st US edn.

This book looks at those study skills and strategies that are relevant to working with the specific technologies covered. It addresses such aspects as time management, critical thinking and collaborating with other students within the context of working with those technologies.

Practical

The book supports you in making practical use of new technologies. You are encouraged to create your own resources to support your studies and, where appropriate, guidance is given on how to do so.

Interactive

Academic study can sometimes draw us into passive ways of taking in information. The most effective learning takes place when we are using our minds actively, followed by a period of relaxation or sleep. Activities of different kinds are used throughout the book to help you to:

- focus your thinking;
- define your viewpoints and choices;
- re-energise;
- evaluate closely how the material applies to you.

🗨 Reflection

This icon is used to indicate a pause for reflection.

Reflective activity is used increasingly within higher education and the workplace. Where relevant to the section, a short reflective activity is provided. This is to help you think through such things as how you would adapt the content of the section to suit your own study preferences, lifestyle or assignment.

Computer literacy and technical skills

A certain level of computer literacy is generally a prerequisite for higher-level study. You can expect, as a general minimum, that you would:

- enrol, register and choose study options online;
- communicate with lecturers, other students and institutional administrators through email and texts;
- produce and submit written work electronically;
- access some learning resources online.

This book is not intended to cover, step by step, the technicalities of using equipment and software. For those, you would need to take a basic IT course or use manuals or online help for the relevant software.

Technical information on the technologies covered by the book

Technical information is provided only where this has been found to be essential to helping students make use of the technologies. Normally, the relevant step-by-step technical advice for using the technologies is provided online and updated on a frequent basis.

How to use the book

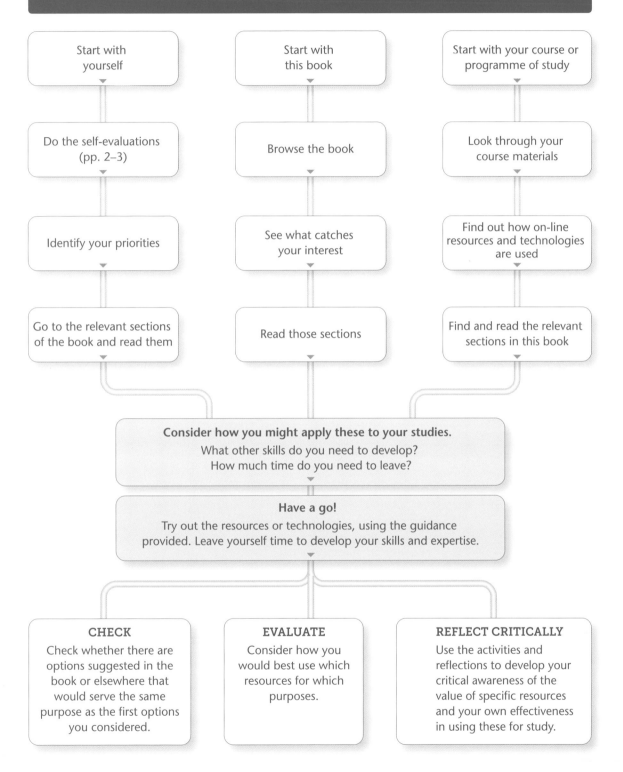

Start with yourself
↓
Do the self-evaluations (pp. 2–3)
↓
Identify your priorities
↓
Go to the relevant sections of the book and read them
↓

Start with this book
↓
Browse the book
↓
See what catches your interest
↓
Read those sections
↓

Start with your course or programme of study
↓
Look through your course materials
↓
Find out how on-line resources and technologies are used
↓
Find and read the relevant sections in this book
↓

Consider how you might apply these to your studies.
What other skills do you need to develop?
How much time do you need to leave?
↓

Have a go!
Try out the resources or technologies, using the guidance provided. Leave yourself time to develop your skills and expertise.
↓

CHECK
Check whether there are options suggested in the book or elsewhere that would serve the same purpose as the first options you considered.

EVALUATE
Consider how you would best use which resources for which purposes.

REFLECT CRITICALLY
Use the activities and reflections to develop your critical awareness of the value of specific resources and your own effectiveness in using these for study.

Chapter 1

Studying with new technologies

Learning outcomes

This chapter provides you with opportunities to:

- identify your priorities for using new technologies for study;
- understand how new technologies are used to enhance learning in higher education;
- familiarise yourself with the culture and netiquette of the online learning environment;
- consider your online presence as part of an academic community;
- consider issues of privacy and security when using new technologies for study;
- identify the technical resources you will need for making use of new technologies as a student;
- consider broader skill sets that you will need as a student.

Introduction

If you are already familiar with using new technologies in everyday life, then you should be able to browse quickly through this chapter. If so:

- Identify your priorities (pp. 2–3).
- Start to take note of the ways that the use of these technologies is different within an academic context.
- Consider your online presence as a student, as well as your responsibilities (pp. 6–16).
- Move on to the chapters that interest you the most.

If you are new to some or all of the technologies covered by the book and to communicating online, then this chapter is designed to help you to:

- make more sense of the culture and language of the online environment;
- become part of the online learning community;
- identify a starting point for using these technologies to enhance your study.

Self-evaluation: identify your priorities

Column A   ✓ Tick/check if the statement is generally true of you.
Column B   Rate on a score of 6–10 the importance of the e-study skill (6 = unimportant; 10 = essential).
Column C   Rate on a score of 1–5 how good you are at this now (0 = very weak; 5 = excellent).
Column D   Subtract score C from B (B – C). Items with the highest scores in D are likely to be priorities.

e-Study skills statement	A True? (✓)	B Importance scale 6–10	C Ability scale 1–5	D Priority (B–C)	E See page(s)
1 I have a **general understanding** of how I can use technologies to enhance my academic study					4
2 I am confident about studying as part of an **online community**					5
3 I have a good grasp of the **language and culture (netiquette)** of online communication					6–10; 173
4 I am clear about the **equipment** that I will need in order to use these technologies for study					19
5 I am aware of the key **security and privacy** issues when working and communicating online					11–13
6 I am aware of the broader **range of study skills** I will need for successful academic study					21–2
7 I am aware of the basic **level of technical skill** that I need in order to gain from this book					23
8 I understand how **virtual learning environments** (VLE) or learning management systems (LMS) are used in higher education					26–7
9 I am confident that I make the most **effective use of our VLE/LMS** (if provided)					29–33
10 I am confident about **writing good threads for discussion boards** for collaborative study					36–7
11 I can **find and recognise good quality material** on the Internet for **academic** assignments					Chs 3 and 6
12 I know how to receive **automated searches** of Internet material relevant to my programme					52
13 I know how to use **bookmarks** to store material for my academic assignments					52
14 I know how to use **reference management tools** to help write references for assignments					52

  Study Skills Connected

e-Study skills statement	A True? (✓)	B Importance scale 6–10	C Ability scale 1–5	D Priority (B–C)	E See page(s)
15 I **use podcasts** effectively to support my study					Ch. 4
16 I can **create my own podcasts** to support the various requirements of my programme effectively					73–5
17 I know how to **use my own podcasts** effectively to support studying for exams					71
18 I know how to **use other people's blogs** effectively in an academic context					97–9
19 I know how to **use a blog of my own** effectively to enhance different aspects of my study					80–7; 90–6
20 I know how to make **constructive comments** on other people's blogs					88–9
21 I am confident about using **existing wikis** to enhance my studies					Ch. 6
22 I understand how to set up and **contribute to wikis** as part of my academic study					109–17
23 I am clear **when to use, and not to use, wikis** as a source of information for academic work.					106–8
24 I know how to **reference** within my academic work materials accessed via new technologies					16; 70; 138–9
25 I am aware of how I could use **social media** to support my academic study					Ch. 7
26 I am confident that I would know how to make good use of **voting handsets** opportunities					143–4
27 I know what is meant by **lecture capture**					149
28 I am aware of ways that I could use **video conferencing** to support my study					150–3
29 I am aware of the range of ways that a **smartphone** could be used to support my study					156
30 I am aware of the range of ways that a **mobile device** could be used to support my study					154–5; 159
31 I am aware of **apps** that can support my study					157–8
32 I am aware of how I can **combine** technologies to support and enhance my academic studies					161–5

Using new technologies at college or uni

Your use of new technologies in support of your academic work will be a combination of the opportunities you create for yourself, depending on how useful you find such technologies, and what you must use in order to participate as required. The following examples give you a flavour of some potential uses, most of which are covered in more depth within this book.

Your choice

You can choose for yourself to use technologies you enjoy using in order to enhance your study. For example:

- downloaded podcasts as a reminder of lectures;
- your own podcasts, made to help preparing for tests;
- your blogs to support fieldwork;
- social networking to help a student team project.

Assessment

As part of a graded assignment, you may be asked to:

- write an online reflective blog to draw together what you have learnt;
- undertake computer-assessed assignments;
- make a podcast for a particular audience as part of a project.

In the classroom

Lecturers vary in how much they use new technologies within class. Your lecturers might:

- put time aside for you to create wikis on a topic being investigated in class;
- use specialist technologies they are using in their research;
- use voting technologies to show class opinions on an issue being discussed.

YOUR VOTING RESPONSES
75% understand bile
10% need to revise
6% have realised they
are in the wrong lecture hall

Guided independent study

Lecturers may use a virtual learning environment or learning management system to provide a range of resources and learning activities:

- back-up notes for lectures and other taught sessions;
- annotated reading lists or syllabi;

- self-assessment materials for you to test your own understanding;
- interactive materials that you complete online;
- structured support for constructing a student wiki.

As support for learning

Teaching staff may provide additional support via new technologies. For example:

- VLE/LMS materials that explain difficult concepts in more detail than is possible in class;
- podcast summaries to reinforce points made in the lecture;
- messaging to link in with students on placement;
- tweets to reinforce a learning point.

@Tutor 761
See VLE for:
Bile - all you
ever need to
know.

Being part of an online learning community

Online learning communities

You can use social media and a range of online tools in order to make connections with:

- students on your course;
- students whose subjects can inform your understanding of your subject;
- students studying the same subject in other universities and colleges;
- study support groups;
- academic staff teaching your course;
- academic staff worldwide if they choose to use these technologies to communicate their ideas and research;
- those working in your professional area interested in, or contributing to, developments in the theory and knowledge base of your subject.

Your role within the learning community

1 **Enjoy the benefits** of sharing your own and others' knowledge and experiences.
2 **Be an active contributor**: contribute material, links and comments.
3 **Respect others** within that community, abiding by ground rules and using good 'netiquette'.
4 **Act responsibly,** taking care of yourself and others (see pp. 12–13).

Building a social community as a student

As students' social and educational lives are closely interconnected, using tools such as blogs, Facebook® or Twitter® to build a social community can also benefit your learning community. These can help you to:

- make more friends on your course or programme, giving you access to a wider community of students to draw upon for support and to discuss areas of interest to your study;
- find clubs or societies at your college or university and receive their updates. This can help you to feel part of campus life, make connections, and open up opportunities that enhance your studies.

Build a larger community

You build your online community through being an active contributor.

- **Select tools that interest you:** you are then more likely to maintain your use.
- **Use these on a frequent basis:** this helps to develop a set of followers.
- **Contribute** opinions, ideas, information, proposed solutions and your own experiences, so that others feel it worthwhile to check in and engage.
- **Engage in dialogue.** When you post comments and responses on relevant blogs, discussion boards and other sites, this indicates your interest in others, who are then more likely to respond to you.
- **Connect to others.** If you follow groups or organisations on tools such as Twitter, look at their followers, and follow them too. Some automatically follow anyone who follows them, building up larger circles of connections (but some discrimination is called for otherwise you may end up following spammers).

Culture, language and 'netiquette'

The online community is dynamic and so the terminology, jargon and customary ways of behaving undergo constant changes.

- To understand the terminology, see the glossary provided on p. 173.
- The informal, widely accepted code of working and communicating online are referred to as 'netiquette': see pp. 6–9.

Basic netiquette

What is 'netiquette'?

Communicating online has its own conventions and culture, known as 'netiquette' (literally, 'Internet etiquette'). You may be familiar with this already. Much will also apply to academic contexts but some will be different.

As in everyday life, be aware that real people receive your communications and are affected by what you say and do.

- *Be sensitive to your audience and the context.*
- *Adapt your style, content and presentation accordingly.*

Common courtesies online

- Offer friendly opening greetings or welcome, appropriate to the context and recipient.
- Introduce yourself to new recipients.
- Sign off at the end of communications.
- Be polite as in everyday life, using please, thank you, sorry, etc. as appropriate.
- Avoid wasting recipients' time: keep messages brief and clear. Get to the point quickly.
- Don't forward emails or other communications to others without their author's agreement.

Show appreciation

- Say thank you when you have enjoyed or been grateful for a post or comment.
- Make a simple brief comment to indicate that you have read a post.

Good point! Thanks!
Nice one. I agree.
I'm glad I'm not the only one!

Check the message

It is easy to send quick responses without having fully understood someone's message. Re-read posts or comments carefully; you might have misinterpreted them, especially if they:

- seem too good to be true;
- appear unexpectedly rude;
- make you want to send angry responses;
- might have misspelt or omitted a word.

You have won a car! Send £100 to claim your gift.

Behaviours to avoid and discourage

- **Rudeness:** Avoid being rude just because you can't see the reaction: send only what you would say in person.
- **Trolling:** Trolls set out to cause nuisance and annoyance, such as disrupting discussion threads.
- **Inappropriate flaming:** Flames express opinions with strong emotion. Avoid using them simply to be provocative, or in ways that cause offence or spoil the atmosphere of an on-site group.

Netiquette: managing your tone

Read for tone

In face-to-face communications, you can use facial expression and gestures to help convey your message. If your phrasing is confusing or inexact, your body language and tone of voice may fill in the gaps, helping your audience to interpret what you really mean.

Unless you are using a webcam when communicating with lecturers and students, you won't be able to rely on facial expressions, body language and tone of voice. You are more reliant on your phrasing and presentation to convey your tone and the nuances of your message.

Do

- Read everything before you send it, checking whether the recipient could interpret your words in ways you hadn't intended.
- Be wary of using irony, sarcasm, humour, innuendo or mock insults unless you know the recipient will find these acceptable – these are unlikely to be appropriate for most academic communication.
- Be aware that the use of capital letters is viewed as shouting or aggression online.

Consider the difference in impact of the use of capitals below.

Lurk a little

Before launching into a discussion group or chat room online, lurk for while to gain a feel of the site, the content covered and the tone and style used. This will help you to communicate in line with the culture of that site.

> ### 💬 Reflection: Tone of communications
>
> In general, what is the main tone of your formal communications (Polite? Chirpy? Cheeky? Friendly? Over-friendly? Complaining? Professional?)
>
> Do you read your emails, messages and other e-communications carefully enough to check for tone, adapting this according to your audience?

Managing emotional content

Messages can come across more strongly than intended when written down and especially if written in brief messages typical of electronic media.

Do

- **Provide explanatory context**
  Provide a brief background and context in order to help recipients interpret your messages in the way you intend.
- **Check for alternative readings**
  Re-read your emails or postings before sending them; check whether the recipient might gain a different impression than you intended. Would the message read differently if read with stress on particular words or with a different intonation?
- **Pause for sensitive communications**
  If you have difficult messages to convey, or are angry or depressed when writing, leave messages for at least an hour without sending. Read these when you feel calmer or in a more positive state of mind, so that you are in a better place to decide whether you should amend the communication before sending.

Netiquette in academic and work contexts

Reasonable expectations

- Be realistic in how often, and how quickly, you expect others to respond to you.
- Don't expect lecturers or other students to respond to you on a daily basis.
- Don't keep sending repeat emails, messages or tweets simply to get a response. Look for other means of gaining the answers you need.
- Don't waste other students' time by copying them in unnecessarily or sending endless trivia.
- Assume that those outside of your circle of family and friends will take much longer to get back to you – and may not do so at all.

First impressions

Much online communication is rough and ready. There is a widespread belief that conventions such as spelling, grammar, punctuation and general care about the technicalities of writing don't matter in emails and online. That is generally the case for friends and family and on many websites or networks.

However, there are situations where good presentation does count. Be aware that your emails and other messages may be used by employers, lecturers and others to make judgements about your personality and the levels of care, commitment, respect and attention you would bring to a job or research project. As in everyday life, aim to make a good first impression.

Avoid

- Don't send rushed, garbled messages.
- Don't send messages with typos and omitted words, that don't make sense.
- Don't use emoticons in academic work and other, more formal, e-messages.

Do

- Use the resources available to help other students. Share ideas and helpful links.
- Ask questions that stimulate genuine intellectual curiosity.
- Proofread for clarity of meaning.
- Read your message through the eyes of the eventual recipients.
- Use a different approach to emails and other communications for work, academic staff and administrative staff than you would for friends and family.
- Write in a friendly, polite but semi-formal style to those in positions of authority and people you do not know.
- Assume that anyone you contact about a job or work experience will be looking at how you present yourself in all of your communications, including your use of grammar, punctuation and tone.

Reflection: Creating impressions

Read through a sample of the messages you sent over the last few weeks to different people.

- How well did you proofread these?
- What impression of you do these messages convey?
- Have could you adapt your communication for people other than friends and family?

Self-evaluation: netiquette

Rate yourself on the following 20 netiquette items, using a scale where 5 represents always using good netiquette for that item and 0 is never doing so. Circle the score that best applies to you.

Netiquette item	Personal rating ☺ ☹					
1 I take care to remember the feelings of the recipients of my online communications	5	4	3	2	1	0
2 I take care of the feelings of others potentially affected by what I write or do online	5	4	3	2	1	0
3 I re-read my messages before sending them, to check that they convey the right message and tone	5	4	3	2	1	0
4 I checked to see whether my college or uni provides its own guidelines for online communication – and adhere to these, if so	5	4	3	2	1	0
5 I adapt the content and tone of my communications to suit different kinds of recipients	5	4	3	2	1	0
6 I am always polite in my online communications, even when I don't like or approve of the other people involved	5	4	3	2	1	0
7 I take care what I send over the Internet so that nothing I say or do could come back to haunt me in future years	5	4	3	2	1	0
8 I avoid trolling	5	4	3	2	1	0
9 I avoid sending flames that might upset or unnecessarily provoke other people	5	4	3	2	1	0
10 I am realistic in my expectations when I ask for information or responses	5	4	3	2	1	0
11 I use the subject line in communications to make it clear to recipients what they are about to open and whether it is urgent or not	5	4	3	2	1	0
12 I say 'thank you' when people take the trouble to send me information, links or support	5	4	3	2	1	0
13 I post helpful comments where appropriate	5	4	3	2	1	0
14 I avoid dominating discussions and message boards with my own issues and points of view	5	4	3	2	1	0
15 I take care not to waste other people's time by sending them unnecessary messages and trivia	5	4	3	2	1	0
16 I check that my emails and posts are reasonably easy to read, adding in words that I may have omitted and correcting punctuation	5	4	3	2	1	0
17 I ask for permission before forwarding communications sent to me by others	5	4	3	2	1	0
18 I respect other people's privacy, taking care not to copy their private information or photographs to others	5	4	3	2	1	0
19 I take care not to jeopardise other people's security through careless use of information online	5	4	3	2	1	0
20 I respect copyright and avoid piracy, paying for legal downloads as required	5	4	3	2	1	0

Your netiquette and ground rules

Self-evaluation: interpreting your score (see p. 9)

Find your percentage score

Add all your scores to find your total. As this is a score out of 100, this is your percentage score.

Interpret your score

Over 80%

If you rated yourself at over 80%, and assuming your judgement is accurate, then you have very good netiquette and people are more likely to want to communicate with you online. Note the pattern of your weaker scores and identify what you could do to improve on these.

Under 40%

If you scored below 40%, it is quite likely that:

- you may be causing offence to others;
- and/or creating unnecessary stress for yourself and those with whom you are communicating;
- and/or you run the risk of other people not wanting to communicate with you or not giving you what you need;
- and/or you run the risk of being barred from chat rooms or other sites.

If you generally consider yourself to have good online communication skills, this is a score to be concerned about. You would be well advised to reflect on your low scores and devise a quick action plan for improvement.

Between 40% and 80%

The closer you are to 80%, the better your netiquette and the more likely you are to receive good communications from others. The closer you are to 40%, the more you need to take care of how you are communicating online. Note the pattern of your weaker scores and identify what you could do to improve on these.

Top priorities for improving netiquette

Identify your lowest scores. Select three items for immediate improvement.

Priorities for improving my netiquette	
1	
2	
3	

Set your own ground rules

As a student, you will be involved in activities where you communicate and share information online. Formulate a clear view on what you find acceptable for yourself – as ground rules for yourself and for groups that you are in.

Ground rules	
1	
2	
3	
4	
5	
6	
7	
8	
9	
10	

Your online presence

Give thought to the amount and kind of information available about you online. Once information is released online, it is very difficult to stop it circulating, even many years or decades later when you may feel very differently about it.

Allowing public access ... to you

If you allow public access to your profile, blog or communications, it is wise to adhere to the following ground rules so as to keep yourself safe and protect your future interests.

- **Be aware of what you send into the unknown.** Keep in mind that if you allow public access to your profile, blog or other online material, you will not know who may see them or use them. Your words or images may be found through search engines and used for a range of purposes that you had not intended.

- **Consider your image.** Consider whether images and words posted in a rash moment might come back to haunt you later, when you might want to convey a different kind of message about yourself.

- **Remember the permanent record.** Bear in mind before posting them that comments in the public arena could be accessed and recycled for many years.

- **Aim to avoid offence.** Think carefully whether your comments could cause unintended offence to other students. As well as being hurtful to others, such comments could be used to make judgements about whether you are a suitable candidate for a job, society, prize or public office. In some cases, you could be sued for damages or prosecuted for breaking the law.

What would a future employer see?

It is not uncommon for employers to research prospective candidates online at some stage in the appointment process. Communications that are intended to amuse friends and colleagues might not remain private. Before sending them, consider whether photos, blogs, postings and other online information about yourself would convey the messages that you would wish to be seen by prospective employers. If you wanted to impress employers or others in future, would the information available on you via Google or other search engines help your cause?

I found this rather interesting photo of you on the Internet. ... Perhaps we should discuss this now in the light of the job description ...

Multiple accounts

If you use Twitter for academic, personal and professional purposes, you could consider setting up multiple Twitter accounts. On a mobile device, you can easily switch between these accounts. The advantage is that your professional 'followers' do not then see the more informal information that you might wish to send to friends and family.

☺ Activity: Employer awareness

What kind of a picture would a prospective employer build up of you from googling you now?

Protect yourself and others

Take care when advertising events

There have been serious cases of house parties advertised on open access sites, resulting in large numbers of uninvited guests and a great deal of damage.

Protect against identity theft

If someone is intent on stealing identities, they may be skilled at assembling and cross-referencing snippets of information from your different communications in order to build up your personal profile.

Draw up a list of the information that could be gathered about you from across the range of your electronic communications and from search tools such as Google. Include such details as:

- where you are studying, what and why;
- your timetable and travel arrangements;
- your likes and dislikes;
- details of teaching staff;
- names and details of friends and family;
- recent purchases, holidays and patterns of spending money;
- when you, your friends or family are away on holiday;
- whether you or someone you know is moving house, when and where;
- places you go out to frequently;
- where you usually get your lunch;
- local events or sights;
- views from your window;
- whether you are feeling vulnerable in any way, and why;
- employment details.

☺ Activity: How much do you reveal?

What kind of picture could a relative stranger build up of you and your life from the information available about you online?

→ What kind of lifestyle does it suggest?

→ What might it suggest about when your home, or that of someone you are writing about, is most likely to be empty?

Protect the identity of others

Chance details that you and others make public can be pieced together to build a profile by identity thieves.

☺ Activity: Can you be trusted?

How much information could a third party find out about your family and acquaintances just by putting together information on them that you have made public?

Be considerate of third parties

Be responsible in how you refer to the words, activities or ideas of other people, even if meant only as a joke. Your comments or photos may be passed on to others or used in ways you hadn't intended. Be careful that you do not cause someone else trouble or harm by what you write, such as through jeopardising their security, privacy, job prospects, relationships, ideas, studies, or general peace of mind.

Show courtesy to staff

It is not good netiquette to complain about college or university staff in ways that identify individuals.

Students have received disciplinary action for comments made about staff on Facebook. There are legitimate, formal mechanisms for providing feedback to your university or college about your experience as a student and for making complaints, if needed.

Taking care of your privacy and security

Your personal security and privacy strategy

How good is your strategy for taking care of yourself online? Evaluate each statement, circling a rating of:

5 for 'always'   3 for 'most of the time'   1 for 'hardly ever'
4 for 'nearly always'   2 for 'sometimes'   0 for 'never'

Statement	Always . . . . . . never					
1 I devise long passwords that include letters, numbers and symbols	5	4	3	2	1	0
2 I change my passwords frequently	5	4	3	2	1	0
3 I gain permission before sharing other people's information with third parties	5	4	3	2	1	0
4 I use privacy settings (see p. 87 in Ch. 5)	5	4	3	2	1	0
5 I adapt my personal settings according to the message I send	5	4	3	2	1	0
6 I use up-to-date anti-virus software	5	4	3	2	1	0
7 I am cautious about sharing personal details with people I know only online	5	4	3	2	1	0
8 If I meet someone I know only from online, I take someone else with me	5	4	3	2	1	0
9 I refuse to share passwords and PINs with close friends and colleagues	5	4	3	2	1	0
10 I never send money to help out friends known only from online communications	5	4	3	2	1	0
11 I would never disclose my password, PIN or similar details to anyone who requested these online or over the phone – even if they sound 'official'	5	4	3	2	1	0
12 I avoid sharing my assignment material before the hand-in date	5	4	3	2	1	0
13 I keep my home address private from people I know only online	5	4	3	2	1	0
14 I keep my landline phone number private from those I know only online	5	4	3	2	1	0
15 I keep family details private from those I know only online	5	4	3	2	1	0
16 I take great care of which photographs I send to others	5	4	3	2	1	0
17 I allow my full profile on social networking sites to be seen only by those I have nominated as friends	5	4	3	2	1	0
18 I avoid making any response to messages I identify as spam	5	4	3	2	1	0
19 I delete spam messages permanently	5	4	3	2	1	0
20 I protect my academic work online, so that nobody but me sees it before everyone's work is graded and returned	5	4	3	2	1	0
Total (add up your scores for the 20 items)						%

Find your percentage score

Add all your scores to find the total. As this is a score out of 100, this is your percentage score. See p. 14 to interpret your score.

Evaluate your score (from p. 13)

In general, the higher your score, the more secure and protected you are. However, anything less than a 100% score leaves you open to unscrupulous use by others.

Err on the side of caution, even if this makes you feel unnecessarily distrustful at times. Loss of control over your information can have serious unforeseen consequences.

There are all too many people worldwide skilled at deceiving even cynical Internet users into believing a false story. Some develop a strategy of building a plausible story and relationship over several years, using convincing false identities, in order to extort money or other benefits once trust has been established.

7 'Nevers'

1   **Never** … assume you know someone purely from online contact.

2   **Never**… share passwords.

3   **Never** … share your PINs.

4   **Never** … meet strangers alone, however well you think you might know them from your online contact.

5   **Never** … send money to individuals you know only through online contact.

6   **Never** … hand in as your own, assignments or parts of assignments that you find or purchase electronically.

7   **Never** … make your own academic assignments available electronically to other students until well after the hand-in date. If other people copy or draw closely on your work, you may be penalised as well.

Sharing personal reflections

It can be useful to share your reflective log with a lecturer or a trusted friend, provided that it doesn't contain personal information. You can ask them to comment on your posts to offer their insights or opinions on your reflection, which may help you to gain a different perspective. However, given the nature of this type of blog you probably wouldn't want to share it too widely.

- **Protect personal information**
- **Protect the information of others**
- **Protect the privacy of yourself and others**

Respect for others' online material

Consent and permissions

Forwarding communications

In general, do not forward email or other communications without the consent of the sender and any others who may be mentioned. Check carefully whom they do – or do not – wish to receive forwarded copies of their communications.

Use of photographs

If you want to send photographs that include anyone other than yourself, always ask their consent before doing so.

Use of audio and video

Audio and video of your lecturers is owned and copyrighted by them and the institution. You should not share, alter or re-post podcasts or videos provided by your lecturers without permission.

Information gained for student projects

If you interview anyone for a project or gain information from them in a survey, they must be made aware, in advance, how you will use it and must give permission for you to do so. Do not use it for other purposes.

Confidentiality

If you are making use of information gained as part of a student or work-based project, always protect the identity of those concerned, unless they give you express written permission to reveal who they are.

Avoid providing details that could, inadvertently, reveal the identity of those mentioned in your communications.

Protect others' ideas

Students and others sometimes develop ideas on their websites or in blogs which they then wish to take forward as business ideas or inventions. Treat other people's ideas with care. Avoid passing them on to others without their permission, in case third parties make use of these to their own benefit instead.

Stay legal

Avoid illegal downloading.

If you want to download material that you find online, do so legally, paying for it if it is not provided as free or 'open source'.

Copyright infringement and plagiarism

Don't pass off as your own the work produced by other people, whether for commercial reasons or for academic use. This applies to any aspect of their work, whether the ideas, their actual words, their photographs, plans, music, drawings or designs.

The work produced by others is regarded as their intellectual property. Just as you wouldn't expect to steal other kinds of property without legal consequences and penalties, you are expected to respect intellectual property or be prepared for the consequences.

If you make money from other people's work, or are found in breach of copyright, you can be sued.

Make correct attributions

If you do refer to material online as a source of information, always say clearly when and where you saw that material online. This is not only fair to the person who first put the information there, it also helps to protect you legally. There have been cases where students have been legally threatened for comments made online.

Plagiarism and cheating

If you draw upon other people's material for academic work, whether or not you have their permission, you have to attribute this to them clearly within your work. There are formal conventions that surround this. In brief, these are that each time you mention ideas or information taken from another source, such as a web page or online journal article, you must:

- **Cite your source**: state the names of the authors and the date of their work.
- **Write out a full reference** at the end of the work or in a footnote, depending on the convention used on your course.

Details of how to do this for different kinds of electronic material are provided in the relevant chapters below. For example, see p. 70 for referencing a podcast and p. 97 for referencing a blog.

The conventions used by your college or university will be available from them. If you do not use these correctly, you will gain low grades and may be found guilty of plagiarism.

How serious is plagiarism?

Universities and colleges take plagiarism very seriously and use software and other methods to check work once submitted in order to identify where students have copied from each other or from material available on the Internet or elsewhere.

Usually, a first offence of plagiarism means you have to redo the work for a low grade. A second offence may mean leaving without any qualification.

The benefit to you of referencing

For academic work it is good to have used many reputable sources, so it is in your interest to state every time that you draw on these, using the system of referencing recommended by your programme.

The various sections of this book give guidance on how and when it would be appropriate to use material accessed via new technologies and how to cite and reference these in your work correctly so that you avoid plagiarism.

Cheating

You are always at risk of low grades, at best, or being caught cheating, at worst, if you use material produced by other students or online essay banks. Detection tools can usually identify where students have borrowed from such materials and made amendments to make it look like their own work.

If you use work by another student, it is likely that they may be penalised as well as you. For the same reason, you shouldn't let others see your work, even in draft, as:

- it may be difficult later to prove that you didn't agree for your work to be copied;
- it may not be clear to your lecturers who has copied from whom.

Using any material other than reputable sources is best avoided. Your lecturers will not be impressed if you use sections from essays or reports purchased online or borrowed from friends, even if these are referenced correctly.

Do not use services which provide student assignments or proofreading.

Using new technologies as a student

Different lecturer approaches

There isn't a standard set of technologies that you will find on every programme. Institutions and individual lecturers vary in their levels of interest and comfort in using these. You may find that your own lecturers are keen to encourage you to use all kinds of interactive learning technologies, from using your phone or a tablet during a taught session to writing blogs and wikis to support group work or class projects. They may provide many opportunities to use voting handsets, collaborative tools and online resources. If you enjoy that, and feel comfortable using these, then you can have a fantastic learning experience.

On the other hand, you may find your lecturers have some of the following reservations. If so, it is good to be aware of these and to consider how you will adapt your own interest in technologies to suit the culture of the course.

Distractions

The use of phones, tablets, chat rooms and other collaborative tools in class can make for a dynamic, exciting learning experience. On the other hand, these can distract from other aspects of the taught session, so that valuable learning opportunities are lost to the user and, sometimes, to those around them. If this sounds like you, then give some thought to when and how you use personal technologies.

Wikis and Wikipedia

Many lecturers are uneasy about students becoming over-reliant on Wikipedia as a resource. Too many students use this as their sole means of searching for material. As a result, they do not develop the search skills that they will need as they move to higher levels of study. Very often, students use Wikipedia and other online sources in an uncritical manner, relying on sources that are inaccurate. Chapter 6 looks at when and how it is appropriate to use this as a resource. However, it is worth being aware of the sensitivities that surround its use.

Concentration and focus

While it is possible to use technologies and online information in an attentive and sustained way, it is more typical to use these in a butterfly manner, landing briefly and flitting to the next bright object. This way of working and thinking can sometimes help creative thinking. You can cover a great deal of information very rapidly in such a way, exposing your mind to many different stimuli with the possibility that this will generate lots of interesting ideas.

However, some students do not balance this way of working with other methods that encourage perseverance and the application necessary to work complex academic problems through from start to finish. That can have a negative effect on their ability to apply themselves to academic work. If this sounds like you, then this is something to work on so that you develop the ability to sustain focus when needed.

Intended learning outcomes

Lecturers will use technologies selectively according to the material they are teaching and what they expect you to learn. In some circumstances, it may be appropriate not to use technology at all to support learning. In other situations, a lecturer may have decided to use one particular technology to help you develop a skill or gain understanding.

> *You should look to develop a critical understanding of which technologies are most useful in which learning situations. This book should help you to develop this skill.*

'Students know this all already'

Although students can be skilled at using some technologies, especially social media and mobile devices, this is far from universally the case.

In addition, when students are asked about which technologies they use and for what, it is clear that:

- many use a relatively narrow range of the functions available to them;
- very few use technologies that they enjoy using for social life in any kind of sustained and advanced way for their studies;
- when they do use technologies that they are familiar with from other contexts, they are not at all clear about how these should be used within an academic context.

Different student approaches

While some students are extremely proficient in the use of IT, this is not the case for everyone. This is worth bearing mind if you are on a programme that encourages the use of IT or if you are keen to encourage others to use IT for group assignments or for student support groups.

Students' approaches may differ for all kinds of good reasons, such as:

- whether they have had easy access to a range of technologies in the past;
- whether they can access and afford some of the high-end technologies that they see other people using;
- their current levels of technical skills;
- whether they have a known or hidden disability that makes it difficult to use certain technologies;
- whether they want to use social media for their studies, or whether they want to keep these for their personal life;
- whether they enjoy using popular technologies: some people love social media and the constant flow of information; others find this banal or oppressive;
- whether they enjoy using technology at all.

What equipment would I need?

Before you can use the technologies, you may wish to clarify what kind of equipment is needed. The following pages provide a template for identifying what is needed for your programme. Look on your institution and programme websites for information about what you will need. If there is a choice about whether you purchase these, check the full costs in detail, including phone and connection charges across the year. Weigh up the relative benefits against the costs. You may also find it helpful to use the evaluation sheets on pp. 19–20.

Which academic skills?

This book assumes that you will already have a good grounding in study skills appropriate for higher level study. These cover such things as honing your skills in time management, group work, writing academic assignments, and critical and analytical thinking. In particular, they focus more on identifying, selecting and using materials that you find online or elsewhere.

If you are new to academic study, then you may find it helpful to complete the checklist on p. 22.

Which IT skills?

If you are interested in using the technologies covered by this book and especially in combining them in multiple ways, you will need a certain level of computer literacy. If you are unsure about whether your IT skills are at the right level, see the self-evaluation sheet on p. 23.

What equipment do I need?

Read each of the following statements and consider whether it is true of you or not. If you answer No, consider what action you will take and jot this down.

Statement	Yes /No	Action I will take
1 I know the kind of computer and other hardware that I will need for my programme		
2 I have access to these		
3 I know the software that I will need for my programme of study		
4 I have access to this		
5 I have checked whether I will be using Flash-based presentations and material		
6 I know whether I am able to run Flash-based materials on my own hardware		
7 I am aware of the Internet connections I will need (such as Broadband to play video files)		
8 I have access to the Internet connections I will need		
9 I am aware of the anti-virus software I need for equipment of my own that I will be using		
10 I have access to this		
11 My computer hardware allows me to listen to sound		
12 I have headphones so that I can listen to sound in computer clusters or public areas		
13 The software on my computer is up to date so that I can view multimedia content		
14 I am aware of what equipment I can use for free through my university, college or workplace		

The following page provides you with a resource for drawing together these requirements, identifying what is provided and what you will need to provide for yourself.

Identifying resource requirements

Read carefully through your programme handbooks and websites and other advance material sent to you about your course so as to identify the requirements. Use the Requirements column to note what is needed. Use the following two columns to clarify what the institution can provide and what you can (or wish to) provide for yourself.

Hardware		
Requirements	Provided by the institution	I will need to provide myself

Software		
Requirements	Provided by the institution	I will need to provide myself

Connectivity		
Requirements	Provided by the institution	I will need to provide myself

Developing the right academic skills

What study skills are covered by this book?

This book is intended as a supplement to standard study skills texts rather than an alternative to them. It starts with the technologies and offers guidance on their use in an academic context. Depending on the specific technology, you will receive guidance with strategies and skills such as those indicated below.

Study skills and new technologies

- **Applying technologies in an academic context:** understanding how to make use of tools such as podcasts, blogs, wikis and social media in the context of academic study.
- **Your online presence:** managing this and your communications as appropriate to membership of the academic community and with your future interests in mind.
- **Gaining from online communications:** using technologies to keep yourself up to date with developments in your subject and career interests.
- **Criticality:** selecting electronic information that is suitable for higher-level academic work.
- **Referencing:** knowing how to reference electronic resources within your academic work.
- **Time management:** managing the time you spend online in research, study and networking.
- **Information management:** managing the information that you find, read, note, store and wish to use for your academic study.
- **Collaboration:** working in a supportive way with other students when using these technologies.

What other skills are needed?

The study skills covered here form only part of the broader set of academic skills required to achieve well in higher education. By contrast, standard study skills books start with the various tasks that students need to engage in and academic skills they need to acquire, such as:

- managing their time;
- developing their critical thinking;
- completing a written assignment;
- or preparing for an exam.

They offer guidance on the strategies and approaches that help students to manage their studies.

Do I need to develop other study skills?

You may feel that your academic skills are already strong, especially if you are doing well at college or university. However, you may benefit from a more through consideration of your academic skills:

- if you are new to higher education: the skills required are different at every level of study;
- if you are transferring from a foundation degree programme to a top-up degree;
- if you feel that there is more that you could do to improve your grades;
- if there are particular areas of your study skills that you feel need attention;
- if, whatever your grades, you think that you could study more efficiently or effectively.

The following page provides a checklist of the key study skills required in higher education. The skills needed will vary to some extent depending on your programme. If those skills are combined with a good use of new technologies, you will be in a strong position to achieve well as a student.

Identifying your academic skills needs

Which study skills do I need to develop?

Thinking skills

- ☐ Skills of analysis and synthesis
- ☐ Critical evaluation skills
- ☐ Critical reflection
- ☐ Memory skills
- ☐ Creative thinking
- ☐ Problem solving

General academic skills

- ☐ Reading effectively for academic purposes
- ☐ Making use of lectures, seminars and tutorials
- ☐ Selecting appropriate information
- ☐ Making and using notes effectively
- ☐ Designing a research project
- ☐ Conducting a literature search
- ☐ Evaluating the literature
- ☐ Formulating and testing research hypotheses
- ☐ Drawing up and presenting your results
- ☐ Understanding plagiarism
- ☐ Referencing your sources appropriately

Writing skills

- ☐ Critical analytical writing
- ☐ Critical reflective writing
- ☐ Applying different academic writing styles
- ☐ Writing for different audiences
- ☐ Writing essays, reports and case studies
- ☐ Writing a research project or dissertation

Managing projects and tasks

- ☐ Planning and managing a project
- ☐ Managing time and resources

Collaborative working and people skills

- ☐ Contributing to seminars and groups
- ☐ Team working and group projects
- ☐ Receiving criticism and feedback from others
- ☐ Offering constructive feedback and criticism
- ☐ Taking a lead
- ☐ Providing support to others

Managing other assessed assignments

- ☐ Oral, poster and group presentations
- ☐ Preparing for, and taking, exams

Managing personal performance

- ☐ Setting personal goals and priorities
- ☐ Keeping yourself motivated
- ☐ Using lecturers' feedback effectively
- ☐ Managing your independent study
- ☐ Developing good study habits
- ☐ Creating the conditions for you to succeed
- ☐ Evaluating your own performance
- ☐ Planning your career and personal success

Study skills: finding out more

As a starting point, the reader is referred to books by Stella Cottrell, all published by Palgrave Macmillan, which cover the above skills and more:

The Study Skills Handbook (3rd edn, 2008) for generic academic skills

Skills for Success (2nd edn, 2010) for life planning and employability

Critical Thinking Skills (2nd edn, 2011)

The Exam Skills Handbook (2nd edn 2012).

See also www.skills4study.com.

Basic IT skills

Which IT skills do I need?

Computer hardware

- ☐ Access the Internet from a computer or mobile device
- ☐ Resolve problems with access to the Internet
- ☐ Plug in and/or configure a microphone on a computer
- ☐ Plug in and/or configure a webcam on a computer
- ☐ Plug in and/or configure speakers on a computer
- ☐ Use a microphone, video camera and speakers on a mobile device

Software skills

- ☐ Install and configure new software on a PC or mobile device
- ☐ Install software updates as necessary on a PC or mobile device
- ☐ Locate and navigate the institution's virtual learning environment or learning management system
- ☐ Create username and profiles for secure online sites
- ☐ Identify an online discussion board
- ☐ Use a word processor to create documents
- ☐ Format documents using icons or special characters
- ☐ Select and copy text from a word processor
- ☐ Create and use an email account
- ☐ Create and use spreadsheets
- ☐ Create and use presentations
- ☐ Save documents on a PC or mobile device

Online searching skills

- ☐ Locate the college's or university's library catalogue
- ☐ Click links in websites and identify new pages/tabs opened
- ☐ Perform basic searches using online search engines
- ☐ Navigate to websites by typing in a URL or clicking a link

Using multimedia resources

- ☐ Use a media player for listening to audio on a computer
- ☐ Play video files on the Internet

Using devices

- ☐ Access Internet services on a mobile device
- ☐ Synchronise a mobile device with your PC or online services
- ☐ Navigate a mobile device effectively

IT skills: finding out more

As a starting point, the reader is referred to Palgrave Macmillan's online resource skills4study. This resource contains a dedicated section on basic IT skills: www.palgrave.com/skills4study/studyskills/personal/it.asp

Summary

This chapter has addressed many of the generic issues that apply when using new technologies as a student. These need to be taken into consideration when using each of the chapters that follow. Many of these issues, such as good netiquette, awareness of your online presence and protection of yourself and others when online, will stand you in good stead as a student, in the workplace and more generally in life. Adhering to these should protect your interests and keep you within the law. They should also make it more likely that others will want to communicate with you and offer you the information or support that you request.

If you already make frequent use of new technologies, you may be familiar with many of the issues covered in this chapter, at least in general terms. If so, bear in mind that there will be subtle differences when using technologies for academic purposes and within online learning communities. In particular, your online presence will be considered differently by lecturers, employers and others than it would have been for communications when you were at school or in informal social settings.

In this chapter you identified your own priorities for developing skills relevant to using new technologies and improving your netiquette. It is now up to you to follow through on the areas that you selected. There was an opportunity for you to formulate your own ground rules for communicating and sharing information online. If you completed that activity, display those ground rules somewhere you will see them. Draw upon them when you set up study groups, discussion boards, blogs or make use of other online tools.

There was also a chance to consider the broader set of academic and IT skills that you will need as a student. Such skills are essential to academic achievement. If you have developed a good foundation in academic skills and combine those with creative use of new technologies, you will be in a very strong position for gaining maximum enjoyment, flexibility and success from your studies.

Chapter 2

Virtual learning environments

Learning outcomes

This chapter offers you opportunities to:

- understand what is meant by a virtual learning environment (VLE) or learning management system (LMS);
- understand the key role played by VLEs/LMSs in higher education and elsewhere;
- gain a sense of some of the many ways that VLEs can be used to support academic study;
- consider how you could make use of a VLE to make your study more enjoyable and to improve your grades.

Introduction

Virtual learning environments, known as learning management systems in North America, are an established feature of the landscape for most universities and colleges and, increasingly, for businesses and other organisations. It is highly likely that you will be asked to undertake part of your study through a VLE/LMS, whether as a student, on work placement or in employment.

As VLEs can be adapted to fit organisations' own operating systems and brands, and can be used in flexible ways, there isn't a single expectation of what these should look like nor how they might be used.

In general, VLEs are very popular with students and trainees, whether they are campus-based or on distance learning or work-based programmes. As VLEs coordinate many different aspects of your study and can generally be used in flexible ways, when and where you choose, they provide convenient additional support for your learning.

Depending on how the VLE is used on your programme, it can provide a single location that enables you to gain access, electronically, to:

- a wide range of materials provided by your teaching staff as a supplement to taught sessions, such as copies of lecture notes;
- generic material about your programme and institution, such as how your work will be assessed and graded;
- a wider range of learning tools and resources provided by or through your institution.

This chapter provides an introduction to some of the key ways that VLEs are used to support learning. It identifies ways that you can make the best use of the facilities available.

What is a virtual learning environment (VLE)?

Virtual learning environments

- Are typically referred to as 'the VLE'.
- Are online sites that, usually, can be accessed only by students registered on the programme or course of study.
- Are provided by many universities, colleges and training providers as a key method for organising a broad range of information, resources, communications, and support for students and trainees.
- Either supplement or replace face-to-face contact between staff and students.
- Provide resources and tools to support the study you do in your own time.

Types of VLE

There are many available, the most commonly used being Blackboard, Moodle and WebCT.

Am I likely to use a VLE?

You are likely to use a VLE at some point in your study – although your institution or organisation may have configured it to look much like other online services, so it may not be obvious that you are using one. You could be required to use the VLE for such essential aspects of your study as:

- accessing all programme materials;
- uploading your assignments for grading;
- receiving feedback on graded work;
- email and announcements;
- online teaching in a 'virtual classroom';
- practice tests;
- linking in to useful information and online resources;
- communicating with lecturers and other students.

Typically, students regard their VLE as an essential feature of their study.

How would I access a VLE?

Once you register on your programme, your university, college or training provider will issue you with a user ID and password.

How is information organised on the VLE?

The VLE is a flexible tool so information provided for you may be organised in many different ways. Typical methods are listed below.

- **By date:** folders of relevant material provided for each week of a course. You might see a list of folders named by week (week 1, week 2) or date (e.g., 14–21 Oct., 22–29 Oct. etc.).
- **By teacher:** a folder for each lecturer teaching on the course.
- **By activity:** there may be separate folders for materials and resources associated with each type of activity used on that programme, with folders named by activity – such as 'Lectures', 'Practicals', 'Tutorials', 'Study sessions' etc.
- **By assessment:** folders with resources for each of your assignments. Each folder might contain such items as the assignment brief, grading criteria, reading lists, lecture notes, podcasts etc.

Get to know your VLE

✓ Tick/check each activity once completed.

- ☐ Read any introductory guidance and help provided.
- ☐ Check how materials are organised within the VLE.
- ☐ Check the tools available to you within the VLE.
- ☐ Identify the Help icon either within the tool or on the main VLE page. Have a go at using this.
- ☐ Browse the range of materials available in the VLE.
- ☐ Use it. Become familiar with your VLE before you are required to use it for an assignment.

How are VLEs used to support learning?

Below are just some ways that the VLE is used. Some or all of these may be available to you.

Connecting you to other students

- Discussion forums
- Student-to-student networking
- Student noticeboards
- Group projects to complete online
- Student support groups
- Links to student clubs and societies

Communications

- Online newsletters
- Student focus groups
- Programme noticeboards to keep you up to date with any changes to the arrangements for your programme
- Health and safety information
- Links to student services

Providing a core grounding in the subject

- Your lecturers' own notes to introduce you to the subject discipline and programme
- A glossary of technical or specialist vocabulary
- Web-based guides to the technical issues or difficult parts of the course
- Web-based clips of demonstrations and practical work

Resources linked to lectures and classes

- Lecture notes, in full or edited, provided either before or after the lecture
- Lab notes
- Podcasts of lectures
- References to sources raised in class so you can look these up for yourself
- Activities designed to help you to follow up on face-to-face taught sessions

Self-evaluation and self-testing

- Self-evaluation checklists, tests or quizzes
- Formative assessment such as multiple choice practice tests

Learning resources and materials

- Background notes provided by the lecturer/ trainer
- Packs of materials, such as extracts from documents, newspapers and books
- Online facilities to order and renew library books
- Links to electronic books, journals and other materials
- Links to other websites
- Links to relevant open source materials
- Material for independent study

Structured independent study

Independent study – the time you spend studying when not in formally taught sessions such as lectures, labs or training sessions.

- Digitised reading lists
- Workbooks to complete
- Mathematical problems to solve
- Structured projects or research to undertake between classes, with step-by-step guidance
- Prompts, questions or reflections to help you get started when you first sit down to study
- Guided reading with accompanying activities to help focus your attention
- Additional notes or activities to help you make sense of material that many students find more difficult

open ...
check ...
read ...
note ...
add ...
complete ...
find ...
build ...

Support from your lecturer

If they choose, lecturers can track your progress using a VLE; they can see if you have used learning resources, handed in work, or completed activities you have been set. They may offer support to you or the class.

General student information

- The student charter or other similar agreement drawn up between the university or college and its students – and how that applies to your own programme
- The regulations that apply to you as a student, including your rights and responsibilities
- Details of student bodies and student representation for your programme
- The support available to you on your programme

The rules
The fun
How we can help
Your life

General programme information

- 'Who's who?' of department staff
- Your administrative contact in the department
- Dates of terms and semesters
- Deadlines for handing in assignments
- How the personal tutor/adviser or year tutor system works
- Who to contact if you are unable to make a session where attendance is required
- Details of rooms used for teaching
- The syllabus or 'programme specification' (the official outline of your programme)
- Programme and unit (or module or class) handbooks
- Details of how you will be assessed and the criteria used to grade your work

☺ Activity: Your VLE

Find out how the VLE is used on your programme of study. In what ways, if any, is it used as a supplement to face-to-face teaching and support? The following pages can help you to:

→ identify what is available

→ consider how you could make use of the opportunities provided.

Using the VLE: interaction and discussion

Below are key ways that you could make use of a VLE if one is available to you. Check whether each facility is available. (Tick/check those that apply and add in any others provided.) Then use the Reflection boxes to consider how you might use each facility more effectively to support your own study.

1 Interaction

- ☐ Students can generate content relevant to the programme, such as through a class wiki.
- ☐ Students can enter a virtual classroom to communicate with teachers and/or peers.
- ☐ Students are provided with online activities to help them work with the material.

Other interactive facilities provided on our VLE:

. . . .

. . . .

Make the most of interactive facilities

- **Take part in a whole-hearted way.** Contribute materials, ideas and links.
- **Work with the material.** Don't just read it: 'doing' as well as reading helps with understanding and recall of the material.
- **Change your pace.** Interaction can change the pace at which you work with material – more quickly or more thoughtfully – depending on your needs and interests.
- **Make the subject your own.** Making use of opportunities for participation and interaction helps you to be part of the learning process rather than simply a passive recipient of what is 'fed' to you.

🗨 Reflection

Three things I could do to make better use of the interactive facilities available on our VLE:

1 . . . .

2 . . . .

3 . . . .

2 Discussion

- ☐ Students can contribute to online discussions.
- ☐ Students can initiate online discussions.
- ☐ Students can comment on ongoing discussions.
- ☐ Students can rate or assess online discussions.

Other discussion opportunities on our VLE:

. . . .

. . . .

Make the most of discussion opportunities

- **Contribute at least one point** to each discussion.
- **Start discussion** threads of your own.
- **Make up your own mind** about each addition to the discussion before looking at what others say; this helps to develop your own critical thinking abilities.
- **Practise giving constructive feedback,** even if you disagree with other people's contributions; this is a useful skill to develop and to take into other contexts such as work.
- **Help draw together the key points** of a discussion – doing this requires you to engage usefully with the material and will help you to check you understand arguments and issues.

🗨 Reflection

Three things I could do to make better use of the discussion facilities available on our VLE:

1 . . . .

2 . . . .

3 . . . .

3 Course learning resources

- ☐ Students are provided with audio files, videos, podcasts, multimedia presentations and other resources.
- ☐ Students can access reading materials online.
- ☐ Students can access resources such as course notes, lecture handouts, slides etc.
- ☐ Students can download learning resources.

Other course resources provided via our VLE:

....

....

Make the most of resources provided

- **Find out** how often, and when, resources are updated. Look at these once they appear.
- **Browse and consider** the reading materials provided; consider why these were selected and which sections to use for assignments.
- **Make your own notes** when using these resources – this helps you to shape and understand the material.
- **Be careful not to cut, copy or paste** materials from these resources into your own assignments either deliberately or accidentally.
- **Print out lecture handouts or notes**, so that you can write on them.
- **Use online handouts before class** if provided in advance, in order to help you understand the topic.
- **Use online handouts after class** to help clarify and reinforce understanding and recall.

🗨 Reflection

Three things I could do to make better use of the course-related resources available on our VLE:

1 ....

2 ....

3 ....

4 Assessment: practice and feedback

- ☐ Students can take online tests or quizzes at the start and end of the course to identify how well they have improved.
- ☐ Students can use online multiple choice tests to test their knowledge; these are graded automatically and provide instant feedback.
- ☐ Students can do a mock test online, with feedback.
- ☐ Students can view their work graded online with electronic feedback.

Other facilities and opportunities provided through our VLE to help improve grades:

....

....

Make the most of practice and feedback

- **Retake the test more than once** if you can, in order to cement your knowledge and memory and improve test-taking speed.
- **Take time to read and think** about whatever feedback you are given.
- **Take note of the positives**, if your online feedback is good. These may help you to remain confident if other areas are difficult.
- **Take seriously suggestions for improvement.** If you don't understand the feedback, ask your lecturers for clarification.
- **Plan to improve your assessment and grades**, thinking carefully about how you will use feedback for future assignments.

🗨 Reflection

Three things I could do to make better use of the VLE facilities available for supporting assessment:

1 ....

2 ....

3 ....

Using the VLE: collaboration and links

5 Collaboration

- ☐ Students are given tasks that encourage them to work together to achieve a learning outcome.
- ☐ Students can set up groups or communities.
- ☐ Students can share files, send each other messages, work on shared documents or view shared resources.

Other kinds of facilities for student collaboration provided through our VLE:

. . . .

. . . .

Make the most of collaboration opportunities

- **Familiarise yourself with the tools**. Find out what all of the collaboration and group tools are for and how to use them.
- **Take part.** Even if you feel other people's contributions are good, offer your own too.
- **Play fair.** Don't make use of other people's contributions without contributing yourself. Share resources and good links that you find as well as using those provided by others.
- **Don't dominate the shared activity**. Give space to others: you don't have to respond to every comment made by everyone else, or always be the first to comment.
- **Be brief.** If you tend to have a lot to say, be selective. Edit your comments and materials.
- **Set up a group online** – or join one – to help keep each other motivated. It can be lonely or difficult, at times, studying on your own.

🗨 Reflection

Three things I could do to make better use of the collaborative facilities available on our VLE:

1 . . . .

2 . . . .

3 . . . .

6 Links to further online resources

- ☐ Students can use web links to other online resources.
- ☐ Students can use links to text-based web pages, multimedia resources, scholarly articles etc.

These are the most useful links provided through our VLE:

. . . .

. . . .

Make the most of links provided

- **Browse** web links quickly to gain an overview of the range of resources available to you.
- **Be selective** in those you add to your 'favourites'.
- **Manage your list of favourites,** browsing it from time to time to look for resources that you might have forgotten. Edit out those that you haven't used.
- **Read them and use them** – set time aside to use them. Make notes. Plan how you will refer to them in assignments or, if relevant, use them at work.
- **Discuss them** with other students.
- **Manage your time**. If you tend to get distracted into unintended browsing, reading or commenting, then:
  Decide how long you want to spend on your planned activity and what time you will stop.
  Set the timer on your phone or computer to alert you a few minutes before the end of that period. This will help you keep focused.

🗨 Reflection

Three things I could do to make better use of the online resources provided via our VLE:

1 . . . .

2 . . . .

3 . . . .

7 Course information

- ☐ Students are provided with all key information such as the programme syllabus, timetable and assessments.
- ☐ Students are provided with administrative information via the VLE through announcement tools or email.

Other kinds of administrative and programme information provided through our VLE:

....
....
....

Make the most of course information

- **Check regularly for information** in your VLE.
- **Look carefully at the syllabus** and any handbooks provided: these give you the best clues to what lecturers are looking for when they grade your work.
- **Read notices and materials provided.** Don't assume that lecturers or anyone else will remind you of dates, deadlines, rules or requirements.
- **Read all course announcements** and/or emails sent via the VLE/email system.
- **Maintain a paper or electronic planner** with details of your classes and assignment deadlines. Update this regularly with information from the VLE.
- **Know your responsibilities** for reading, making sense of and acting upon the information provided.

💭 Reflection

Three things I could do to make better use of the information made available on our VLE:

1 ....
2 ....
3 ....

8 Submitting assignments online

- ☐ I am required to submit my assignments online, via the VLE.

Understand the requirements

- **Understand the term 'deadline'** as used in higher education. It means you MUST hand in work by the required date and time unless you have permission, in advance, to extend the deadline.
- **Find out how to do it.** Ensure you know exactly how to use the VLE to submit your work – well before the deadline.
- **Leave extra time.** Complete and submit your assignment well before the deadline, to allow for technical difficulties.
- **Be aware of the regulations.** Note that faulty equipment or connections are not accepted as excuses. Marks are usually subtracted for late submission.

Student comments about VLEs

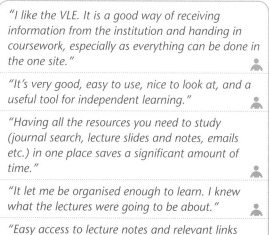

"I like the VLE. It is a good way of receiving information from the institution and handing in coursework, especially as everything can be done in the one site."

"It's very good, easy to use, nice to look at, and a useful tool for independent learning."

"Having all the resources you need to study (journal search, lecture slides and notes, emails etc.) in one place saves a significant amount of time."

"It let me be organised enough to learn. I knew what the lectures were going to be about."

"Easy access to lecture notes and relevant links has enabled me to add to the notes that I have made in lectures and given me useful pointers to the types of articles and text books that I should be reading."

Case study: a student's use of the VLE

Sasha is a second-year undergraduate student studying law at a large university in the UK. Her university has a virtual learning environment which is accessed from a student portal. She uses it almost every day.

As part of her programme of study, Sasha takes options taught by three academic departments from across her university: law, business and politics. Each uses the VLE a little differently.

> *"I love the VLE. Everything I need to study is available and it is really easy to access. My only wish is that all my teachers would organise things in the same way!"*

Resources Sasha uses through the VLE

Some of Sasha's lecturers provide lecture notes in the VLE in advance of her classes, which she downloads to read the day before. She prints these out so that she can write supplementary notes on them during the lecture whenever an interesting new point is made. This is useful, she feels, as it makes each set of notes look more distinct, helping her to find them and remember them when she needs to. Reading lecture notes beforehand helps her make sense of the lecture.

> *"Reading the notes in advance helps me to follow the lecture. If the lecture covers complicated ground, it is easier to work it all out if I have read the notes."*

In addition, Sasha reads various notes and summaries her lecturers provide on the VLE about topics that her class is studying. These are posted as web links, and she normally makes notes on paper while reading these on the screen. She does this by hand as it helps her keep her own notes short and to the point.

Group work

One of Sasha's business studies assignments was a group project on marketing. For this, she and three other students had to promote a fictitious new product. Her group were able to use group tools in the VLE to help them communicate and to coordinate the project.

Typically, while working on the project, Sasha checked the group discussion board several times a day for updates. If the other students from her group posted updates, she commented on these, asking for more details if needed. She posted her own new threads, keeping her group members informed about the work she had done for the project over the weekend, checking that everyone agreed with direction of travel, asking for advice, and detailing what remained to be done.

> *"The group tools in the VLE are really useful for this project. We can keep in touch easily and share our ideas. The assessment is a group assignment and the wiki is much better than emailing a document around all the time."*

Virtual classroom

The professor who teaches one of Sasha's subjects in law is also contributing to an international research project. One week, he had to be overseas when her class was scheduled, so he arranged to use the VLE for a virtual class instead. For this, Sasha logged in to the VLE at a pre-arranged time and entered the virtual 'classroom'. The professor and some of her classmates were already online. Sasha used the chat function to introduce herself. The professor used a video conferencing tool to speak to the group and wrote notes on a virtual whiteboard. During the class, students could click an icon to signal that they wanted to contribute, in place of 'putting up their hand'.

> *"The live video lecture worked fine. It was useful to be able to chat to other students online and we could watch the video again after the class, which was useful when preparing for exams."*

Online assessment practice

Online quizzes and other practice tests

Your lecturers may provide online quizzes, self-assessments and practice tests to help you to:

- check your understanding for yourself;
- go over the material from different angles;
- help you to prepare for tests and exams that will count towards your marks and grades.

Typically, these are:

- provided through the VLE, although they may be made available through separate software;
- in the form of multiple choice question (MCQ) tests as these can be graded automatically, giving you the results straight away.

Treat them as a real exam

Take them seriously. Treat them as you would a real examination. Put time aside to study the material and then take the test in conditions as near as possible to those of your formal exam.

Select an appropriate environment. Choose a place where you can complete the test at one sitting without distractions and interruptions.

Set a time to start and finish the test. Start at the time you decided and stop as soon as your time is up. This will help you to practise time management for exams.

Focus. If you choose the right environment and approach the task seriously, it will be easier to concentrate. You will also be able to see more closely how well you would have succeeded on a real test.

Read the instructions and questions carefully. Read every word of every question rather than browsing the text in a more general way. It is tempting to skim-read online, so be aware of your own reading habits when reading on-screen and compensate for any that are unhelpful in exams.

Follow-up. Make notes of any areas that you feel you need to study in more detail.

Use the feedback

If feedback is provided following a test, use this to see where you lost points. Plan how to avoid losing such points in the real exam. Note where you:

- had gaps in your knowledge;
- misunderstood any of the material;
- made unexpected mistakes;
- misinterpreted the questions;
- failed to follow the instructions correctly;
- made other kinds of mistakes.

Retaking practice tests

If you are allowed to retake the test:

- Check how many times you are allowed to do this so that you do not waste practice opportunities.
- Print out any feedback, if you can. Note the points you received for each section and the areas where you got questions wrong.
- Go over the course material that is being tested until you feel confident that you understand it and can remember it. Then take the test again.
- Compare the results of each attempt in order to check where you are improving. If some areas remain problematic, look for a different way of working with that part of the course material before taking the test again.
- Ask for help if your practice points are weak and do not improve.

🗨 Reflection: Online practice tests

Consider how well you use online practice tests. For example:

- Do you treat them seriously, as you would a real exam?
- Do you put time aside to work through the feedback provided and use this to improve your understanding?

How could you make better use of the online practice tests and quizzes available to you?

Making effective use of online feedback

Many VLEs allow teachers to provide areas for students to upload electronic copies of their assignments. It is now common practice for this to be required and for lecturers then to:

- check submitted work electronically for copying and plagiarism, using software that can do this quickly and easily;
- grade the work online and provide electronic feedback (this has the additional advantage of being legible);
- link their feedback more closely to the learning outcomes and/or grading criteria for the assignment;
- archive copies of all students' work.

What is electronic feedback?

Electronic feedback can take many forms, such as:

- standardised comments provided automatically through the VLE in response to certain mistakes or errors;
- standardised comments chosen by the lecturer from a series of options; their selection depends on what you did well and what needs further work;
- detailed comments inserted within an essay, report or other written work you have submitted;
- audio or video feedback on assignments or examination questions.

Detailed electronic feedback

Depending on the VLE, the lecturer or trainer may be able to:

- add comments throughout written work, much as you would use *Insert comment* or *Track changes* in Microsoft Word;
- provide a list of comments at the end of the piece of work;
- provide overall feedback on your assignment.

When the assignment is returned to you, there should be a grade and a copy of your assignment with the electronic feedback.

Using electronic feedback

Keep copies

Download your graded assignment and keep a copy. Store it where you will find it easily for your next assignment, such as:

- in a dedicated folder for all feedback;
- in a folder of materials you use for preparing your next assignment.

Think about it

Take note of the written feedback as well as your overall grade. Many students focus only on the mark or grade and miss the chance of thinking about how the feedback could be used to improve their grades on future assignments.

Note your ideas for using it

- Jot down notes about any aspect of the feedback that you find particularly useful.
- Consider how you will apply this to future assignments. This makes it much more likely that you will really take in what the feedback suggests and apply it to your advantage to produce better work and gain higher grades.
- Store these notes and thoughts with the feedback.

Follow up feedback that you don't understand

If you really cannot make sense of feedback even after giving it some thought, contact the course leader. He or she should be able to help or to direct you to the lecturer who graded it.

Plan how to use it

- Return to the feedback and your notes before you start your next assignment. Use the feedback to change how you approach your assignment.
- Check through the feedback and your notes again before completing and handing in future assignments to see that you made full use of previous feedback.
- Compare the feedback you receive for each assignment to see if there are any patterns to your strengths in gaining marks or areas you need to develop so as not to lose marks.

Using discussion boards for study

What are discussion boards?

Discussion boards are straightforward to use. They are online sites where you can generate or take part in dialogue or debate, by posting or responding to messages.

Features of a discussion board

- **Threads:** Discussions are organised by topics, each known as a 'thread'. For example, there could be a thread for every lecture, allowing students to discuss each in a separate area of the discussion board.
- **Posts:** This is a message on a discussion board. It can be the first message in a thread, or any reply or comment on a message.
- **Reply:** This is how you respond to a message on a discussion board. It is much like replying to an email, except that the response will be visible to all discussion board members.
- **Moderators:** Some boards are 'moderated', meaning that a lecturer or administrator can oversee the discussion, encouraging new lines of debate and ensuring that netiquette is observed.

Discussion boards within the VLE

Discussion boards may be contained within the VLE or separate to it, and are likely to be restricted to the students and staff for each course. If one is provided for your course or programme, you can usually:

- initiate new discussions;
- ask questions that interest you;
- ask for help and support from other students;
- respond to questions and comments already raised through the discussion board;
- help to build a dialogue about the thread;
- Take the discussion in a new direction.

Support and administration

Discussion boards can be provided for students to ask each other questions, to help each other clarify their understanding of course material, and to resolve administrative difficulties with modules or courses.

'Frequently asked questions' (FAQs)

You may be offered the option of using a discussion board to post questions about the course material, assessment or administration. The question and replies would be seen by all the students on the course so all can benefit from the advice given. If your course has an FAQ discussion board, check it regularly to keep up to date with course news.

Discussion boards on placements

Discussion boards can be helpful for students who are on a work, industrial or other placement. Before going on placement, check whether the department has provided a means for you to keep in touch, share experiences and to ask questions of the lecturer and others.

☺ Activity: Find out how to ...

→ check discussion boards for updates;
→ post a new thread to a discussion board in your VLE;
→ post a comment on an existing thread;
→ rate or comment on other students' posts in discussion boards.

Using discussion boards for assignments

Assignments using discussion boards

Lecturers may require you to use discussion boards as part of an individual or group assignment. They can then:

- *either* rate your individual comments;
- *or* award grades for your overall contribution to the discussion.

They may also use ratings from other students on the course to contribute to the overall grade.

Typically, to gain good grades, you would:

- **take an active part** in the debate and, if possible, start a relevant line of discussion on the issue;
- **research the subject,** using authoritative sources, so that your input comes across as well informed;
- **read and comment** upon other people's contributions, picking up on points they make;
- **offer helpful, constructive comments** that support and encourage other contributors;
- **find a good balance** between dominating the debate and not contributing enough.

When rating discussion board postings, teachers (or peers) would look for the following:

- **the relevance** of your contribution(s) to the discussion;
- **critical thinking and insight** in your contributions;
- **use of strong evidence** from the literature;
- **evidence of problem solving** in your contributions;
- **the novelty** and **practicality** of your ideas;
- **attention to** detail;
- **breadth of understanding** of the topic;
- **openness** to others' ideas and suggestions.

🚶 Case study: Problem-solving assignment

The assignment

Izzy was a geology student taking part in a group assignment to write a geological report for a company planning major construction work on a new site. Their report was to be modelled on an actual report produced for a company in recent years. The lecturer provided each group with the report, and guidance on sources they could use for background information. As part of the assignment, students had to post their comments on a discussion board in the VLE; these were assessed as part of the assignment.

Clarifying the nature of the task

Izzy started reading the material provided. She used the discussion board first to help her identify what exactly they had to do and to make sure that she was interpreting the assignment brief in the same way as the rest of the group. At times, it became clear that the group had differing views of what was required; the discussion board helped to tease out confusions and to identify the questions they wanted to check with the lecturer. Izzy summarised these and the lecturer was able to respond to the whole group through the VLE.

Izzy and the other group members used the board and other collaborative tools on a daily basis to discuss local data, maps and the company's plans in order to arrive at the essential issues. An extract of one thread is provided on pp. 38–9.

How the discussion board helped Izzy

"I found the posts most useful in helping me to think more clearly ... It wasn't the discussion of the technical matters that helped me most, though that was good. There were aspects to include in the survey that only emerged out of our discussions. If we hadn't investigated and included these, our overall report would have missed out an essential perspective – this would have made the report unhelpful if it had been for a real business." 👤

Case study: discussion board thread

Thread

Tom: Why are they asking us do this? We haven't been taught any of this stuff yet! LOL

Xiang: We have just been looking at the sub-strata from the point of whether the company could build ON it. What about building WITH these rocks?

Suniti: Is that the point of a geological survey? Would we be going off-brief?

Izzy: We may be. But it would be good for the company to think about this. It could add value to the report?

Suniti: In general that might be a nice idea but the 'client' is a construction company so they would know about that, wouldn't they? They may feel we were patronising them.

Xiang: All true, but they may not know what aggregates are down there. That is what our report will be showing …

Tom: Has anyone looked at their plans to see how deep they want to go down there?

Izzy: Good point. We have to think about the cost of building. On that point, actually, I have been reading the Nordic Geological Surveys which has a really good section on using geological surveys for decisions about land use. It made me think about a range of other things we should consider, such as whether the cost of building on this land might be much higher than building in other areas. Even if they can do it, they may think it would cost too much.

Tom: I'm getting lost here.

Izzy: I'll quote you: 'The overall costs of a construction process are firmly fixed in the initial stage of the process, where geology-based land-use planning may lead to substantial reduction of construction costs.'

Commentary on the thread

Remember that lecturers may well be reading any comments you make – including any cynical comments.

Even when they do not agree with each other completely, the students are constructive in acknowledging each other's posts. Nobody's ideas are dismissed without consideration.

Suniti is demonstrating a good awareness of the client for whom they are writing the report. This is important to do: even if your lecturer is the only person who will read the report, they will be looking at such things as client focus.

Izzy broadens the group's thinking by referring them to a new source. This is a good quality source and raises a number of new questions for the group to consider.

The students here have used the board well to try out ideas, and to bat these back and forth to test them out. In doing so, they raise important questions about what is required of a geologist, what should go into a geological report, and the roles of other experts that they may need to work with as part of their professional lives.

Izzy refers the group to the sections of the survey that are directly relevant to their own project. Tom may sound rather negative here, which can be discouraging for others. However, Tom is helping the group by verbalising when he is getting lost because, online, you wouldn't otherwise know whether everyone is clear about the direction of travel.

Case study: discussion board thread (continued)

Thread

Xiang: That's probably true, but is it our job?

Tom: Is it for us to include the costing, or do we just provide the geological information, and then the company uses their engineers and accountants to work out the cost implications themselves?

Izzy: I'll add that to the list of questions to put up for our online tutorial with Geoff.

Suniti: This is all good stuff but why don't we look first at the report we were given as a model. Let's see if they include the costings. I'll go look now and come back to you. That might be quicker than waiting for the tutorial …

…

Tom: I remembered that we can use GeoScholar through the library. I have been searching it for maps and photos of our site. I was getting really lost looking at all the words in the report but now that I can actually see what we are working with, it is clicking …

Xiang: Nice one Tom. I'll take a look …

Tom: Can you all have a look? I think there may be an issue with access to the site. Think: big equipment; heavy goods vehicles; look at the substrata to the proposed main routes …!

Izzy: Thanks Tom. I followed that up. Are you referring to the area of soluble rock to the east of the site?

Tom: Bingo!!!

Xiang: What about access from the north of the site – it's a longer route but it's possible. Let's extend our survey in that direction.

Commentary on the thread

The important thing is that Tom does continue to contribute and looks to find a different way to understand the issue without expecting others to sort this for him. His questions can help the group members to clarify their remit for the project.

Izzy is helpfully maintaining a list of the questions that arise – this keeps the group organised. It also means that the lecturer can look to one place to see quickly what the students are struggling with.

Suniti makes a very helpful contribution here by encouraging the group to do things for itself, rather than falling back on the lecturer.

Note that the lecturer here isn't jumping in to help – he is giving the students space to work out the issues for themselves, as they would need to do in employment.

All of the students are good at volunteering to look up information, suggest ideas, or look for materials that add to their thinking.

Using a new resource that presents the material in a different way can help make sense of a difficult topic, as Tom found here. Sharing this with the group helped to develop its thinking.

The students have thought around the task and used a range of materials and approaches. As a result, they came up with a new angle on the project that will probably convert to good grades for the assignment.

Summary

It is probable that your programme will use a virtual learning environment, either as a key tool for programme delivery or as a supplement to other methods of teaching. You may find that some or all of the learning resources, administration and support for study are coordinated via the VLE. As the VLE is such a key tool on most programmes, it is worth putting time aside early in your programme to find out:

- whether your programme has a VLE;
- what it uses it for;
- how it works;
- how often you are expected to enter it;
- what optional resources and tools are made available to you through the VLE – and how to use these.

Decide for yourself:

- which devices you prefer to use in conjunction with the VLE;
- which resources you prefer to use within the VLE;
- how you can combine these in ways that suit your personal style and circumstances.

Aim to use the opportunities that are made available to you, whether these are organised via the VLE or independently of it. For example, make full use of online reading materials and activities, lecture and lab notes, resources provided for test preparation and self-testing, lecturer feedback and for working with other students.

In particular, it is worth finding out what is provided by way of feedback and practice for assessment. These are an invaluable way of making sure that you have interpreted the requirements of the programme correctly and of testing out that you understand, and can recall when needed, the material you have covered.

Chapter 3

Managing online information for academic study

Learning outcomes

This chapter provides you with opportunities to:

- understand how to conduct effective searches for the information that you need for your assignments;
- recognise sources of appropriate academic quality;
- find out about tools that can assist you as a student, such as for making automated searches and writing the references for your assignments;
- understand how information management tools can help with collaborative group work that you may need to undertake as a student;
- use YouTube as an additional resource for study;
- consider how to produce video of appropriate quality for student assignments and load these onto YouTube if required.

Introduction

Whilst most students are already familiar with using search engines such as Google, Yahoo or Bing to search for information on the Internet, there are different approaches and resources which help when using the Internet for academic purposes. The assignments that you are set in higher education are likely to provide significant challenges in searching for, recognising and using good quality, relevant material.

This chapter looks at what counts as good quality material for academic purposes. It provides information about search strategies and online tools that can assist you in finding the material you need.

Use this chapter to undertake such tasks as:

- conducting online searches, including limiting and filtering search results, using Boolean operators, accessing bibliographic databases and digital repositories;
- automating searches and having results delivered directly to you, for more convenient study;
- aggregating news feeds;
- managing your academic references for use in your assignments;
- using online tools to share information for group assignments;
- making use of video material.

Self-evaluation: what would be useful to me?

For each of the following statements:
(1) Tick ✓ if you consider that this is something you need to know (items that are likely to be essential to all students are already ticked).
(2) Tick ✓ those you want to find out more about, either because you feel you need to or because you think it would make your study more interesting or effective.
(3) Look up the item on the pages indicated.

Statement	(1) Need to know	(2) Want to check	(3) See page
1 Understanding the nature of the challenge of managing information for academic study and the stages involved	✓		43
2 Understanding how to recognise material of appropriate academic quality for assignments	✓		44
3 Understanding of what is meant by 'peer reviewed'	✓		44
4 Knowledge of the key locations of suitable material online			45
5 Awareness of the pros and cons of using the Internet for academic study	✓		46
6 Understanding of how to develop a search strategy			47–9
7 Ability to limit and extend searches			47–9
8 Understanding of how to use Boolean operators			47–9
9 Awareness of how bibliographic databases could help me			50
10 Awareness of how digital repositories could help me			51
11 Understanding of the potential benefit of automated searches			52
12 Knowledge of reference management tools for helping to put together references for assignments			52
13 Knowledge of tools that I can use to store information so that I can find it again			52
14 Knowledge of tools that I can use to share information with other students			52
15 Knowledge of Delicious as a bookmarking service			52
16 Knowledge of Google tools that could help my study			47; 53
17 Reading case studies of how other students use the tools available			54–6
18 Use of YouTube for educational resources			57–8
19 Making videos for YouTube as part of an academic assignment			59
Decide which topic you will look at first, or whether you need to work through these issues in order.			

Stages in managing information for study

The nature of the challenge

It can be a challenge to manage information for study because:

- there is a great deal of material available, far more than you could read for an assignment;
- not all the material that you will find will be suitable for academic study.

It helps if you know:

- what kind of information you are looking for;
- suitable online locations for finding it;
- methods of finding these;
- tools that can help filter and store information;
- what is available to you as a student to help you access information you need.

Defining the task

Before you start your search, your first task is to:

- look carefully at assignment briefs to make sure that you understand as precisely as you can what it is that you are looking for;
- look for clues about key terms and dates that can help you define your online search as closely as possible. This will save you a great deal of time later.

Selecting material of appropriate quality

To help ensure that your material is a reputable source for academic purposes, it helps to:

- understand the importance of peer-reviewed material;
- develop a feel for the kind of things you need to look out for when selecting books to read.

Locations and tools

There are mechanisms that you can employ to make it more likely that your searches will yield suitable resources. These include:

- using key locations to sources of academic information in general and for your subject;
- using tools that help you with various stages of finding, storing and using the information.

Methods

There are strategies that you can apply to help you conduct efficient searches and avoid wasting time on information that you cannot use. In particular, it is useful to know how to:

- limit your searches, so that you are not overwhelmed by unhelpful or irrelevant material;
- extend your searches, so that you can look further afield if you haven't found what you are looking for;
- use Boolean operators in useful combinations so that you limit and extend searches effectively.

Storage and retrieval

Once you find the information you need, the next stage is to tag or store this so that you can retrieve it again easily when you need it for your assignment. This may be through a combination of downloads to your hard drive or memory stick, emailing to yourself, bookmarking or tagging.

Sharing with other students

You may be required to take part in collaborative group assignments or, alternatively, you may form part of a study group where you decide to share good resources. There are tools that can help you to do this.

Referencing your sources

Tools are also available that help you to retrieve information in such a way that it is easy to use when you come to write references to your sources for your academic assignments.

Finding suitable material for your assignments

It isn't always easy to judge the academic quality of material. You are more likely to draw on good quality material in your assignments if you use journal articles, as these tend to be peer reviewed. For books, you would need to look for other quality indicators, as suggested below.

What does 'peer reviewed' mean?

The term 'peer reviewed' is used when subject experts evaluate a piece of research to decide whether it should be published, and identify potential flaws, errors, inconsistencies or confusions so that these can be addressed prior to publication. This process is not infallible. Peer review does not guarantee the accuracy of information, but the high level of scrutiny helps to ensure that material is accurate, clear, well researched and original.

Peer-reviewed journals

There is a great deal of competition to publish new research in good specialist journals so only the best tends to get into these. The journals call upon experts to check and select articles – that is, to put the articles through a process of peer review.

Such research articles can sometimes be rather advanced, especially for undergraduate use. If so, look at reviews, summaries, and letters about the research, often to be found in journals too. These items are usually selected through a rigorous editorial process. They provide useful insights into the research and how it is being received by other experts.

Where do I find good journals?

Your lecturers will indicate the most reputable journals in your subject. Use these as your starting place to find others.

- When you find a new journal, check its ranking within its subject area, using a Journal Citation Report tool.
- Look at the list of references within journal articles to identify other journals referred to on a frequent basis.
- Search for related articles on that topic: you may be able to click links to these.
- Use bibliographic databases to suggest 'related articles' when you have found a relevant article; check whether these appear in reputable journals.
- Search for additional articles by authors of articles you have selected.
- Use articles to find keywords for additional searches.
- Look at which articles have cited the article (many bibliographic databases will list these, or you can use citation index tools).

How do I identify books of academic quality?

It can be more difficult to identify whether a book is of good academic quality until you become more familiar with the discipline. Weigh up a combination of the following factors:

- the number and quality of the references;
- whether the book makes reference to original sources or data;
- the reputation of the author in this field;
- whether the book or the author's work in general is reviewed in reputable journals;
- the qualifications of the author;
- whether the author is employed by an academic institution or equivalent professional organisation;
- the reputation of the series or the series editor, if the book is part of a series;
- whether lecturers, other books or good journal articles make positive references to the author's work.

What students say about finding material

"In the first year, I used anything relevant I could find on Google … I soon learnt it was wiser to rely primarily on well-known journals for assignments."

"I have bookmarks on my browser for the databases I use to find journal articles."

Locations for finding academic material online

When you are looking for information for use in academic research or for assignments as a student, start with the following locations.

Library catalogue

Usually, you can use your library catalogue from anywhere that you have access to the Internet. The library catalogue is likely to be able to help you find:

- **Books** held in the library, or available as online e-books, or which can be accessed via an inter-library loan.
- **Journal articles** held in the library or available online.
- **Theses** produced by PhD students, some of which may have been digitised.
- **Magazines and newspapers** held by the library in print and online form.
- **Special collections,** such as diaries, letters, prints, photos, paintings, posters and personal papers.

The university librarians can offer excellent advice on how to complete a thorough search for an academic assignment.

Search engines

Search engines can help you find useful background information when researching topics for assignments. See p. 46 for tips on searching the Internet for academic purposes.

Consider using Google Scholar as your main online general research search engine (scholar. google.com). This searches scholarly literature and provides results from journals, book publishers and other authenticated sources. See p. 53 for Google Tools.

Bibliographic databases

These are databases that help you to search for journal and newspaper articles, conference proceedings, reports, government and legal publications, patents and books. Bibliographic databases may be broad, such as: www. webofknowledge.com or more specialised and discipline-specific, such as, for medicine and biomedicine: pubmed.com.

You can access these from the library catalogue at your university or college or via the Internet.

Subject gateway services

These are dedicated, subject-specific sites to help you find detailed and relevant information within your discipline. They are maintained by professionals and validated by academics, so you can have a reasonable level of confidence in the quality of the information.

You can find a list of subject gateways relevant to your studies through your library website.

Using the Internet for academic purposes

Pros and cons of searching the Internet

Pros

- Vast amount of information available – you are likely to find something relevant if you look long enough.
- A wide range of search engines available to help search, limit and filter results.
- Information is available from all over the world.
- Resources are available in a wide range of formats (e.g., text, images, video etc.).
- Information from the past is archived.

Cons

- Anyone can publish information on the Internet without it being checked.
- Information may be untrue or difficult to verify.
- Information may be outdated.
- Information can be changed or removed from the Internet at any time.
- Information may be presented in a biased way, but the bias may not be evident.

Tips for searching the Internet effectively

Search engines

When using search engines such as Google, Google Scholar, Yahoo or Bing to search the Internet:

- use keywords, Boolean operators and date ranges in combination with each other in order to limit your searches (see p. 47);
- consider whether your search results are best presented as web pages, news, images or videos;
- check for 'sponsored links' and 'ads' in your search results – these may not be objective sources of information (see below);
- critically review the title, URL and preview of the link before selecting an item, rather than clicking on every result.

Evaluating websites

When using any online resource, consider the quality of the material using the following prompts.

Authority Is this a reputable source of information written by subject experts? Look for references to original research, links to other information and author credentials. See p. 44.

Objectivity Does the information on the website read as even-handed and neutral? Consider the potential motivations of the author(s). Consider, too, the type of URL as this gives you clues about whether the website is reputable or may have specific agendas. For example:

- .org (non-profit organisation such as charities);
- .gov (a government site);
- .ac.uk or .edu (academic or educational institution);
- .com, .net or co.uk (company or commercial site).

Relevance Is the information focused on aspects, examples, locations, populations, time periods etc. that are relevant to your assignment? Is it pitched at an appropriate level for higher education studies?

Timeliness Is the information up to date? Check the date that the website was last dated. Is it an archived website that hasn't been updated recently? If so, the information may well be out of date.

Developing the expertise

Inevitably, you will find inaccurate information on the Internet at some point, so it is important that you are able to recognise it as such and avoid using it in your assignments. You will become practised at sieving good information from bad.

Narrowing or extending your online search

Advanced searches

You can conduct an advanced search in Google by clicking the 'advanced search' link on the home page. This enables you to refine your search in a number of ways: you can limit your search to information to that:

- in specific languages;
- between specific dates;
- at certain reading levels.

You can decide whether the words or terms you are searching for appear:

- anywhere on the web page;
- only in the title of the web page;
- or a variety of other options.

Searching with Google Scholar

scholar.google.com

When searching for academic material, it is likely that you will find it more useful to use a dedicated search engine such as Google Scholar. Using this, you can refine your results by searching within one or more of the following categories:

- Keywords
- Date
- Author
- Collection

Refining your search using *keywords*

You can opt to search for articles that contain:

- a single word: *Spider*
- a combination of keywords: *Spider Widow Black*
- an exact phrase: *Black Widow Spider*

Refining your search by *author*

You can search for authors in a number of ways:

- by surname: *Smith*
- with initials if known: *FR Smith or F Smith*
- by multiple authors: *Philips Hogg Smith*

Refining your search by *date*

You can search for articles published:

- within an individual year: *1975*
- between a range of years: *2000–2010*.

Refining your search by *collection*

You can choose to only search for articles in specific subject areas: *Life science, Business, Science, Engineering, Medicine, Social science, Arts and Humanities.*

Using Boolean operators

When AND, OR or NOT are used to limit and extend searches, they are referred to as Boolean operators.

In some tools, including Google Scholar, your results would be different if:

- you do/don't use these actual words in your search query;
- you do/don't use capital letters for them.

What will happen if I use these?

OR search: *Spider OR insect OR carnivorous*

The search will reveal a relatively high number of results as it will look for items that contain any of these items.

NOT search: *Spider NOT Tarantula*

This gives fewer results as it cuts out items that contain those words or phrases. However, you may find that this is not always in operation – that is, you may find that the number of results does not decrease and the search still retrieves items containing that term.

AND search: *Black Widow* AND *Spider*

This also gives fewer results as every item needs to contain the terms *Spider* AND *Black Widow*

The impact of your search strategy

Depending on your research strategy, you may be faced with an unmanageable number of items, or a realistic number of relevant items. The following searches were undertaken on 17 February 2012 using advanced search options in Google and Google Scholar; the table illustrates how a good search strategy, coupled with the use of Google Scholar, results in a more manageable number of results.

Strategy	Results on Google	Results on Google Scholar
OR search: *Spider OR insect OR carnivorous*	2.1 billion	1.35 million
Single word search: *Spider*	495 million	672,000
An OR search: Spider OR *Black Widow*	51 million	167,000
AND search: *Spider AND Black Widow*	12.1 million	31,400
NOT Search: *Spider –Black Widow (note: if you don't use the advanced search option, you need to include a dash directly before the word to be excluded)*	1.3 million	2,820
Searching research on antidotes to the venom of Black Widow spiders, effective for children		
Keyword combination: *Spider Widow Black*	8.9 million	27,200
An exact phrase: *Black Widow Spider*	946,000	27,300
One of a number of words: *Spider, insect, carnivorous*	1.3 million	10,700
Keyword combination: Black widow spider eggs	315,000	20,300
Keyword combination: Spider, insect, carnivorous, venom	655,000	1,500
Keyword combination: Spider, insect, carnivorous, venom, Journal, Entomology	37,000	258
Keyword combination: Spider, insect, carnivorous, venom, Journal, Entomology, fatalities	27,400	69
Keyword combination: Spider, insect, carnivorous, venom, Journal, Entomology, fatalities, antidote	8,700	**14**
Keyword combination: Spider, insect, carnivorous, venom, Journal, Entomology, fatalities, antidote, effective in children	5,410	**11**

Developing your search strategy

You can see from the table on p. 48 that, depending on your research strategy, you might achieve hundreds of millions of results, or a handful. It is evidently a much better use of your time if you design an effective search early on.

Thinking through your strategy

The following example illustrates how your research strategy using Google Scholar could help or hinder you in finding relevant information for an assignment. In this case, the assignment is on the significance of an aspect of childhood immunisation in the United Kingdom.

- Searching for "immunisation united kingdom" returns over 35,000 articles, far too many to use.
- Adding *MMR* as a keyword only reduces the number of articles to 7,300.
- Limiting the search to subjects in biology and medicine reduces results to 3,400.
- A quick Google search reveals that the MMR immunisation programme was introduced in 1988 in the UK. Limiting your search results to the date range 1985–1995 reduces the results to 206.
- Including *United States* as a NOT keyword (to exclude articles from there) reduces the results to 58.

You can save time and effort by giving initial thought to the particular focus of your assignment:

- which type of immunisation to cover;
- which time span to cover – a shorter time span could further reduce your results;
- excluding areas other than the UK;
- focusing on a specific aspect, such as mortality rates, or a specific age group.

This search strategy may not provide exactly what you need immediately, but should yield sufficient relevant articles to track down more useful keywords, authors and dates for a further advanced search. Once you have created an advanced search, you could create an email alert to receive the results. You may need to widen your search later, based on the information you find. For example, the safety of the MMR vaccine was questioned in a controversy that began in 1998 and this would not be captured by the search described above.

Strategic searching

The clearer you are about what you want to find, the easier it is to conduct a search that gives you:

- what you really want and need *and*
- only what you want and need.

Before you launch into your search for material, it is worth pausing to consider:

- what exactly you want to find;
- what else you might retrieve if you search in an unstructured way;
- how you could avoid retrieving a mountain of unwanted information.

Efficient searching

1 Use tools designed for academic study rather than a generic tool – such as Google Scholar rather than Google.
2 Use repositories and databases designed for academic purposes, and select those relevant to your subject.
3 Make full use of lecturer guidance, and to passing references to sources in the writing of eminent scholars in your field.
4 Give advance thought to working out what you want before commencing your search.
5 If you are using a search engine new to you, experiment with different kinds of search to test which strategies yield the best results.
6 Use Boolean operators and combined keyword searches to limit the number of results – or to extend them if you are having trouble finding what you want.

Bibliographic databases

Examples of bibliographic databases

There is a wide range of bibliographic databases available to help you search for journal articles in your subject. Some widely used examples include:

- **Web of Knowledge**
  Searches across a wide range of disciplines including science, medicine, social sciences, arts and humanities.

- **Pubmed / Pubmed Central**
  Biomedical literature, including medicine.

Your lecturer will direct you to specialised bibliographic databases relevant to your discipline.

How would I conduct a search on these?

You can vary your search on bibliographic databases depending on what you are looking for:

- **Keyword search**: Use relevant terms to find articles of interest.
- **Author search**: Search for all the articles available by a single author.
- **Journal search**: Search for all the articles published in a specific journal.

Limiting your search

In order to limit the number of items generated by a search, and to keep your search focused on relevant items, you can refine your search further in one or more of the following ways. You may need to perform an advanced search to use these (see p. 47).

- **Date of publication:** Specify a particular date range to search.
- **Boolean operators:** Use AND, OR or NOT terms to limit a keyword search (see p. 47).
- **Subject:** In a general database, you may be able to limit or extend your search by specifying a subject area.
- **Type of article:** Limit your search only to journals, or reviews, books, newspapers, etc.
- **Language**: Limit your search to articles in a specific language.
- **Article options** Limit your search by access to items offering the free full text.

Once you have performed your search and generated a manageable number of articles to look at, you can review these and decide which ones to read fully.

Can I access the full text?

When you find a journal article that interests you, check whether you can read the full text. You may be able to access some journal articles for free, depending on arrangements at your college or university.

- To gain access to articles online for which your library has paid a subscription, log in using a password from your college or university.
- If you find a journal article that you want to read but can't gain access to online, check whether your library has a hard copy or can order you one via an inter-library loan.
- Alternatively, you can pay to view the full text if it looks worthwhile.

Reflection: Conducting better searches

Take one assignment for which you have already conducted a search. Conduct a new search using a combination of the routes outlined on p. 45.

- Which routes did you find easiest to use?
- Which yielded the best information?
- What kinds of good quality material did you find that you hadn't the first time around?

Digital repositories

Information in digital repositories

Universities and organisations are building digital repositories which, typically, contain:

- digitised versions of books, printed material (e.g., newspapers), theses and papers;
- multimedia resources, such as images and videos.

As a result, each year, more resources become available online that would, traditionally, have been available only in hard copy in libraries.

Accessing and searching digital repositories

Many digital repositories are free to access and search. However, you do need to enter the repository in order to be able to search it: the resources cannot always be found by Internet search engines. Content in digital repositories has metadata tags to help users find the most relevant information.

Using information from digital repositories

When using a digital repository, check the authenticity of the source. Most digital repositories are managed by universities or organisations linked for academic purposes. Content from digital repositories must be referenced as usual and may be subject to copyright limitations.

Examples of digital repositories

The Universal Digital Library (Million Book Collection) available at: www.ulib.org

This digital library has digitised versions of printed books and is aiming to offer 10 million books online within the next 10 years. Searching for "Jane Eyre" produces 12 digital copies of the Charlotte Bronte book published in 1907.

JSTOR available at: www.jstor.org

JSTOR is a digital repository providing access to over 1000 academic journals, over a million images, primary sources and other scholarly content. Searching is free but access to some content is by subscription through your library.

British Newspapers 1800–1900 available at: http://newspapers11.bl.uk/blcs/

This digital library was produced by the British Library and offers some free content. Other content is available by subscription through your institution's library or via pay-per-view services. Searching for "Crimean war" and ticking the "Display only free content" box returns 665 newspaper articles published between 1865 and 1900 (from a total of 21,084 articles).

New York Public Library available at: digitalgallery.nypl.org

This digital library provides free access to over 700,000 images from manuscripts, maps, posters and photographs.

Finding more

For a comprehensive list of digital repositories available around the world, search Wikipedia for 'List of digital library projects'.

Saving, retrieving, sharing and using information

As well as tools that help you to find information on the Internet, there are tools that help you to mark or store that information for future use. These are also tools that help you to produce references or bibliographies.

Saving and automating searches

If you are working on several assignments on a related theme or undertaking a student or work-based project over some time, you would need to check the same locations more than once, in order to capture new publications that appear during that time. One way to do this is through repeated searches of bibliographic databases, search engines and digital repositories etc.

Alternatively, most bibliographic databases will allow you to save a search and return to it at a later date, saving time in typing in the search variables. They may also allow you to save the search and request details of any publications that meet your search criteria. These might be sent to an email address that you specify.

Receiving journal information automatically

If you find a journal that is particularly relevant to your studies, you could sign up for an 'eTOC'. This is an electronic copy of a journal's table of contents which can be sent to your email address and has direct links to the journal articles. You may be able to receive updates via social networking tools.

Reference management tools

Your institution may provide you with a tool to use to collate references and produce bibliographies. If not, one of the following may be of help.

- **Mendeley:** This is a free research management tool that you can use on the Web and on your desktop and mobile devices. You can import references (including PDFs) from bibliographic databases and digital repositories. You can also share references with peers and produce bibliographies in word-processing tools.
- **Zotero:** This is a free reference management tool accessed via the Web, with features similar to Mendeley's.
- **CiteULike:** This is a free online tool for storing your journal articles. You can add tags and notes to citations, rate articles, make connections with other people and share references.
- **Endnote:** Once installed, this tool allows you to import references (including PDFs) and create bibliographies.
- **Reference Manager:** This software tool, if installed on a PC or institutional server, allows you to import references (and PDFs), share these and produce bibliographies in word-processing tools.

Storing and sharing bookmarks

As you progress in your studies, it is likely that you will come to draw mainly from a collection of websites that you trust and use regularly. To find these sites easily when you need them, just add them to the Favourites list on your browser.

However, if you need to use a different computer those bookmarks will not be available to you. You can get round this by using a social bookmarking tool such as Delicious.

Delicious available at: www.delicious.com

Delicious is a social bookmarking service, free to users. It enables you to save all your bookmarks online and gain access to them from anywhere in the world. Using Delicious, you can:

- create collections of related bookmarks;
- tag bookmarks with appropriate keywords;
- share bookmarks via Delicious or other social networking tools;
- search for popular bookmarks.

Using Google tools for study

Google

Google is currently one of the best-known search engines for searching the Internet in general. It also offers a number of free tools that are useful to your studies. For a full list of the tools and services available, see www.google.com/options.

For full functionality:
- create a Google username;
- log in to these services.

Google Reader

The advantage of news readers such as Google Reader is that they enable you to see updated content from many websites in one place without the need to visit these individually. They use the real simple syndication (RSS) system, which lets them receive, automatically, updated content from multiple computer servers.

With such news readers, you can subscribe to news feeds by clicking 'Subscribe' on the RSS icon which you can find on many websites. Each time you log in to Google Reader, you will see updated content from the websites to which you have subscribed. You can also access news readers on your mobile devices.

Use Google Reader or other news readers to receive updates from:
- news or information websites;
- electronic tables of contents (eTOCs);
- journals;
- blog postings;
- social networks;
- posts on discussion forums;
- social bookmarks on Delicious;
- podcasts;
- search engines.

Google Docs

Google Docs is a free online system that enables you to create, store, edit and share files. You can:
- create or upload documents, presentations and spreadsheets;
- edit files online so that you can access them from any computer anytime and anywhere;
- share documents with any other person, who can edit them simultaneously with you;
- access files from mobile devices;
- track previous versions of your documents. (You are advised to keep local copies and backups of important documents.)

Academic uses for Google Docs

You can use this tool to:
- write collaborative reports by sharing a single document with other students – this may be useful and appropriate for some kinds of group project;
- share and manipulate data in spreadsheets for group projects by sharing a spreadsheet;
- prepare group presentations which can be modified by all group members.

It is easy to share a document you create with your group members; you just need to add their email addresses to the list of people you share a document with and they will receive an email with a link to the document.

☺ Activity: Using Google tools

If you have a group assignment to complete:

→ take a look at Google tools available online;

→ discuss these with others in your group;

→ clarify which uses would not be appropriate for the kind of group assignment you have been set;

→ decide which, if any, you wish to trial;

→ experiment to see how well they would suit your assignment and group.

Online tools for study: group presentations

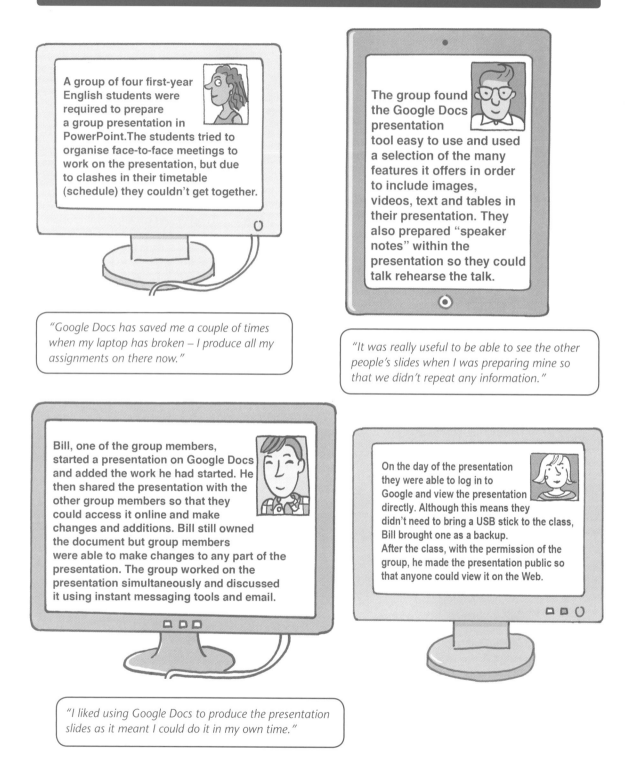

A group of four first-year English students were required to prepare a group presentation in PowerPoint. The students tried to organise face-to-face meetings to work on the presentation, but due to clashes in their timetable (schedule) they couldn't get together.

"Google Docs has saved me a couple of times when my laptop has broken – I produce all my assignments on there now."

The group found the Google Docs presentation tool easy to use and used a selection of the many features it offers in order to include images, videos, text and tables in their presentation. They also prepared "speaker notes" within the presentation so they could talk rehearse the talk.

"It was really useful to be able to see the other people's slides when I was preparing mine so that we didn't repeat any information."

Bill, one of the group members, started a presentation on Google Docs and added the work he had started. He then shared the presentation with the other group members so that they could access it online and make changes and additions. Bill still owned the document but group members were able to make changes to any part of the presentation. The group worked on the presentation simultaneously and discussed it using instant messaging tools and email.

"I liked using Google Docs to produce the presentation slides as it meant I could do it in my own time."

On the day of the presentation they were able to log in to Google and view the presentation directly. Although this means they didn't need to bring a USB stick to the class, Bill brought one as a backup.
After the class, with the permission of the group, he made the presentation public so that anyone could view it on the Web.

Online tools for study: written group report

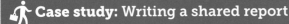 Case study: Writing a shared report

Alena and Etsuko were assigned to a group to produce a report for their second-year history module (course). Their lecturer suggested that they use Google Docs to produce a collaborative document.

Etsuko had used Google tools before to create and share a questionnaire so was familiar with the idea. She helped Alena to set up a Google account and become familiar with using Google Docs. They created a document and shared it so they could both edit it.

At first Alena was apprehensive about writing the assignment using the online text editor and she preferred to copy text from a Word document stored on her home PC. However, she soon began to edit the online document directly, especially when she was away from home and couldn't access the files on her PC.

Alena and Etsuko worked well together on the collaborative task because they had planned their approach and divided the sections before starting writing. They were also able to see all the revisions to the document using the revision history and could restore previous revisions if required.

Alena's comments

"I found it so much easier to work with Etsuko on this report than when I worked with people on previous group assignments.

The big difference for me was using Google Docs. Before, we used to be continually emailing each other new versions of the document. For me, this was confusing, because I couldn't always remember which was the most up-to-date version. In Google Docs, we both use the same document so I know which one to use. For me, it is important that I can change back the revisions if I change my mind, without having to remember what I said or go searching for the original document.

Working with Etsuko on this has also encouraged me to have a go at using other tools that let me share documents, like Dropbox … I suppose it has changed the way I think about working with others.

The only possible drawback for me is that I enjoyed working so much sharing tools and seeing our ideas evolve that I need to remember not to share my work for assignments that are not meant to be collaborative!"

Using Google tools

If you have a group assignment to do, consider how you could use online resources more effectively. Tick all of the boxes that apply:

- ☐ I will learn how to use Google Docs to manage collaborative files.
- ☐ I will experiment with using Google tools for making a group presentation.
- ☐ I will encourage group members to communicate using instant messaging or social networking tools.
- ☐ I will take a constructive approach to working collaboratively with others in using these tools.
- ☐ I will store references and bookmarks that I find using reference management and social bookmarking tools so they are easy to find.

💭 Reflection: How I would use these tools

How do you think these tools could make a positive difference to the way you work with others?

What are the risks involved? How would you deal with these?

Case study: conducting literature searches for projects

The project

Calum was a materials science student who had to undertake a literature search for his final-year research module. The module was worth a third of the marks for the year. He had to produce a 10,000-word dissertation on his chosen topic of 'Future uses of polymers in plastic production'. He had weekly meetings with his academic adviser/supervisor who guided his project.

First searches

Calum started by conducting a number of online searches using Google but struggled to find relevant research-level information appropriate for his dissertation. He also searched the institution's library catalogue for books on plastics and plastic production, without any success. He found hundreds of thousands of results. He looked at some of these, but they were of varied quality and relevance.

Guidance received

Eventually, Calum visited a librarian in the engineering library to get help with searching appropriate databases. She recommended that he use Google Scholar to find general journal articles and directed him to a number of bibliographic databases that searched relevant engineering and technology journals.

The impact of using bibliographic databases

Using these bibliographic databases, Calum identified a range of relevant bibliographic databases, subject gateways and web resources to help him with his research. He started to find many journal articles relevant to his topic and began printing out papers. As he began to browse and read the articles, he started finding a great amount of relevant material, much of it specialist.

Using literature searches to focus the project

From his searches and reading, Calum realised that the angle he had taken for the project was too broad to cover in appropriate depth within the word limit. It was unrealistic to think that he could cover more than a small fraction of the required reading. As a result, he used his search results to give him ideas on how to narrow the scope of his project. He used his meetings with his supervisor to refine his dissertation title, narrow his focus, and to discuss the ideas he gained from reading journal articles.

Preparing citations and references

Calum found it boring and onerous to type out the information he would need for the references section of his dissertation. Errors were creeping in and he didn't like the process of correcting these. His lecturer told him about a reference management tool installed on the institution's computers that he could use to produce a bibliography automatically from a list of references. When he realised this meant he wouldn't have to type out all his references, Calum was keen to use the tool and added all the journal articles that he had already found.

> "I really struggled with my dissertation. Some of this was about the way I approached the task academically – not thinking sensibly about what would be a realistic project. As well as that, I jumped in without finding out about the tools that I could use to help me along the way. I didn't have the skills to handle the volume of information that I found. I wasted a lot of my dissertation time by not learning how to search databases and manage references earlier."

Longer-term value of his new skills

By the end of the research project, Calum had gained skills in information retrieval, storage and manipulation that would prove invaluable when he started on his Master's degree.

> "I feel much better equipped now to undertake a piece of research, academic or commercial, knowing there are good tools that I can use."

Evaluating material on YouTube for study

You are probably familiar with YouTube (www.youtube.com) as a video-sharing site that you can use to watch entertaining clips from home-made videos, TV programmes, sport, music, films and more. YouTube can provide an additional tool for supporting study.

Searching for educational videos

Searching on YouTube

You can search YouTube for almost any topic that you are studying and find a video on it. As you type in a search term into YouTube on a browser, you will be offered suggestions to assist you. You may see 'Featured videos' at the top of your search results. These are not adverts but could be videos from YouTube's commercial partners or currently popular user videos.

Educational material on YouTube

YouTube provides facilities to browse videos by category; you can see these on the home page or by typing youtube.com/categories. The Education category contains videos of university lectures within a number of subject areas: mathematics; science; business, engineering, humanities, law, history, social sciences, medicine, arts and education.

A number of international universities have 'channels' where they upload all of their video content. You can search for an individual institution such as University of California at Berkeley and browse all of their videos. You can subscribe to their channel so you see any updated content instantly.

Evaluating video quality for academic use

Most of the videos uploaded to YouTube are from members of the public and would not normally be suitable for academic study.

However, many clips, even on non-educational sites, contain material that could be cited in essays, to support an argument or illustrate a point. You need to weigh up the probabilities of whether the information is accurate, relevant and the best source to use.

For example, clips of politicians speaking about the economy in Parliament or in a serious documentary could provide information that is suitable for you to refer to in an assignment. The politician is likely to have given thought to what she or he will say. Their own advisers will normally have researched the issue and provided them with the most up-to-date information from official sources.

However, if the same politician is caught on camera and asked questions they were not expecting, it is likely that their answers will be less prepared and less reliable than in the previous instance.

Quality considerations

As with any source, when using YouTube clips weigh up the following considerations.

- **Accuracy:** Is the video material accurate?
- **Authenticity:** How likely is it that the presenter is suitably expert in the subject?
- **Relevance:** Is the video material relevant to your studies and pitched at an appropriate level?
- **Currency:** Is the video content up to date?
- **Comprehensive:** Are all of the key considerations covered? Does the clip offer a balanced, neutral view?

Popularity considerations

Although these are not indicators of academic quality, you can see others' ratings of videos via:

- number of views;
- number of Likes/Dislikes;
- comments from users;
- number of times listed as Favourite.

Using YouTube for study

YouTube tools

When you create a free username on YouTube you can use the following functions:

- **Share** videos with your friends via social networking tools, such as for use in a group project or discussion group.
- Add videos to your **Favourites** list for future viewing.
- Create **queues/playlists** of videos to watch continuously or share.
- **Subscribe** to a YouTube user's channel to see future content and activity.
- **Like/Dislike** videos you have watched.
- **Comment** on videos you have watched.

Student comments

"I am a really visual learner and I find it very useful to watch animations on YouTube."

"My lecturer posts links to videos on YouTube and shows some in lectures – it helps to understand the concept."

"I had to produce a video diary for my research project. I uploaded it to YouTube for my lecturer to assess. I got loads of views and Likes from my classmates so I could see how well it was received."

Using educational YouTube videos

If you enjoy using video content, search the educational videos for items such as:

- videos of lectures;
- videos of assignment instructions;
- practical demonstrations;
- interviews or formal conversations;
- animations or multimedia presentations.

World-class material

Some of the educational videos on YouTube are from presentations by world-leading researchers. As such, they can provide insights into the latest thinking and cutting-edge research in the subject.

For your own programme

Extend your awareness of what is happening worldwide in your subject.

Extend your thinking

Such videos can be an excellent way of finding out about developments in other disciplines, extending your knowledge base. This can offer new perspectives that stimulate your thinking about your own subject.

Using videos from other universities

Check the level Is the video material appropriate to your level of study and the learning outcomes for your programme?

Use before or after your class? Check the purpose of the video to decide on the best timing for viewing it. Some, such as practical demonstrations, may be intended for viewing in advance of a class; others, such as videos of lectures or animations, may have been designed to help reinforce learning following class.

Time and planning Work out how much time to allocate to watching the lecture without distractions.

Apply study skills

- **Make notes** to help you focus on the essential material and to retain a record of what you felt was most important.
- **Use the pause and rewind** to check for definitions or meaning if you don't understand or need to find a missed piece of information.
- **Listen for meaning** If the video seems difficult, avoid stopping and starting frequently the first time round. Keep going in order to gain a sense of the whole. Then check back on the sections or details that appear most important, summarising these in your notes. Your note making will help you sort out whether you have really understood, need to check further, or if the video is too advanced for your year of study.

Making YouTube videos for assignments

Videos as assignments

You may be required to produce a video for an assignment for your programme:

- a video diary about a project;
- material related to a field trip;
- interviews with project participants;
- group discussions;
- learning resources to help other students;
- reflections on your learning experience;
- practical techniques;
- art or visual productions;
- performances;
- poetry readings;
- translation or interpretation.

Guidance

It is likely that you will be given advice on how to produce your video and criteria for assessment. You may be asked to upload the video through YouTube or via a facility at your college/ university.

Producing the video

Equipment

Unless you are on a specialist programme in film or media, you can usually record video of sufficient quality for a student assignment on devices such as video cameras, cameras, mobile/cell phones and smartphones.

Before filming

- **Content, length, and sequence** Plan out what you will include in your video. Decide how much time to give to each topic or question, the order to film, and how your video will start and finish.
- **Sound** Check you can record sound that is audible and clear.
- **Light** Check that the light level is correct; avoid recording people sitting in front of a window.
- **Scene** Consider the background scene for your video, such as where and when to record your video for best angles, lighting and content.
- **Editing decisions, continuity and structure** Decide whether you want to edit your video, and how. If you are not editing it, plan how you will film it so as to maintain continuity, focus, time scale and a sensible sequence.
- **Participants** Make sure participants are well briefed and relaxed: be encouraging and supportive.
- **Permissions** Obtain written permissions (1) for recording people and (2) for uploading their contribution to YouTube.

During filming

- Stabilise the equipment, using a tripod if needed, to reduce unwanted movement.
- Keep the subject in focus.
- Avoid quick camera movement.

Uploading to YouTube

- **Log in to YouTube** to upload the video. Follow the straightforward, step-by-step instructions.
- **Edit** your video within YouTube with its easy-to-use editing tools.
- **Size and length** To upload to YouTube, your video must be a maximum of 2Gb and no more than 15 minutes long.
- **Profile** Decide if your video will be public, private or unlisted.
- **Add keywords (tags)** to your video so that other users can find it easily.
- **Name it** Give your video an appropriate title.
- **Copyright** Check you have copyright permission to upload the video. This is particularly important if you are uploading a video that contains other people's intellectual property (such as a university lecture).
- **Sharing** Decide if you are going to share your video using social networking tools (see Chapter 7).

Summary

Managing information is now essential to study. You will need skills in finding, evaluating, selecting, storing, applying, citing and referencing, creating, editing and sharing information – all from an academic perspective. You may need to do all of this on your own for some assignments and collaboratively in pairs or in groups for others. In each case, the skill set required can vary. The demands of your higher-level study mean that it is especially important that you can:

- undertake information management tasks at speed;
- identify the right kinds of information for the purposes of your assignment brief;
- understand what counts as material of a suitable level of quality for your subject discipline.

All of this is a challenge – and the nature of the challenge increases with each level of study and beyond into professional life or for research-based posts. As the information available online continues to increase at a rapid pace, it becomes all the more important to be able to:

- hone your skills in information management for academic purposes;
- develop and extend your knowledge of, and skills in using, online tools designed to help with such information management.

Although most students have excellent skills in finding certain kinds of information online already, it can be difficult to apply those skills from an academic perspective. This chapter has provided an overview of the issues, some of the key tools that are available to help you to manage information as a student, and guidance on ways of using these to support your studies. You will find further information on using specific online tools and resources in the following chapters.

Chapter 4

Podcasts

Learning outcomes

This chapter offers you opportunities to:

- understand what is meant by 'podcasts';
- find out how to locate academic versions of these online and download them;
- identify how to use podcasts to support different aspects of study;
- apply study skills effectively when using podcasts;
- learn how to go about creating your own podcasts.

Introduction

Podcasts are widely used in colleges and universities as well as more generally in the workplace and the media. Many students are used to downloading podcasts and use them for personal enjoyment.

This chapter looks at the use of podcasts from a study skills perspective. It offers guidance on how to:

- find podcasts appropriate to higher-level study;
- use podcasting in order to enhance different aspects of study;
- apply study skills and thinking skills effectively when using podcasts;
- make your own podcasts, either to support your learning or for assessment purposes.

If you are already familiar with podcasts, you may

wish to skip the next two or three pages and focus on their use in academic contexts.

However, if these are relatively new to you, then you may find the first few pages of this chapter helpful. These provide an introduction to what podcasts are, where you can find them, and some basic technical background so that you can become more comfortable and confident in working with them to support your studies.

What are podcasts?

The word 'podcast'

The word *podcast* originally comes from two words:

- 'pod' (from 'Playable On Demand', later used in iPod®);
- 'cast', from 'broadcast' (which means 'to transmit information')

What are 'podcasts'?

- A podcast is a file containing audio material, normally accessed via the Internet.
- Video podcasts are files containing Video On Demand content (often shortened to vodcasts). Increasingly, the term 'podcast' is used to describe both audio- and video-containing files.

You can save and download these to your computer or a portable device such as a smartphone or MP4 player.

What material do they contain?

Almost any audio or video material can be made into a podcast or vodcast, including:

- radio programmes and TV clips;
- news, comedy, extracts of sports fixtures;
- club and society updates;
- lectures from universities around the world.

Episodes

Podcasts are commonly provided as a series of *episodes*, rather like the episodes of television programmes. When you view a podcast file, you see a list of all the episodes available, details of when each was posted and how many minutes each lasts.

Are podcasts easy to use?

If you already download music from the Internet to a portable media device, you will be able to do the same with podcasts very easily.

Even if you are new to downloading audio or video content to your computer, you should find it relatively straightforward. For example, if you come across a podcast episode on a web page you are using, you should be able to open it and listen simply by clicking the 'play' button on the screen.

Alternatively, if you prefer to listen to the podcast later or away from your computer, you can download it onto a portable device. Right click on the file, select 'Save as', and choose where you wish to save it.

What equipment do I need?

To listen to a podcast, you need access to a computer (with built-in speakers or the facility to use headphones) and Internet access.

If you wish to listen to the podcast on the move, you need a portable media device (e.g., iPod, iPad, smartphone, or other MP3 or MP4 device).

- *MP3 files*, which store audio, can be played by most media players available within Internet browsers on computers and portable media devices.
- *MP4 files*, which store audio, video or still images, can be played on computers and modern portable media players or smart phones which have a video screen.

Navigating a podcast

There is no universally agreed format to a podcast episode. Many use a musical jingle and an introduction to the content; these help you to navigate them.

Academic podcasts on the Internet or provided by your course may not contain any navigational features, apart from their title and a description. Sometimes, these start when the lecturer begins the lecture and end with the sound of students leaving an hour later. These may contain information intended only for students at that lecture, such as announcements or references to assignment deadlines – you can just ignore these.

Finding and subscribing to podcasts

Podcasts and vodcasts are widely available: on the websites of artists, musicians, comedians, publishers, universities, colleges, radio and news stations, charities, local and central government – or the website of your academic department. Many websites have audio or video content available; these usually give you instructions on how to listen and watch, or subscribe.

Podcatching programmes

These are programmes that you can use to search for, and subscribe to, podcasts. They can normally be installed directly onto PCs and Macintosh computers. Popular podcatching programs include:

- iTunes
- Podnova
- Juice
- podcast.com

Finding academic vodcasts and podcasts

iTunesU

Academic material on iTunes is contained in a dedicated area called *iTunesU*. Through iTunesU, universities and colleges make lectures and other information available for free as open source material.

TED www.ted.com/

Initially focusing on technology, education and design, TED now provides free vodcasts across a range of disciplines including business and science.

'Subscribing' to podcasts

Subscribing is a process that enables you to request that new podcast episodes are downloaded to your computer as they become available. They are then moved automatically onto your mobile device when you next plug it into your computer.

On smartphones (mobile or cellular telephones that have more computing ability and connectivity), you can also download podcasts without the need for a computer. This gives you the freedom to listen to podcasts anywhere.

Information provided about the podcast

The programme which manages your podcasts will also provide details about all your podcast episodes, including:

- the title;
- the author;
- the publisher;
- keywords and a summary of content;
- the length of the podcast;
- the date of the podcast;
- a link to more information.

Selecting episodes to download

You can control how many episodes you have on your computer or portable media device at any one time. When you subscribe to a podcast, your podcatching software will:

- ask you whether you want to download all the previous episodes or just the most recent;
- advise you how often to check for new episodes;
- give you release dates or publication dates for every podcast episode.

Listen direct

Internet sites such as podcast.com allow you to access and listen to podcasts without the need to subscribe or download them to your computer.

> ### ☺ Activity: Exploring podcasts
>
> → Browse the websites mentioned above, such as iTunesU.
>
> → Select various podcasts that catch your interest.
>
> → Listen to each for 3–4 minutes.
>
> → Take note of the differences you find in the quality and style of these.

Evaluating quality for academic purposes

A variety of podcasts available on the Internet can be used for academic purposes, such as:

- recorded lectures from your academic course;
- lectures relevant to your course but produced by other universities for their students;
- recordings or clips of academic discussions between lecturers, students or other experts;
- course instructions provided by teaching staff;
- student-produced material;
- online learning resources provided by publishers of academic material;
- public lectures or talks by professionals;
- series produced by television or radio stations.

Podcasts vary greatly in quality: some indicators are outlined below to help you to judge whether a given resource is likely to be right for your needs.

Provenance

Knowing who produced a podcast can help you to evaluate whether it is suitable for your purposes. A podcast may be made simply by someone recording themselves, so it may not be easy to tell who produced it, or their expertise or motives. You may be able to Google the podcaster if details are provided.

A podcast with video material gives a better indication of its provenance. You can see more of the context – whether it was filmed with a reputable audience, on location in the workplace or the field, or in a student bedsit. Visual information such as body language and context helps you judge whether it is intended as a serious clip or a spoof.

Activity: Checking podcast provenance

(a) Check whether an organisation such as a political party, religious body or lobbying group made the video.

(b) Google them to find out more about their aims and motives.

(c) What groups or bodies disagree with their point of view, if any?

(d) In the light of your investigations, consider how their interests and viewpoints might influence the ways they select and present information in the podcast.

(e) Where could you find further resources so as to increase the likelihood of your gaining a rounded and accurate knowledge of the issues?

The academic reputation of the speaker

Consider whether the speaker (or speakers) in the podcast has a strong academic reputation. You can check, for example, whether they have published books and peer-reviewed journal articles or receive good reviews.

Use a combination of your library catalogue, reviews in peer-reviewed journals, and search engines such as Google to check this information.

Selecting podcasts for academic use

Relevance

The value of the content depends on your purposes. Specialist podcasts can help you to broaden your understanding of your topic, even if you don't understand every detail. However, these may be too technical for your needs. Conversely, student podcasts of their experiences, such as how they manage independent study, applied for jobs, coped on a year abroad or organised a gap year, can be invaluable for providing insights, tips and reassurance to others.

Professionally produced versions

Journals, publishers, broadcasters, professional bodies and others produce professionally made podcasts showcasing recent research. These are generally of good sound quality, easy to navigate, and with material of publishable quality. They can be easier to use than podcasts made in lecture halls or on location.

Currency

You need to know when episodes were published, to help evaluate whether they are still current and relevant. This is especially important in areas of fast-moving research.

- Check how many episodes are available in a series and when each was published.
- Check whether they are still 'active' – that is, whether the series is still being produced and updated. To do so, check the release date of the most recent episode.

Podcasts from other universities

Podcasts can be of value for your own programme even if produced by lecturers at other universities for their own students. Many universities, including the world-leading universities or departments, put their lectures on the Internet for free access via iTunesU. You can use these to supplement your course material and gain a deeper understanding of your topic.

Select to your level of study

Each year of full-time study is the equivalent of a 'level' of higher-level study. The first year of a degree is referred to as HE level 1 (or NQF level 4). Start with podcasts produced for your level of study. If you are interested in the topic, you may find inspiration in podcasts produced for higher levels of study. Academic podcasts on iTunesU usually state the target audiences.

Look for edited versions

If lecturers make a separate recording of their lectures, or edit longer lectures down to 5–20 minutes, this suggests thought has gone into their production and that they may be more useful than unedited podcasts.

Quality of production

Podcasts of lectures may be quite 'rough and ready', made using a lapel microphone or webcam in the lecture theatre itself. These were intended mainly for the use of students attending the live lecture. The contents may be excellent but you may need to adjust volume levels, and ignore silences where the recording equipment failed to pick up audience contributions.

Student podcasts/vodcasts

Students may be required to produce podcasts as part of an assignment, and these can be available on the Internet. These often present subject material in accessible language and from interesting angles, reflecting the perspectives of students at similar levels of study. As with all resources, these should be cross-referenced with other sources of information, especially primary resources.

User ratings and reviews

Some podcatching software and websites use a rating system so that subscribers can rate the quality of the podcasts. See iTunes for examples.

You may also be able to see reviews by previous users. Ratings and reviews can help you decide whether it is worth using the podcast.

Podcasts made specially for your course

As support for live lectures

Lecturers may provide full or edited versions of lectures as podcasts. If so, these are usually available within a few days of the live lecture.

Why do lecturers make these?

These are generally intended to help students to:

- reinforce their recall of key points from the lecture;
- listen again to parts of the lecture that contained difficult or complex material, to help them make sense of it;
- revisit parts of a lecture for which they might not have made good notes;
- review the lecture material in conjunction with other learning resources;
- provide an additional support for students with a preference for auditory approaches to learning.

Be there in person ...

The live lecture can help understanding and recall. You pick up on other students' responses to the material, hear their questions, and can ask questions yourself. The best lectures tend to be interactive, engaging students in thinking and working through issues collectively. This means podcasts are not normally good substitutes for attending lectures in person, unless they were designed specifically for that purpose.

As a supplementary resource

Podcasts can be excellent supplements to reading, lectures and taught sessions, especially if:

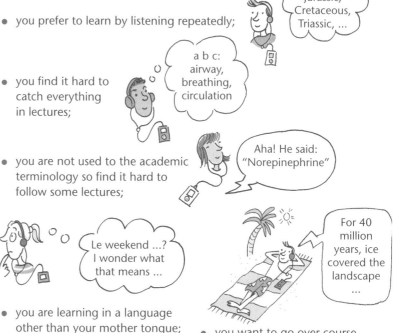

- you prefer to learn by listening repeatedly;
- you find it hard to catch everything in lectures;
- you are not used to the academic terminology so find it hard to follow some lectures;
- you are learning in a language other than your mother tongue;
- you want to go over course materials whilst out running, travelling or waiting around.

Triassic, Jurassic, Cretaceous, Triassic, ...

a b c: airway, breathing, circulation

Aha! He said: "Norepinephrine"

Le weekend ...? I wonder what that means ...

For 40 million years, ice covered the landscape ...

As core course material for your course

If podcasts have been designed especially for your programme, take care to use them as intended, whether for information, guidance or for exam preparation.

Make full use of accompanying resources, such as guidance notes, course handbooks, printed or electronic notes, computer-assisted self-testing material, digitised texts, links to reading lists and others.

This is especially important for online and other distance learning courses where there is little, or no, direct face-to-face teaching.

☺ Activity: Find course-related podcasts

→ Check which podcasts are produced for your course. Find out when these are made available to students and for how long.

→ Visit iTunesU and see what kinds of podcasts are available in your subject.

Organisational skills for using podcasts

Organise your podcasts

If you build a collection of podcasts from the Internet, check that you have complete sets of the episodes to which you subscribe and that these are up to date and organised. Programs such as iTunes will do this for you automatically and will let you know when your new episodes are available.

- Organise podcasts into collections according to categories to make it easier to find them. This helps if you need to find an episode quickly when making a reference in an assignment or to check information before an examination.
- Sort through your podcast collection regularly; delete podcasts that are no longer needed.
- Cease to subscribe to podcasts that you no longer wish to receive.

Choose your location ...

- so that you can combine podcast information with that from other resources. Most students use podcasts in a place where they can move quickly between these and other relevant resources available through a computer, such as lecture notes, web-based course materials and digitised texts;
- so that you can truly concentrate and make notes;
- so that you can cut down on other distractions;
- so you are comfortable and able to maintain your focus and note making for a reasonable time, whether in a library, study area or at home.

Vary your style of working

Work differently with a podcast depending on what you are using it for.

- Listen to the full episode from start to finish so as to gain an overview of a topic.
- Pause it to make notes, think about the content, or follow its instructions.
- Pause, stop, rewind and fast-forward podcasts to listen to parts that you found especially interesting or difficult, just as you would a video or other recording.
- Skip over material that you don't need or that you want to come back to in more detail later.
- Pause and summarise information if you are revising for an exam.
- Pause and repeat information such as quotations or formulas that you need to learn by rote.

Manage your time

- **Balance study methods** Listening to podcasts has many advantages for recall and understanding. However, listening takes much longer than working with the same information visually. This means that you need to balance use of podcasts with other study methods.
- **Be selective in your use of full podcasts** Choose which lectures you listen to again in the form of a full podcast. If you listen to them all in full, this will take considerable time and is unlikely to be the best use of your time.
- **Choose your moments** Use free time when travelling by bus, coach or train or when doing mundane tasks in your room or around the house to listen to podcasts.
- **Don't use as a replacement for lectures** Use time productively in your lectures and only use the podcasts to reinforce your learning; avoid using podcasts as a replacement for poor attention and note making in lectures.

Making notes when using podcasts

Making notes: Listen out for ...

Podcast purpose: whether it is meant to be a reminder of the lecture, an aid to understanding complex material, supplementary material, or a guide to help with your assignments. Is that what you need? What do you need to listen for specifically?

References to other resources: listen out for ideas on useful websites, reading and podcasts.

Your purpose: jot down a quick list of things you want to note for your own purposes. This will help you catch that information when you listen or watch.

Headline messages: the one main message the podcaster wants to get across. Is this relevant for your needs?

Making notes of lectures and podcasts

- **Use a podcast to write up your lecture notes**, adding to notes you made during the live lecture. Do this soon after the lecture, whilst it is still fresh in your mind.

- **Supplement with further reading and notes** Read broadly around the subject to develop your knowledge base and understanding.

- **Engage with the material** Think through for yourself the issues and debates that are current in your subject discipline.

- **Select the significant** Make notes of the most relevant material. Whittle down long sets of notes into a more concise set that is meaningful to you.

- **Organise to help your memory** For exams, your memory is assisted if you organise your notes well. Draw these together into a single summary of the key material, organised under relevant headings. You could make an audio file of your notes to use as a podcast (see 'Using podcasts for exam preparation and recall', below).

Note making and time management

Leave enough time to listen

Podcasts can be of any length so check in advance how long to leave to listen at your own pace. As a rough guide, set aside study time equivalent to almost twice the length of the item. This gives you time to listen, make notes, think about what you have heard, jot down your thoughts, and listen again to complex material.

For example, give yourself 2 hours to work through a 50-minute lecture podcast and make notes. If you know the material well, leave less time. Over time, you will get a sense of your own work pace when working with podcasts.

Select the highlights

Podcasts are often produced as edited highlights. You can edit down the material yourself, noting just the key points.

Note-making strategy

One of the advantages of podcasts is that, if you have a portable device and headphones, you can listen to them anywhere – whilst walking, on the bus or train, at a café, in a study group, whenever and wherever suits you. If you do this, then carry a notebook and pen, or a suitable mobile device, to note any points that you find important.

Applying critical thinking to podcasts

Criticality

Apply a critical approach to your use of podcasts just as you would to your reading and use of other resources. Where relevant to the type of podcast, consider the following:

- the strength of the argument being proposed;
- the reasons being given to support the podcaster's position on an issue;
- the quality and relevance of the evidence being put forward;
- whether the reasoning supports the conclusions or recommendations that are being made.

Take a questioning approach

Avoid taking material simply at face value, even if it is provided by your lecturer. The lecturer is likely to have provided a very good, reasoned approach with a sensible selection of material. It is fine to assume that they know what they are talking about.

However, there is usually more than one way of looking at the issues. As a student, you are usually expected to engage with the material, going over the main arguments for yourself and considering whether these would hold up to closer scrutiny. As a starting point, question the position taken by the podcaster. Consider what other points of view might have been presented, and weigh up the quality of the evidence.

Questions to ask

What is the message?
What is it that the podcaster is aiming to convey to me? What do they want to persuade me to think or do or feel convinced about? What arguments do they want me to take on board?

Am I convinced?
If so, why? Is it for good academic reasons such as that the podcasters' arguments are compelling or the evidence supporting the case is so strong? Or am I persuaded for the wrong reasons, such as because they are very impassioned speakers or sound like they know what they are talking about, or because they confirm my own beliefs? If I am not convinced, is this because they haven't made their case – or I just don't want to hear it? How can I be more objective about what I am hearing?

What were the alternative messages?
Could the material have been used to support alternative arguments if other details had been selected, or if the material had been presented in a different order, or the emphasis on particular details or evidence changed? If so, is that significant?

Listen for persuasion strategies

Repetition
As the section below on good podcast design indicates, repetition is a legitimate way of helping the listener. However, from a critical perspective, consider whether repetition is used as a persuasive device. For example, it is a well-established device in politics and advertising to repeat a phrase three times: this appears to have a strong psychological impact on listeners if delivered with good timing and emphasis before a point in an argument is fully established.

Emotional persuasion
Many legitimate arguments have inherent emotional content. However, check whether the podcaster is deliberately using examples and details that appeal to the emotions in order to persuade you of a relatively weak argument. Check whether you are being convinced by logic and good reasons and not emotional content.

Flawed logic
It can be hard to follow a sequence of points by ear. Check whether the podcaster takes advantage of this, assuming you will not notice. For example, look for gaps in reasoning, or jumps to new points before a point in an argument is fully established.

Referencing podcasts in your work

Detail to include

As general rule you should include all of the following information in the reference:

- author's name followed by initials;
- year (in parentheses);
- title of podcast followed by [online];
- [Date accessed]. Available from World Wide Web: <URL>.

Give details of where the podcast or vodcast was published or is available for download, rather than referring to your own portable device.

Order to present reference details

Your department or institution may have specific instructions about how to reference podcasts in your work. The Harvard method is used widely and would require these details in the following sequence.

The Harvard method for referring to podcasts

Provide the details in the exact order given below, and using brackets and punctuation as in the examples that follow:

- author or presenter: surname(s), initials;
- year the podcast was last updated;
- title of the podcast;
- name of Internet site;
- day/month that the message was posted;
- available at: URL;
- accessed: date.

Referencing a podcast (1)

The following example uses the Harvard referencing system. The podcast episode is from the University of Oxford and is about Shakespeare's play, Henry V.

Citation in the text

Shakespeare depicts the life of King Henry V of England and raises questions about whether Henry was admirable or deplorable in his actions (Smith, 2010).

Reference in full

Smith E. (2010) Henry V [online]. Wednesday 20th October. Available at: http://media.podcasts.ox.ac.uk/engfac/approachingshakespeare/02_henry_v.mp3?CAMEFROM=podcastsGET. [Accessed: 20th June 2011]

Referencing a podcast (2)

The following example also uses the Harvard referencing system. The podcast episode was produced by the BBC about the Severn Barrage.

Citation in the text

Recent research has simulated the ecological impact of a barrage on the Severn estuary (BBC Radio 4, 2009).

Reference in full

BBC Radio 4. (2009). Material World: Severn Barrage introduced by Quentin Cooper [online]. Thursday 12th November 2009. Available at: http://www.bbc.co.uk/programmes/b00nrrd3. [Accessed: 19th May 2011]

Using podcasts for exam preparation and recall

If you remember things best when you repeat them aloud or in your mind, then podcasts can help you to take advantage of this auditory preference – either for exam preparation or to assist recall of material for professional practice.

How podcasts can help

- **As a reminder** As you can listen to podcasts anywhere and skip easily over sections that are irrelevant, they are an excellent way of reminding yourself of material covered during your course.
- **Rehearsal** We tend to remember better when we hear material three times or more. As it is easy to go back over sections of podcasts, they are an excellent way of helping to reinforce the memory, especially for complex material, formula, technical terms, poetry, etc.
- **Spaced rehearsal** If you can, it is better to review material initially soon after you first covered it. This gives your brain time to absorb the material, find connections with other course material and make sense of more complex material.
- **Filling the gaps** If you missed a lecture, then listening to a podcast of it helps you to catch up. It is not ideal to cover new lecture material just before an exam.

Making your own podcasts for exam preparation

There are two main ways of making such podcasts:

- Make an audio file of yourself or others reading or talking aloud about the course material.
- Use software that will turn your word-processed notes into audio files that you can use as podcasts (see 'Useful resources', p. 178)

Organising material for podcasts

Below are some ideas for preparing material for podcasts used to revise for exams. If you are likely to rely heavily on this method when studying for exams, then experiment with a range of methods. This helps you to maintain attention and interest for longer, which in turn helps you to recall it later for exams or work.

Be selective

It would eat into your exam preparation time disproportionately if you listened to podcasts of every lecture in full. Be selective – so that you make best use of your time.

Organising material for your own podcasts

Headings and key points
- Make a list of headings for the material you are covering for an exam topic.
- Beneath each heading, make a numbered list of key points (organising your material in this way is, in itself, likely to help you to recall the material later).

Questions and answers
Write out the material you want to study as sets of questions followed by succinct answers.

Rap, sing, act
Whether you are talented musically or not, you can use varied ways of recording material so that different sections stand out. Singing, chanting, raps, or using different dramatic characters and intonation can all help to make the material memorable.

Summaries
Write a summary of the topic in a few sentences. Sum up the complex material as if you were explaining it to a non-expert.

Readings
Depending on what is relevant to your course, read aloud short extracts from course texts, your notes, formulae, poems or other materials so that you can hear these in your own voice.

How helpful are podcasts?

What students say

"I listen to podcasts by my lecturer straight after the lecture – they are really helpful for writing up notes."

"I used the podcasts for exam preparation – they were great for remembering key concepts and facts."

"Podcasts are the best learning resources available to us on our course."

"I download podcasts of my lectures to my phone before going home on the train … it is a great way to use the time effectively."

"I sometimes go to sleep listening to a podcast of my lecturer!"

"I have found open source podcasts from lots of different universities. I quite like listening to these as it makes me feel I am gaining from the best of many universities and not just one."

Professor Patel notes that modern sewerage systems, unlike the Victorian …

What staff say

"Students tend to use podcasts right before the exams – I wish they would integrate them into their studies earlier in the course."

"We received a petition from students asking for all lectures to be podcasted – luckily, they are simple to produce and make available to students. It is great that students find these resources so useful for their studies."

"I produce short summaries of course materials before the face-to-face teaching begins. I have found that students who listen to these podcasts engage much better in the course."

What the research says

Recent research has investigated how podcasts affect students' learning. This has indicated that students who engage with podcasts tend to improve their examination results.

For example, a study by Dani McKinney at the State University of New York in Fredonia found that students who listened to podcasts did better in their exams (McKinney et al., 2009). The researchers concluded that the improvement in scores was due to students replaying the podcasts multiple times and taking detailed notes.

Another study, by Neil Morris at the University of Leeds, found similar improvements in examination results when students were given access to lecture podcasts, along with practice exams, which they answered with their mobile/cell phones (Morris, 2010).

Good podcast design

Tips for successful production

1 **Content:** Plan what you want to say before you start recording so that the recording flows well.
2 **Use of script:** Consider writing notes or a script to help with fluency. Aim to use these in such a way that you don't sound as if you are just reading them out.
3 **Quiet:** Record in a place where you won't be interrupted. Remove all unnecessary sources of noise.
4 **Position:** Position your mouth about a hand's width away, below and to one side of the microphone.
5 **Articulate:** Relax. Speak clearly and slowly, with regular pauses.
6 **Volume:** Check the sound quality before publishing. If you can't hear it on your computer, your listeners won't be able to either.

Audience-friendly podcasting

What would make your podcast most effective? Bear your listener in mind from the planning stage, thinking through what would really encourage and assist them in listening to the material. This is true even if you are the sole audience, such as if you make podcasts to assist your exam preparation.

How can you best design the podcast to help your audience to:

● find what they need?
● remain interested?
● absorb the material?
● remember what they heard?

Podcast design	
Aspect	**Details**
Your style or 'brand'	What makes your podcast stand out from others? Think about whether to use common elements in all of your episodes, such as a jingle or specific ways of opening or closing each section.
Title	Give the podcast series and each episode a clear succinct title that indicates its content clearly. Consider whether the title would help your audience to find it easily if they did a search on the Internet. Avoid being too general or too obscure.
Opening	Introduce yourself and state briefly the purpose of the podcast and who it is designed for.
Content	Give the listener details and examples that illustrate your point vividly, so they can paint a picture in their mind whilst you talk.
Structure	Many people can find it hard to remain focused for long when listening – shorter sound bites can help concentration. You can help the audience to focus if you use devices such as question-and-answer formats, or using short sections separated by a pause, example or jingle. Consider asking others to help out: it is easier to listen to a variety of contributors each speaking in short bursts. Unless someone is telling a story or has an especially good reading style, it is hard to listen for long to text being read aloud.
Navigation	Use sound cues, pauses and titles or clear introductions to sections to help the listener locate material easily.
Access	Give good descriptions as well as good titles to your podcast episodes so that people can find them easily. Also, make sure others can subscribe to your podcast using your podcatching software.
Repetition	Repetition reinforces a point and also assists memory. As many people find it harder to capture, by ear alone, complex information and specific details such as names, dates, numbers, formulae and technical terms when listening, skilful use of repetition can help the listener to take in and make sense of such material.
Follow-up	If appropriate, say where you can find more information (for example, your blog or website).

Producing your own podcasts

It is relatively easy to produce your own podcast episode, either for personal use or to publish on the Internet so that others can subscribe to it. You may be required to do this as an assignment for your course. For example, you might be asked to produce an audio diary every day for a week, and publish it as an assignment for your course. The following steps take you through the process of producing your own podcast.

Plan

Content	• Decide on topic and what you want to say about it. • Do you need to find out more about it – or research any specific aspects of the topic?
Audience	• Who is your intended audience? Consider your audience at the planning stage so that you collect and organise material appropriate to its needs and interests. • What will your intended audience find most useful and interesting about the topic? • For how long will they listen to this topic? What style and tone is appropriate?
Length	• How long will your podcast be? • Do you have the right amount of good material for the intended audience and length? Do you need more? Or do you need to sort through your information to edit it down, picking out the most interesting and important material?
Organisation of the material	• For your intended audience, what is the best way to sequence the material? What is the most important material to start with? • Into how many sections will you divide the information? Consider whether this is the best way to present the material to the intended audience.
Structure	• Consider how you will plan to introduce the podcast – will your audience need any background information? • How will you signal to your audience that you are moving from one section to another? For example, will you use a sound cue such as a short jingle? Or will you give each section a heading? Or introduce it by asking a question?
Production planning	• Consider when and where you will undertake each stage of the production process. For example, how long will you need for each stage of researching, writing and recording it? Do you need to arrange for a quiet time and place to record it?
Design	• See 'Good podcast design' (p. 73).

Write

- If you think it will help you, write out what you want to say before you record it. Consider whether this works best for you if written out in full or as a set of key points.
- Even if you do not wish to write out your podcast in detail, you will probably find it helpful to have a written running order, or checklist, of the material you want to cover.
- Don't spend too long perfecting the exact wording. Move to the trial run stage to see if your material works.

Trial the material

Does it sound right?
- Read out your material to see whether it sounds right to you.

Use a trial audience
- Encourage a friend, student or someone similar to your intended audience to listen to the trial.

Record

Tools to record and edit
The simplest way to record your voice is using a microphone attached to your computer, or an inbuilt microphone. If you do not already have sound recording software on your computer, there are some free tools available, such as Audacity, which allows easy audio editing.

Rehearse
Rehearse the material as a recording. Decide what adjustments are needed. Make these and record again.

Production
See 'Tips for successful production', p. 73.

Edit
Edit out pauses, background noises, coughs, 'ums' and 'ers', and superfluous material. Good quality can depend on what you leave out as much as on what you include. Assume your audience has little time to listen.

Release

Save the file as an MP3
Save as a WAV file, using computer software to convert to an MP3 file.

Upload your audio files to the Internet
At this stage, you will need to decide if you are going to put your files on a computer server with a web feed, or upload them to an online tool such as iTunes or another online service for hosting podcasts. Getting audio files on iTunes is a simple process but takes some time. Putting the audio files on a computer server and producing a web feed (RSS) is a little bit trickier, but there are tools available online to help you. You may also be able to do this in your institution's virtual learning environment. You can also host or link podcasts using social networking tools, for example Facebook, blogs, MySpace® or Twitter.

Update
Add new audio files (podcast episodes) and update the web feed so that listeners and subscribers get new content regularly.

Summary

Podcasts are an ever-expanding resource available through the Internet. As they are in audio or video form, they add to the variety of ways in which you can study, and can help to make learning easier and more enjoyable. They are especially useful if you like to learn 'by ear'.

As with much information available on the Internet, podcasts vary in terms of the quality of the product and the reliability and currency of the content. You will need to be selective in what you choose to listen to and how you combine and cross-reference podcast material with that from other sources. You are likely to develop, very quickly, a sense of differences in quality and style and whether a specific podcast is likely to suit your preferences.

Podcasts are also easy to produce and you may be required to make them as part of your course. Depending on the purpose of your podcast, you may wish to spend more time and consideration on aspects of good production and design. It is worth giving some thought to a few of the basic listening needs of your intended audience so that your podcast is easier for others to find, use and enjoy.

If you like using podcasts as a study aid, or need to use them for your course, then there are study strategies that you can apply so that you make efficient and effective use of your time. As with any area of study, good organisation, planning, time management and a constructively critical approach are essential – and there are particular ways of thinking about these strategies when using podcasts.

Chapter 5

Blogs

Learning outcomes

This chapter offers you opportunities to:

- identify how you might use blogs as a student;
- find out how to create, design and publicise your own blog;
- consider ways of attracting a readership for your blog and becoming part of a blogging community;
- apply study skills when using blogs for academic work;
- consider matters of blog netiquette such as privacy, confidentiality and constructive commenting.

Introduction

Weblogs, or 'blogs', are a type of journal. Unlike traditional journals or diaries, which are usually written as private documents, blogs are designed to be read by one or more people online. They are easy to create, share, edit, update and customise.

Blogs are believed to have first appeared on the Internet in 1994. Tools to make them more readily available to the general public began to proliferate from 1999; since then, they have become a popular means of sharing news, thoughts, ideas and feelings with others. Approximately 70,000 blogs are created every day around the world.

Many universities and colleges now provide a blogging service for staff and students. Depending on your programme, you may be directed to read blogs written by experts in the subject, your lecturer, other students, or the general public. You may be asked to maintain one or more blogs for personal development or for specific academic purposes. In addition, some of the administrative information for your programme or institution may be provided via a blog.

This chapter provides guidance on how to:

- create and maintain your own blog;
- apply good design principles for your purpose and intended audience;
- make effective use of blogs as a student;
- think critically about the design and content of blogs, whether written by yourself or others.

What is a blog?

The word 'blog'

Blog is an abbreviated blend of 'web' and 'log'.

- 'To blog' means to post or edit an entry on a blog.
- 'Bloggers' are people who create blogs.

What are blogs?

Like a journal

Blogs are diaries or journals created on websites; they can be easily edited, updated and shared. Just as people use diaries in different ways, bloggers develop distinct blogging styles and habits. As with diaries, people tend to update their blogs regularly.

Easy to use

It is straightforward to create, maintain and share your own blog. Reading someone else's blog is as easy as reading any other content on the Internet.

Is it expensive?

Free tools are available to help you get started.

The structure of a blog

Blog entries appear in reverse chronological order, so that your most recent entry, or 'posting', appears first.

Sharing the blog

Bloggers can either keep their blog postings private, share these with a single close friend, or with many people of their choosing, or even open the blog worldwide to anyone surfing the Internet. You can also enable your readers to post comments or messages about the blog.

Format of blogs

Blogs are usually text-based, but can include images, movies, hyperlinks, podcasts or access to other content, including uploaded files. They may contain links to other online content, helping the reader to find related information.

Personalise it

Blogs vary greatly in length, style, frequency and appearance – it can sometimes be hard to tell when a web page is a blog. Many tools are available to create blogs and these, in turn, provide a variety of templates, backgrounds, fonts and tools for you to choose from. This means you can be creative in the design of your blog, and personalise it to suit your style or purpose.

Where do I find blogs?

Blogs are widely used, so you are likely to come across them by chance on the Internet. When you use a search engine such as Google or Yahoo! to look for a particular item on the Internet, one or more of the results of your search are likely to be links to blogs. You can find blogs written by celebrities from all walks of life. Businesses and charities also use them because they can give a more personal touch to otherwise impersonal websites.

What equipment do I need?

The only equipment you need to read or create blogs is a computer device connected to the Internet. This could be a personal computer (PC), laptop or a mobile device such as a smartphone.

> ### 😛 Activity
>
> Search for the blogs of your favourite bands or singers. Look at the way the blogs are formatted and how the posts appear. Make a note of your favourite parts of these blogs to help guide the design of your blog.

What students say about blogs

Students spend much of their time searching for information on the Internet. Sometimes, these searches will lead to blogs. Here, students reflect on their experiences of reading blogs and using them in their academic studies:

"As a political studies student, I find that blogs are a really useful source of information and opinion. Some of the main political commentators update their blog every day and their comments end up making the news the next day."

"I had to prepare an assignment on the ethical issues surrounding genetic modification of crops. Whilst it was fairly easy to find scientific information about GM crops to help me formulate my 'for' arguments, I needed to read and understand the more personal and emotive issues to get a sense of the 'against' arguments for this assignment. I found a number of really well written, and referenced, blogs from anti-GM activists which helped me to understand both sides of the argument."

"As a fashion student, media and celebrity are really important to me. Last year, I had to critique the new season's clothes at London Fashion Week and I read blogs written by the designers, the fashion critics and the media. It was useful for me to see a wide range of opinions from key commentators and I was able to use quotes from their blog posts to support my own opinions about the new designs on show."

Many students are required to complete a blog as part of their course. For most, this will be their first time writing a blog and it can be a daunting experience. Here, students share their experiences of writing blogs associated with their academic studies:

"I had always kept a diary, so for me blogging was just a more public way of doing the same thing … In fact, it was actually better than writing a diary as I could share my thoughts with other people!"

"At first, I was scared about writing anything in my blog because it would be permanently recorded on the Internet, but I soon learnt to respect this and to write thoughtfully and carefully. It must have worked because I got a really high grade for my reflective blog."

"I was so pleased my lecturer taught us how to use a blog … I had wanted to keep an ongoing record of my progress with my project and didn't know how to do it on the Internet. I received lots of useful comments and ideas via my blog that influenced my research."

Reasons for creating a blog

Below are some reasons for creating a blog. Read through these to gain ideas for how you might use a blog to support your study or work – or just for pleasure. To help focus your thinking, put a tick or check mark ✓ beside those that you want to come back to consider further, before starting out on your blog.

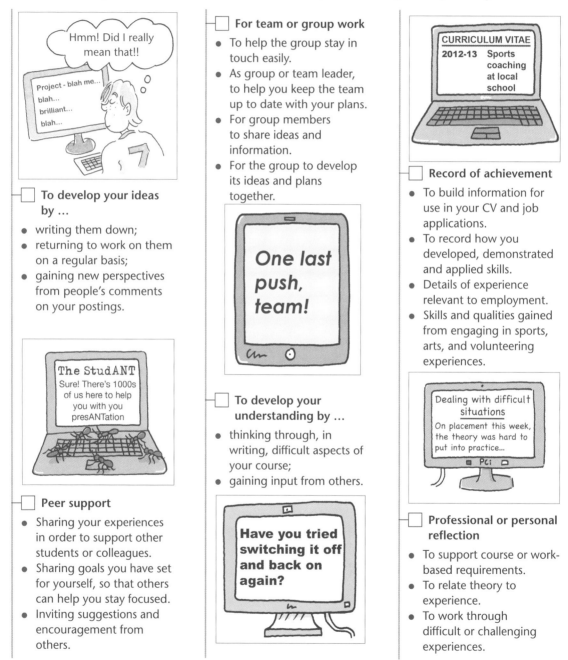

To develop your ideas by ...

- writing them down;
- returning to work on them on a regular basis;
- gaining new perspectives from people's comments on your postings.

Peer support

- Sharing your experiences in order to support other students or colleagues.
- Sharing goals you have set for yourself, so that others can help you stay focused.
- Inviting suggestions and encouragement from others.

For team or group work

- To help the group stay in touch easily.
- As group or team leader, to help you keep the team up to date with your plans.
- For group members to share ideas and information.
- For the group to develop its ideas and plans together.

To develop your understanding by ...

- thinking through, in writing, difficult aspects of your course;
- gaining input from others.

Record of achievement

- To build information for use in your CV and job applications.
- To record how you developed, demonstrated and applied skills.
- Details of experience relevant to employment.
- Skills and qualities gained from engaging in sports, arts, and volunteering experiences.

Professional or personal reflection

- To support course or work-based requirements.
- To relate theory to experience.
- To work through difficult or challenging experiences.

Reasons for creating a blog (continued)

As a diary of events

- Regular updates of your experiences and thoughts so that you have a historical record for the future.
- A log to support a project or research.

> Day 1 Fed plants with Solution X
> Day 2 Plants grew 1cm
> Day 3 Plants died
> Day 4 Put solution X in bin

To get to know others by ...

- telling them about you so they get a sense of who you are and your interests;
- replying to posts so that you start a 'conversation';
- creating an opportunity for making contact with people you might not otherwise get to speak to in class;
- opening the blog to contacts outside of your usual circle of friends and acquaintances.

> Kim: Sorry to hear about your disaster with solution X...
> Ty: Yeah! I loved those plants.

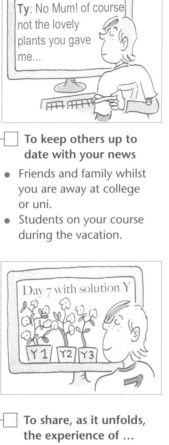

To keep others up to date with your news

- Friends and family whilst you are away at college or uni.
- Students on your course during the vacation.

To share, as it unfolds, the experience of ...

- a field trip or expedition;
- a work placement;
- a year abroad;
- a show, performance or exhibition you are putting on;
- a challenge such as running a marathon;
- a project that you are undertaking.

To develop skills in ...

- using a new technology;
- writing for an audience;
- writing in English if it isn't your first language;
- writing in a language you are learning.

To create shared memories of an experience by ...

- writing an account of it;
- posting relevant photographs, clips or music;
- encouraging others who were there to do the same.

Creating a blog

Steps in creating a blog

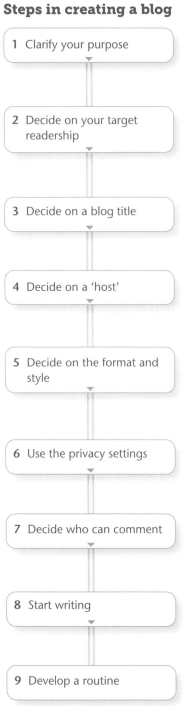

1 Clarify your purpose

2 Decide on your target readership

3 Decide on a blog title

4 Decide on a 'host'

5 Decide on the format and style

6 Use the privacy settings

7 Decide who can comment

8 Start writing

9 Develop a routine

1 Clarify your purpose

Decide first on your reasons for creating a blog. There may be more than one. The prompts on the previous 2 pages may help clarify your thinking.

The purpose of my blog

✓ *Tick/check the responses that apply*

- ☐ Just to give it a go
- ☐ To network and keep in contact with others generally
- ☐ To share ideas with students on my course
- ☐ To share thoughts on a personal project
- ☐ To fulfil course requirements to keep a blog
- ☐ Other reasons (give details)

....
....
....

2 Decide on your target readership

You need to consider the content, design and style of the blog in terms of who you want to read it and how you want them to engage with it – so take time at the outset to think through who is your intended audience.

My blog is going to be read by:

✓ *Tick/check the responses that apply*

- ☐ Just me
- ☐ Me and close friends/family
- ☐ People with a common interest
- ☐ My lecturers/tutors/ examiners
- ☐ Other students
- ☐ My employer, supervisor or academic adviser
- ☐ Work colleagues
- ☐ Anyone on the Internet
- ☐ Other defined group(s) (give details)

....
....
....

3 Decide on a blog title

The title of your blog will usually appear across the top of the page and will influence who reads it. Consider what the title says to potential readers: does it give the right impression of the blog's contents and purpose?

☺ Activity: Blog titles

Jot down a list of titles used for 'academic' blogs on university department websites or by authors of books in your subject. Compare these to titles used for personal blogs and blogs used by celebrities.

→ What differences do you notice?

→ What would make the title of your own blog stand out for your target audience?

→ Does your intended title set the right tone for the audience you wish to attract?

4 Decide on a 'host'

Through your college or university

For course assignments, check whether your university or college provides tools for you to create blogs on its website. If so, it will provide information on how to access these and start your blog.

Through a free host site

For a personal blog or to reach a larger audience, the Internet is preferable. Navigate to one of the free online services described below and create an account. You can be up and running within just a few minutes.

Free online blogging tools

There are many online tools to choose from when creating a blog. Useful starting places are:

- Blogger
- Wordpress
- LiveJournal

If you have a Google account, you could use that for your blog account. Alternatively, type 'free blog' into your favourite search engine. Free blogging services are sustained through advertisements so be prepared to see these appearing on your own blog pages.

As you become more experienced you may wish to pay to upgrade your account, receive better services and tools and to remove the advertisements from your site.

5 Decide on the format and style

If you are setting up a blog on an Internet site, you will be assisted through the process of making choices to customise your blog. There are usually various templates available so select one that fits the aims of your blog and conveys the right messages.

Plants...blah etoliated... ...chlorophyl photosynthesis

Or maybe not ...

☺ Activity: Blog design

Take a look at several blogs to note the differences in design. For each blog, note:

Overall impression

→ What is your first impression? What created that effect? Did your first impression make you want to stay on that page or to move on?

Details

→ Use the table on the following page to look at which design features appeal to you and could be used to inspire your own design.

Blog design: what works?

Look at several blogs then jot down the design features that appeal to you and those that you find off-putting. Draw on these observations to consider how you will design your own blog.

Aspect	Features I like	Features I dislike	How I will adapt these for my own blog
Overall layout of screen Is the page dominated by text, by images or by empty space? How big is each chunk of text? Does that work? Is it easy to find the different features?			
Use of images Number and type of images? Positioning of these on the screen? Do they draw you in or distract? Do they help make sense of what is written?			
Size and style of font Consider how these are used for: • the title • headings • text • links • effects			
Colour How is colour used to create an effect?			
Signposting How are headers, font, highlighting and other features used to make key messages stand out?			
Multimedia What media are used? Do these enhance the blog or distract from it?			

Good blog design

All blogs are different and can be customised according to the user's preferences. However, there are a number of common features shared by all blogs that you should think about when designing your own.

URL You may get to choose part of the URL for your blog. Choose this wisely as it will appear in links to your blog and may form part of a potential reader's decision to visit your blog or not.

9 Post title Each blog post should have an informative, clearly visible title that informs the reader about the contents of the article. You might want to consider using different coloured text to make the title stand out from the background.

1 Title The title of the blog should be clearly visible in large font across the top of the page.

2 Author The author of the blog should be obvious at the top of the page. Some bloggers do not use their real name for their blog, but most professionals do and will also describe their affiliation (e.g., place of work).

3 Links Depending on the blog, you can embed links to other websites within your blog post or have them as a separate part of the blog. Be sure to add a description of your links so your readers will know what they are linking to.

8 Post content Posts can be text, images, movies, links, interactive content or a mixture of any of these. The most popular blogs use a combination of text and multimedia content to keep readers interested.

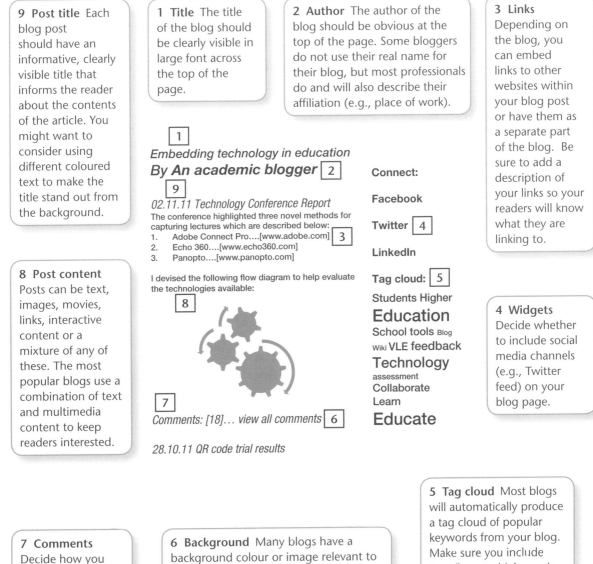

4 Widgets Decide whether to include social media channels (e.g., Twitter feed) on your blog page.

5 Tag cloud Most blogs will automatically produce a tag cloud of popular keywords from your blog. Make sure you include tags (keywords) for each of your blog posts, to build the tag cloud.

7 Comments Decide how you want comments on your postings to be visible to readers.

6 Background Many blogs have a background colour or image relevant to the topic of the blog. Choose a striking background that will catch readers' attention, without being too distracting.

Writing blogs for an audience

Creating expectations

Your target audience will view your blog with certain expectations. This is the case whether the audience is just you reading it back in a few weeks' time, or your lecturer grading it, or a special audience you have been asked to address, or the general public. Some of these expectations will be created by you through:

- the title you chose;
- where you hosted or publicised your blog;
- the template and design you selected;
- the first content that your audience sees, which will always be your most recent posting.

Reflection: Setting expectations

→ How does each of the above aspects apply to a blog that you have set up already, or that you intend to create?

→ Do these work effectively for your purposes?

Style and tone

For your intended audience and purposes, which tone or style of writing is most likely to encourage readers to keep reading and to return to your blog?

For each attribute below, indicate with an X where along the spectrum it is best to position your blog.

Informal .... Formal
Friendly .... Neutral
Subjective .... Objective
Emotional .... Detached
Opinionated .... Factual
Reflective .... Informative
Humorous .... Serious
Personal .... Academic

Brevity

- Keep posts short – aim for a maximum of 1000 words.
- Be concise: if you can use fewer words, then do so.

Signposting

- Use headers, bold, colour or other effects to signal new sections or themes in the posting.
- Highlight key words, themes or conclusions to maintain readers' attention.
- Link to other sites to help readers access information related to your post.

Adding multimedia content or links

Most tools will allow you to post images, videos and hyperlinks, which can make your blog more informative and interesting.

- Keep image file sizes reasonably small so that they will load quickly onto the page.
- Respect copyright permissions for images and other multimedia content.

Edit

Check for spelling, grammar and sense. Your readers are more likely to stay with your blog if it looks as if you have taken care with its presentation.

Keep your blog up to date

Update regularly, ideally at least once a week. Readers won't return if the information looks stale.

Sharing and publicising your blog

Choose your audience

The nature of a blog as an online diary or journal usually means that you want other people to read it. However, give careful consideration to exactly who might have access to what kinds of information. See 'Your online presence', pp. 11–13.

For academic assignments

Unless you are required to share your blog with peers, it is usually important that material that contributes to a graded assignment cannot be seen by others prior to it being assessed. If another student used your ideas or text, you might not be able to prove this. Blogs you create within your institution's VLE/LMS are likely to be private to you and your lecturer.

Use the privacy settings

Depending on the tool you are using, decide how to publish each blog post – be it private, restricted access or public.

Private

This means that the post (or the whole blog) can only be seen by you.

Restricted access

This means that you decide who will be able to read your post (or the whole blog). This level of control is normally available within academic learning environments and may have been preset by your lecturer(s).

Public

This means that anyone will be able to read your post (or whole blog). However, there may be control over who can post comments on your blog (see below).

Make sure you are aware of the privacy settings for your blog before you start posting entries.

Publicising your blog

Your blog will be competing with many others for a share of readers' online time. If you wish for a large public readership, the following actions can help.

Be audience aware
Use the guidance in 'Writing blogs for an audience' (p. 86).

Focus
If your blog has a theme, always check that this is evident in your most recent posting. As blogs usually publish posts in reverse chronological order, the reader may miss information provided in earlier posts.

Use tags or keywords
Include tags for each blog posting, as this helps users to find your blog when searching for a particular topic.

Be current
Add a new blog post every few days to maintain readers' interest in your thoughts. If a topic is live in the public arena, then update more frequently. Little and often maintains interest.

Design and links
A well-designed and attractive blog using multimedia and relevant links is likely to attract more readers.

Use social networks
You can use social networking tools such as Facebook or Twitter to link to your blog postings, attract a wider audience, and gain followers interested in the topic of your blog.

Become part of the community
You gain publicity for your blog if you comment on those of other people, providing a link from their blogs to your own. If you link your blog to others' blogs, their authors are likely to do the same in return, broadening your potential readership.

Comments in blogs

One key difference between blogs and traditional journals is the practice of opening up blogs for readers' comments. This enables online conversation with others about your thoughts and findings.

Select who can comment

When you set up your blog, configure the commenting tools to suit you. Normally, this facility would be open to anyone you have allowed as a reader. However, you may be able to require readers to log in to – or register on – your blog so you have a record of who posts comments.

Trackbacks and pings

Many blog tools have built-in features such as trackback or pings that alert bloggers when other authors have linked to their post or blog. This works as an acknowledgement, telling you that someone has referenced you in their writing.

Encourage readers to comment

In general, most readers don't post comments. If you wish them to do so, the following can help; it encourages others to comment if they can see that you engage actively with your readers.

- **Ask a question** Include a clear question in your blog posting so as to show that you welcome comments and to provide a focus for these.
- **Respond to comments** If readers do comment on your post, show appreciation by responding back.
- **Show interest** Ask relevant follow-up questions when people comment. Consider reading their blog and let them know if you do so.
- **Show respect** The nature of blogging encourages people to give opinions on topics they find emotive. Show respect even if those commenting hold strong opinions that differ from your own. Avoid responding in a defensive or angry manner as that may discourage further comments on your blog.
- **Don't require registering** You may wish to register readers, but be aware that this does discourage comments.
- **Consider using a comments policy** Some blog tools will have a policy for comments which you can use for your own blog. If not, you could set ground rules for how you want commenters to interact with your blog.

Generally, bloggers encourage comments but respond only to contructive, useful and well-phrased comments. Most bloggers will be happy for you to include a 'signature' in your comment, which links to your own blog, as long as it is relevant.

Comment on the blogs of others

For blogging, as for other aspects of behaviour, treat others with respect and consideration. People may spend a great deal of time and care on their blogs even if this isn't apparent to the reader. Aim to:

- give appreciation and thanks if you enjoy a posting;
- let them know what you found interesting;
- word comments carefully and respectfully;
- check whether comments could be misinterpreted;
- avoid firing off responses to opinions that annoy you;
- find constructive ways of wording disagreement.

Dealing with spam

Spam is an inevitable feature of blogging. Individuals or companies use the comments features of blogs to post links or content to encourage readers to visit their own sites. These are often completely irrelevant to the topic of your blog. Most blog tools have built-in spam filters to prevent automated commenting on your blog, but you may have to manually remove some spam comments from your blog.

Constructive commenting

Checklist for a comments policy

The following are things you might like to cover if you decide to include a comments policy:

- **Approach**: Request or encourage a constructive approach within comments.
- **Length:** Suggest a maximum length for comments.
- **Rules:** Provide rules or guidelines that you have on respect, privacy or the conduct of blog discussions.
- **Editing:** State whether you reserve the right to edit comments.
- **Abusive comments:** State what kinds of comments, if any, you would delete.
- **Links:** State whether comments can include links back to their poster's own blog.
- **Your use of comments:** Clarify whether you would use, in current or amended form, comments that appear on your blog.
- **Duration:** Clarify whether you will leave comments up indefinitely or delete them periodically.

Constructive comments and responses ...

- make the blogger feel that you have respected their blog;
- leave bloggers and posters of comments on the blog feeling respected;
- generate positive feelings and emotions;
- add something to the discussion or open up a new area for consideration;
- use any humour in a positive way;
- respect privacy and confidentiality;
- help the blogger to improve their blog;
- provide insights or suggestions which help the blogger or other posters to develop their ideas or postings, without pointing out negatives.

Destructive comments and responses

- give excessively negative messages;
- include abusive or unkind language;
- ignore the blogger's comments policy;
- leave bloggers or posters feeling disrespected, angry or uncomfortable;
- invade personal privacy and don't respect confidentiality;
- use humour in an unkind way.

☺ Activity: Constructive comments

Read through the following comments and decide whether each is constructive or destructive, and why. Compare your responses with those on p. 181.

1 Great tips on how to survive first day of teaching practice. Here's one of my own. Carry a bottle of water – in case you don't get time for a coffee break!

2 Loved your blog on volunteering in a local school. I am so inspired I am going to look into whether there are any schemes I could join at my college!

3 So, big deal! You missed out on the view on your field trip up Mount Snowdon! It isn't the end of world so why moan about it? And what did you expect, going in winter?

4 I have been following your blog so as to get updates on your research. I have to say I find your methodology a bit behind the times. I would have thought you would have been familiar with work by Jim Jones which shows you need to take an ethnographic approach to these issues.

5 I had the same experience in my exam! Nice to know I am not alone!

Creating blogs for academic assignments

Reasons blogs are set as assignments

The rationale for asking students to complete a blog for an assignment will vary greatly depending on your programme of study. Usually, your lecturers will explain their reasons in the programme materials. Check these so that you focus your blog appropriately. Some reasons are listed below.

✓ *See if any of these apply for blog assignments you have been set.*

- [ ] To encourage reflection
- [ ] To help students to form a learning community
- [ ] To help overcome student isolation
- [ ] To encourage students to think about a particular issue on a regular basis or over time
- [ ] To help develop writing skills
- [ ] To encourage students to work together on developing their understanding an issue

Grading criteria

Check whether your blog assignment is:

- optional;
- compulsory but not graded;
- compulsory and contributes to your grade.

Check carefully for how grades will be allocated. For example, you may receive a percentage of your grades for some or all of the following:

- for active engagement in writing the blog;
- for how far your blog meets the objectives set out for the assignment, such as how well it addresses a particular target audience;
- for particular kinds of content within the blog;
- for your comments on other people's blogs;
- for providing a critical commentary on how your thinking, understanding or a particular project developed through your use of the blog;
- for drawing on your blog entries to illustrate developments in your thinking;
- for presentation, style and tone.

Follow the guidelines

If your blog is for an assignment at university or college you may have been given very specific instructions about what to write and when. If so:

- Check these from the outset.
- Check them again from time to time to make sure you are still fulfilling the assessment criteria.

In particular, check whether any of the following apply:

- *Word limits*: are you required to write postings of a particular maximum or minimum length?
- *Frequency*: how often are you required to write in your blog?
- *Timing*: are you required to make blog postings at particular times?
- *Style and tone*: are you required to address any particular audience apart from your lecturer? If so, 'Writing blogs for an audience may help' (p. 86).

Edit for accuracy

Edit for grammar and spelling (the spell checker may be outside of your blog tool). You can normally go back and edit blog posts that you have already published if you notice a mistake.

Check it makes sense

Read it aloud – this is the best way of checking that it makes sense. When reading silently from the screen, it is easy to overlook omitted words, oddly phrased passages, or even where you forgot to paste a crucial part of a sentence.

Using blogs for academic reflection

Creating space for thought

Increasingly, students are being asked to maintain a blog for one or more of their assignments. One reason for this is that writing regularly on a theme provides opportunities for your mind to generate different perspectives. In the time between each posting, your brain may still be working away at an issue, and you may then find ideas forming more fully the next time you sit down to write.

Mulling it over

Writing is a relatively slow process, so when you write, the mind has time to let ideas develop.

For academic assignments

You may be required write a reflective blog as part of a research or work-based project. This is to encourage you to give thought to one or more aspects of how you:

- conceptualise the task or project;
- plan your work or project;
- apply your learning to new contexts, such as applying theory learnt in class to practical work or life settings;
- work with others, manage difficult or complex tasks, deal with challenges and take responsibility for the consequences of your own actions;
- evaluate what happened and draw lessons from the experience, so that you do things even better next time.

First stage reflection

The initial reflections that you make in a personal blog are likely to start in a rough and ready way, combined with emotions, observations and 'stream of consciousness' thoughts. Writing in an unedited way is helpful, as it allows your ideas to flow.

Second stage reflection

Before presenting your blog to others, it is useful to edit and rework your reflections so that they are fit for purpose. For a graded assignment, you may be asked to write a short piece that draws your thinking together.

- Edit out rambling and vague thoughts.
- Synthesise scattered ideas.
- Relate your ideas to relevant theory.
- Draw out what you have learnt.
- Identify clearly how you would approach the task, project or issue differently as a result of what you have now learnt.

Blogs to support project development

Student projects

At some point in your studies, it is likely that you will be asked to undertake a project. Typically, this will be a project that you are asked to design yourself, so that you get practice in managing a project from start to finish. You will need to show that you can:

- identify a project relevant to your studies, of a manageable size for the time scale and with reasonable levels of challenge;
- build on the body of knowledge already established within your subject discipline;
- collect, analyse, present and write up a set of data that you have generated;
- apply relevant theory;
- demonstrate that you can generate ideas and manage them to a successful conclusion.

Reflection prompts for each project phase

As you work through your project, the nature of your reflection will change. The following prompts can help structure your reflection at each stage.

Choosing a project

- Which previous studies inspire your own project? Why do these interest you?
- What do you want your project to achieve?
- How would you be able to build upon this topic for a larger project or dissertation later in your programme, or for higher levels of study?

Ethical issues

Typically, student projects will involve ethical considerations. Use your blog to consider these and to weigh the arguments on both sides.

Skill set

- How will you use your current skills and qualities to complete the project?
- What new skills are you likely to develop through undertaking this project?

Motivation

Academic or work projects can be complex and multi-layered, creating challenges and frustrations. Consider whether writing a personal blog would help you to:

- [ ] remain focused on your aims;
- [ ] identify and build on aspects that you enjoy;
- [ ] identify potential barriers and deal with these;
- [ ] pinpoint the exact nature of what you find difficult;
- [ ] think through the meaning of complex material;
- [ ] manage feelings, emotions and frustrations;
- [ ] weigh up pros and cons of potential solutions so as to tease out strategies that could work for you.

Background reading

- What impresses and interests you most in the background reading for this project?
- What lessons can you learn from previous studies?

Evaluating your project management

How well did you manage each stage of the project?

- Planning: setting time scales and milestones?
- Finding the right project design?
- Collecting and analysing data?
- Working with others?
- Keeping to deadlines?
- Writing your project report?

Evaluating the project as a whole

- Did your project achieve what you set out to do – meeting the lecturer's (or client's) brief?
- What went well?
- What could have worked better?
- Where could you take this idea next?

Blogs to support professional development

Increasingly, students see a degree as an important route towards a good job and career. Reflective journals or blogs are used in a number of ways to help support personal and professional development.

Tick boxes (a) or (b) in the sections below as appropriate.

(a) Blogs are used this way on my programme.
(b) It would be useful for me to use blogs in this way, even if I am not required to do so.

1 Planning towards a career

(a) ☐   (b) ☐

Within most programmes of study, there will be choices to make within the curriculum and supplementary to it, which may ultimately have an impact on:

- the careers open to you later;
- the knowledge and skills you bring with you into job interviews and future roles;
- the impression you will make on potential future employers, as someone with particular specialisms or a broad range of interests.

A reflective blog can help you to think through your potential options, teasing out the benefits of different choices.

2 'Reflective practitioner' approaches

(a) ☐   (b) ☐

Increasingly, professional and vocational areas varying from medicine and the caring professions to business or engineering, require staff to undertake ongoing professional development by engaging actively in critical reflection of their work – or an agreed aspect of it. Even if you are not already required to do this, regular structured reflection on your performance is likely to shine through in the quality of job applications that you make.

3 Evaluating your education and training

(a) ☐   (b) ☐

Reflect on how these contribute to improvements in how you approach your work and achieve planned objectives.

4 Reflective case studies

(a) ☐   (b) ☐

You can use a personal or shared blog to work through the issues related to an ongoing issue at work, study or extracurricular activity such as volunteering. Frequent reflection on a specific case study, issue or example can help to develop your understanding over time of how to manage a complex or difficult problem.

5 Identifying skills application

(a) ☐   (b) ☐

It is easy to work through a programme of study, even when skills have been carefully planned into the curriculum, without pausing to reflect how your skills profile would appear to a prospective employer. You could use a reflective blog to consider:

- which skills you have developed recently;
- whether these would be relevant in that form in other contexts, such as in particular kinds of work;
- how you would apply your current skills within new contexts;
- where there are gaps in your skills that you could address through taking particular study options or undertaking activity outside of the curriculum.

6 Tracking development

(a) ☐   (b) ☐

Over time, if we apply skills, reflect on them, and learn from our reflection, we can become more adept at managing increasingly complex and difficult problems and interactions. Reading back over previous blog entries can help you to track changes in your expertise over time. These observations can prove helpful both in writing job applications and in job interviews.

Checklist: creating blogs for academic study

Assignment brief

- [ ] All aspects of the assignment brief (if any) are met.
- [ ] The blog fulfils the purpose of the brief.
- [ ] The assignment deadline(s) are met.
- [ ] All sources are properly cited and referenced.

Audience awareness

- [ ] The blog is clearly designed for the intended audience.
- [ ] The tone and style of the blog take the target audience into consideration.
- [ ] The core themes of the blog are evident to the reader in each posting.
- [ ] Background explanations are provided when needed, to help the reader make sense of the content.
- [ ] Privacy settings match the intended audience.
- [ ] Proper care has been taken to ensure confidentiality.

Design and structure

- [ ] The colours and graphics used are fitting, given the purpose and focus of the blog and intended audience.
- [ ] The template used is fitting, given the purpose and focus of the blog and intended audience.
- [ ] The text is broken into sections that help the reader.
- [ ] Points made in each posting are grouped well and presented in a sensible order.
- [ ] Headers or other signposting helps the reader to find what they need easily.

Length and frequency

- [ ] Each posting is of a reasonable length for the intended audience (in line with any guidelines).
- [ ] The blog is of the right length for the assignment brief.

Content

- [ ] The content is focused on the blog theme(s).
- [ ] The content is pertinent to the discipline.
- [ ] For my subject, the blog has a suitable balance of personal opinion and academic content.
- [ ] The blog makes reference to theory (if relevant).
- [ ] The blog includes critical self-reflection.
- [ ] Where other sources are referred to, there is evidence of critical engagement with these.

Features

- [ ] Links useful to the reader are provided (if relevant).
- [ ] Multimedia are used where appropriate.

Style and editing

- [ ] The blog is written in a way that makes it easy and interesting for the target audience to read.
- [ ] Postings have been read aloud to check they make sense to the reader.
- [ ] Postings have been proofread for accuracy in spelling, grammar and typing.

If a reflective summary was required, this …

- [ ] is focused on the assignment brief;
- [ ] synthesises thinking from across your postings;
- [ ] links theory to your experience (if relevant);
- [ ] makes considered use of comments and feedback;
- [ ] draws out the lessons you have learnt ;
- [ ] uses clear cross references to postings (if required).

Other checks relevant to this blog

....

....

Case study: blog to support a student project

The project

Jasmine, a final-year chemistry student, was required to maintain a blog as part of her research project. Her project was spread out across the whole final year and she spent one or two days a week in the laboratory with her academic supervisor or his PhD research students. Jasmine's blog contributed 10% to the final grade for her research project and it was visible to all other students on the research project module (course), her project supervisor and his students and the course leader.

Jasmine's initial reluctance

Jasmine was initially sceptical about the value of the blog for her research project. Her academic supervisor required her to keep a detailed laboratory book to record her activities in the lab and she felt maintaining a blog would be like the lab book. She also didn't welcome the idea of her blog being seen by others in case they were critical of her ideas. However, as it was a compulsory activity she reluctantly began posting on the blog:

> "I spent the whole day in the lab today and didn't get any results … I'm worried about what I am going to write about in my dissertation if this continues …"

Support through the blog

When Jasmine next logged into the blog a few days later, she discovered that she had three comments on her initial post. Two were from fellow students on the module, reassuring her that she had plenty of time to collect data, and that they were also having some initial difficulties. The third post was from her academic supervisor who suggested that they meet up to discuss progress. Jasmine noted that she felt less alone with her anxiety about the project, as others knew what she was going through and her lecturer was there to advise and support. The supportive comments made her feel more positive about using the blog.

Developing her thinking about the project

Jasmine's next blog post was more considered and detailed. She included examples of experiments she was planning.

> "I had a productive chat with my academic supervisor's PhD student, Malik, today. We talked about my project and, as a result, I came up with three new ideas to test out over the coming weeks. I am going to summarise them here so I don't forget them. First, from talking to Malik, I realised that I would get stronger reactions if I worked with industrial-strength liquids rather than the ones I had been using from the lab. This led naturally to a second idea which was to trial the solution on a metal that had already been galvanised … I am not sure I quite grasp the third aspect, now that I come to write it down here …"

Jasmine noticed a few days later that the PhD student she had spoken to in the lab had commented on this blog posting, clarifying what he had meant about how to approach one of the experiments and this now made much more sense.

Extending use of the blog

Jasmine began to value her blog as a way of clarifying her thinking and receiving occasional feedback. She set aside at least 30 minutes per week to reflect on her experiences (both good and bad) in the lab, to share tips with other students about data analysis and to ask questions about writing up her dissertation. She found that the more interesting and reflective her blog posts were, the more comments she received.

Jasmine's final blog post contained an extract which really summed up her experience:

> "The blog made me feel that I was part of a whole community of people who were there to share the highs and lows. I have learnt a lot about my own abilities and skills by writing this blog and it was also really useful when I wrote my dissertation. I will be back when I do another project."

Case study: work placement blog

The placement

Doug was a healthcare student who opted to do his work placement project in a hospital in Germany. Doug was fluent in German, and was excited about the prospect of working in a large hospital for 6 months. Before leaving for the placement, he was told he had to maintain a blog for the duration of his placement to keep a record of his activities, professional development and skills training. His blog was to be monitored by his personal tutor/academic adviser, who would also use the tool to keep in contact and check on progress. However, Doug's college didn't have a blogging tool, so he was asked to set a blog up on a free site and inform the department of its whereabouts.

Setting up the blog

Doug was reasonably IT competent and was familiar with the structure of blogs, although he had never started one from scratch. He spent a few hours searching the Internet to find a good hosting service for blogs and set one up using a simple wizard. He posted a "Hello World" message to check it was working and then sent the URL to his personal tutor. Doug didn't log in to his blog again until he was settled in Germany.

Tagging the posts

After 2 weeks of his placement, Doug remembered that he was required to post on his blog. He had a bit of trouble remembering the username and password to log in to his account, but eventually managed to post an update on his placement. He tagged the posts in several ways, so that they would be automatically organised:

(1) general posts;
(2) training log;
(3) skills developed;
(4) work completed;
(5) fun stuff.

Professional development posts

At first, Doug couldn't really see the point of spending time writing his blog. He didn't get any comments on his posts and the tracking tools indicated that only one or two people had read them. However, he persevered as it was building up a complete record of his professional development activities and would be useful later when he had to update his curriculum vitae.

The impact of receiving posts

After about 2 months on his placement, Doug's personal tutor posted a comment on his blog.

> "Hi Doug, glad to see that you are making the most of the placement. You have gained really relevant experience in a short space of time – keep up the good work. I have been checking your blog every week or so and it sounds like you are enjoying your trip and gaining new skills. I spoke to your placement supervisor at the hospital last week and she is also really happy with your progress. Well done."

When Doug saw this comment, it gave him a strong sense of achievement. He continued to keep his blog up to date and started to write longer posts about his experiences of working and studying abroad.

Developing a following

Over the months, Doug built up a following of people who regularly commented on his posts – some were from the hospital where he was based and others were students in the UK who were due to embark on overseas placements in the next year. He felt a duty to make his blog as detailed and informative as possible to help other students. When Doug returned to the UK after his placement, he talked to his personal tutor about the experience of blogging.

> "I have been looking back through the posts recently. It was really interesting to see how my language and writing changed after I realised people were actually reading my blog. It went from a diary for myself to a story about my experiences written for others. Students from loads of other unis commented how useful it was to read about my trip before going on their placement."

Using other people's blogs for academic study

Blogs written by experts

Blogs are used by academics, critics and commentators in all subject disciplines. As a student, these can help you to learn about:

- newly published material;
- controversial findings and hot debates within the discipline;
- trends, gaps and concerns;
- future directions in the discipline.

You can also gain interesting perspectives on the broader academic community of which you are part. For example, you can see:

- who tends to have interesting things to say on new issues;
- the ways that academics analyse and think about each other's work – what they notice and the level of detail that they go into;
- how academic debate develops, from one comment or blog posting to another;
- who tends to be first with useful comment;
- which issues tend to generate what kind of comment;
- where your discipline is developing, which may help in planning for your own future career or research;
- references to materials that you might find useful for your current academic study.

☺ Activity: the best subject blog?

Browse the blogs written in your subject area.

→ Who writes the best blogs in your subject? What appeals to you about those blogs?

→ Which characteristics of these would you want to include in your own blog?

Blogs as a primary source of information

As there are now many blogs being written, these offer us a large and increasing amount of information about how individuals think and live. Potentially, blogs are primary source materials that could provide rich insights into areas such as:

- which issues captured the public imagination at a given time;
- the kinds of information that were circulating in the public domain at a given time;
- how ideas developed on an issue over a particular time frame;
- minority interests that do not make it into mainstream publications;
- how public opinion is influenced.

Source material on trends

Data collated across many blogs could generate factual information for a student project, as long as reliable and acceptable metrics were used to classify the data. These might indicate, for example, trends in levels of interest in issues such as global warming, or how well advertising in blogs correlates with sales patterns.

Referencing blogs in academic work

You may wish to acknowledge a blog as the source of an idea, opinion, or perspective that you draw upon in your academic work. In that case, cite the blog as your source within your work. At the end of your work, write the reference in full, just as for any source material.

Reference sequence	Citation
Author surname Author initials Title of blog posting Date blog entry written Title of blog Date blog post accessed Available at: URL.	*Social proof, or informational social influence, is used to great effect by many online companies to improve their customer base and sales (Lee, 2011).*

Reference

Lee, A. Social proof is the new marketing. 27/11/11. Techcrunch.com. Accessed 28/11/11. Available at: http://techcrunch.com/2011/11/27/social-proof-why-people-like-to-follow-the-crowd/

Applying critical thinking to blogs

Critical evaluation of perspectives

Blogs are sources of personal opinion. They can be useful in providing different perspectives on an issue, which, in turn, can develop your thinking as a student.

However, for academic work, it isn't sufficient simply to outline all perspectives as if each is automatically of equal validity. It is expected that you will analyse each perspective from a number of angles, in order to see which has most merit.

Which perspective is best?

It isn't always easy to determine whose point of view should carry the most weight. It is likely that in any source, there are gaps, omissions, things not yet known, some compelling arguments and some that are hard to verify completely.

Critical questioning when using blogs

About expertise

1 What do I know about the blogger? What are their credentials as an expert in the subject?
2 What sources of information does the blogger use? Are these produced by subject experts?

About intention and influences

1 What do I know about the political, commercial or other interests of the blogger that might influence what they are writing?
2 Why is this blog being written?
3 Why is it being written in this way?
4 Who is the expected readership? How might the choice of target audience be influencing the blogger's choice of contents and approach?
5 Is the blog being sponsored? Could that be influencing the contents or direction of the argument?

About the evidence

1 Does the blogger provide good evidence to support the points that they make?
2 Do they make clear references to their sources?
3 Can you track back to their source materials?

Check the source of information

A blogger can simply write a post and click 'Publish' for it to appear on the Internet. Blogs may be interesting and entertaining, even informative, but they are not reviewed by a subject expert in the way that books or journal articles are scrutinised before publication.

That means that if you wish to use, in your academic work, factual information that you came across in a blog, you need first to verify it by going back to the source. An expert writing a good quality blog is likely to provide a reference or link to the source material.

- Check the source to see that it is good quality in its own right – such as a journal article, research paper or an academic textbook.
- Consider whether there is any reason why the source might weight its findings in any direction – such as for political or commercial reasons.
- If the source looks reputable, read it for yourself, checking the information carefully.
- Make sure that, when read in context, the information still means what you had originally understood; it is possible that it was misrepresented in the blog for some reason.

☺ Activity: Broadening your critical perspective

Browse for blogs on an issue relevant to your study.

→ Select three that approach the issue in different ways.

→ Jot down your thoughts on how these different approaches influence your own thinking.

If your thinking is not changed at all, is this:

→ Because you hold too rigidly to your own ideas?

→ Because you can identify clear flaws in the argument and evidence of the alternative viewpoints. If so, what are these?

Thinking critically for academic blogs

When writing a blog for academic purposes, bring a critical eye to the material just as you would for any other academic activity. If your blog forms part of an assignment, the following questions can help to structure your critical analysis of it before you hand it in.

Fitness for purpose

The brief: Does my blog match the assignment brief in all respects?
Focus: Is it focused on its declared theme(s)? Have I remained on topic? Could I remove tangential material?
Balance: Does its content maintain the right balance for my subject between my personal opinion and consideration of evidence from reputable sources?

Is it right for the intended audience?

Your assignment brief may specify an audience for the blog, such as work colleagues, a segment of a market for a product or a performance you are planning, members of the public with a particular health concern, or students in the year below. If not, the assumed audience may be your lecturer and the external examiner.

Writing for an audience helps to develop critical alertness to the messages that you convey. Your lecturers will be looking to see how well your blog takes your intended audience(s) into account. Consider:

- Does the style and tone of my blog suit the intended audience(s)?
- Will the content make sense to them?
- Have I provided sufficient background information so they can understand the issues?
- Can they tell how and why my thinking changes from one posting to another?
- Is it obvious why I believe this / did this / plan to do this / said this / feel this?
- Would everyone agree with me on this? Have I covered alternative perspectives fairly?
- Have I taken on board fully any critiques that have been raised in audience comments?

Academic rigour

- Is it clear that I have researched and given thought to other people's views and findings?
- Does my blog demonstrate that I have read reputable sources on the subject?
- Do I demonstrate a critical approach to my sources rather than taking them at face value?
- Have I written out all references in full according to the system required for my programme?
- Are the points that I make well substantiated by evidence or supported by my reading?

Clarity and presentation

- Is my writing clear, coherent and unambiguous?
- Do my headings provide the right structure?
- Does it all make sense when read aloud?
- Are there any rambling or over-lengthy sections that I could edit down or rewrite so that my points stand out more clearly?
- Is this free of spelling and other errors?

Confidentiality

- Unless I have explicit written permission to use this in my blog, have I removed all information about other people that might identify them?
- Have I removed all information that is, or might be considered to be, confidential?

Summary

Using blogs for academic purposes

It is likely that you will be asked to use blogs at some point during your studies. These can bring a great deal of enjoyment and provide you with many new perspectives that stretch your mind. However, make sure that you use blogs in the specific ways required for your assignments. In most instances, that will be different from using blogs in your personal life.

Using other people's blogs for study

Select wisely

As anyone can produce a blog without scrutiny of their expertise, select wisely from experts in the field when using blogs for academic purposes.

Apply critical analysis

If using material from a blog for an academic assignment, take a constructively critical approach to it, evaluating the perspective taken, the direction of the argument, the supporting evidence and source materials much as you would for any other source.

Engage with other people's blogs

If a blog interests you, let the blogger know. Post comments in a constructive way, honouring the comment policy if there is one. You may find that you develop a good dialogue between yourself, the blogger and other posters, as part of a blogging community.

Creating your own blog for study

Follow the brief

Take care to design your blog in line with the assignment brief, taking particular note of the marking criteria and the intended audience(s).

Bring academic rigour

Unless you have been asked to design a blog aimed at a particular public readership or client, or to use 'stream of consciousness' writing, then take an academic approach. Show that you have read around the subject and are aware of relevant research and theory, and have thought about the strengths and potential gaps or flaws in these. Reference all sources fully and correctly.

Apply critical analysis

Take a critical approach to your own writing, just as you should for sources or blogs upon which you draw. Stand back from your own writing and critique your argument. Check carefully that the points you make are well supported by evidence or your reading.

Write clearly

Keep your audience in mind at all times and check that whatever you write is clear and unambiguous. For blogs, you can use headings to help develop and structure your thoughts in a coherent way. Read your blog aloud before submitting it to check that it makes sense. Edit any unnecessary anecdotes and wordy sections that might obscure your point. Check for spelling and errors that could distract your reader.

Ensure confidentiality

Check that you remove all references that could help identify third parties, unless they have given you written permission for that information to be used.

Chapter 6

Wikis

Learning outcomes

This chapter offers you opportunities to:

- familiarise yourself with wikis and how they work;
- find out about the principles that underpin the writing and editing of wikis;
- understand when and how it is appropriate to use wikis as a source of information for academic study;
- understand how to create your own wiki pages;
- learn how to write wikis collaboratively with other students for group projects.

Introduction

Wikis are web pages that anyone can edit. They can provide a helpful addition to your toolkit as a student. Many lecturers now actively encourage their use, provided they are employed in combination with other resources and used in ways appropriate to higher education. In particular, students are being asked to contribute to the writing and editing of wikis, and opportunities to do so are, increasingly, being built into programmes of study.

Collaborative writing is an increasingly important aspect of working life and as part of funded research projects. For these reasons, collaborative writing activities such as those required for wikis are also becoming more popular as part of the undergraduate curriculum. These may be assessed as one of a number of graduate writing skills that support employability.

This chapter looks at how you can make use of wikis to support different aspects of your learning. It helps you to:

- understand the basics of navigating a wiki;
- recognise the benefits and limitations of wikis as a source of information for academic assignments;

- understand when and how to use Wikipedia as a means of identifying sources for your studies – while recognising the drawbacks and hazards of over-reliance on it for academic work;
- edit a wiki if required to do this as part of an assignment;
- work with other students on creating your own wiki pages or writing a wiki as part of a group assignment.

Wikis work to a given set of principles. Through this chapter, you can learn about these so that you gain a better understanding of why and how wikis are edited in the way they are. Applying these principles yourself can also assist you in your academic writing in general and, in particular, for online collaborative writing projects.

Wiki 'health warning'

Some uses of wikis, especially the improper use of Wikipedia as a source of information for assignments, are widely frowned upon in higher education. While creative use of wikis can greatly enhance your study, the poor use of wiki-based sources is one key reason why students lose points for assignments.

What is a wiki?

The word 'wiki'

Wiki is a Hawaiian word for 'fast' or 'quick'. The first wiki, launched in 1995, was named WikiWikiWeb and the term wiki-wiki was chosen as an alliterative substitute for the word quick.

- Wiki page – an individual web page that can be edited by multiple users.
- A wiki – a collection of interlinked wiki pages.

What is a wiki?

A wiki is a website to which many people can make contributions, adding new material and editing the material already there. In other words, it is a group collaboration in creating knowledge. The key features of wikis are that:

- they consist of a series of wiki pages which can be edited by a number of users;
- users can create new wiki pages within a wiki;
- hyperlinks are used to link wiki pages on the basis of associated topics;
- they are regarded as always being 'a work in progress' – wikis can be updated and edited continually.

What do wikis look like?

At first glance, wikis look much like any other web page, with text, hyperlinks and images. Wiki pages usually have tabs at the top of the page which allow you to:

- sign in or register;
- 'view history';
- see 'page discussion'.

Types of wikis

Wikis are versatile and used in many contexts.

- Public wikis such as Wikipedia are available to all users on the Internet.
- Student or lecturer wikis can be found within virtual learning environments, where they can be public or private to a defined group of users such as students on the same programme.
- Corporate wikis, which may take the form of intranets, are knowledge management systems or documentation systems for businesses and other organisations.

The best-known wikis

Wikimedia commons

Wikimedia commons, or simply 'commons', is a repository for media file images, sounds and video. Its materials are free. It allows content to be used as it stands or in altered form, as long as appropriate credit is given.

Wiktionary

Wiktionary is a free online dictionary and thesaurus of over 2.5 million entries. It can be edited by the public but there are strict guidelines on layout and content.

Wikipedia

Currently, the best-known wiki is Wikipedia, launched in 2001. This is hosted by the Wikimedia Foundation, a non-profit-making organisation. More details are provided below.

Wikiversity

Wikiversity contains a wide range of learning resources for use by schools and universities. These are open source and promote and support collaborative learning by students, researchers and teachers, across all kinds of learning communities.

> **Activity: Explore Wikiversity**
>
> → Go to www.wikiversity.org/.
> → Select your preferred language.
> → Select the guided tour.
> → After you complete the tour, select "resources by level" and go to Portal: Tertiary education.
> → Use its guide to select topics that interest you.

Wikipedia: the five principles or 'pillars'

Wikipedia is an online, free resource available in over 280 languages. It can be edited by any user. At the time of writing, the English version hosted over 3.5 million pages and this continues to rise daily.

The five pillars of Wikipedia

Wikipedia has five important principles that guide its development and use:

1 It is an encyclopaedia.
2 It has a neutral point of view.
3 It is free content.
4 Wikipedians should interact in a respectful and civil manner.
5 Wikipedia has no firm rules.

1 Wikipedia is an encyclopaedia

As an online encyclopaedia, Wikipedia is a reference source that provides information on many branches of knowledge. The main difference between Wikipedia and a traditional encyclopaedia such as the *Encyclopaedia Britannica* is that Wikipedia changes constantly as it is updated frequently by numerous users. This has implications for academic study:

- As such a vast store of information, Wikipedia is a useful starting place for finding at least basic information on almost any subject.
- Updates may be made by experts, but they may be made by anyone with a superficial knowledge of the subject too.
- You can add to it yourself.

2 Wikipedia has a neutral point of view

Encyclopaedias are a source of information and knowledge. As such, they must provide a balanced, verifiable and impartial coverage of topics, and avoid showing preference for one point of view over another.

The editors of Wikipedia take care to ensure that contributions to wiki pages:

- present the different points of view fairly;
- avoid engaging with the debates;
- provide appropriate reference.

Normally, any changes to a wiki page which offer opinion or do not provide a balanced view are removed promptly.

For more about what is meant by 'neutral point of view' see http://en.wikinews.org/wiki/Wikinews:Neutral_point_of_view

3 Wikipedia is free content

All Internet users can access and read any Wikipedia page for free. Any Internet user who registers can edit wiki pages, also without charge. Wikipedia content is publically licensed, which means that it can be reused, adapted and distributed by anyone who uses it.

4 Wikipedians should interact in a respectful and civil manner

A 'Wikipedian' is anyone who creates and edits the wiki pages on Wikipedia. The site expects all users to behave appropriately when making changes to wiki pages or creating new content. Most users respect this and it is rare to find wiki pages with inappropriate content. If this is abused, Wikipedia editors can opt to step in to prevent edits to a page. They may choose to do so if the language or content is inappropriate or does not maintain neutrality.

5 Wikipedia has no firm rules

Wikipedia expects that its rules will evolve and be modified over time, just as its content also evolves. Users are encouraged to be innovative and bold when writing and editing articles on Wikipedia. There are not rigid rules for users to follow although there are guidelines to help and support users to maintain the principles of Wikipedia and produce useful pages.

Searching on Wikipedia

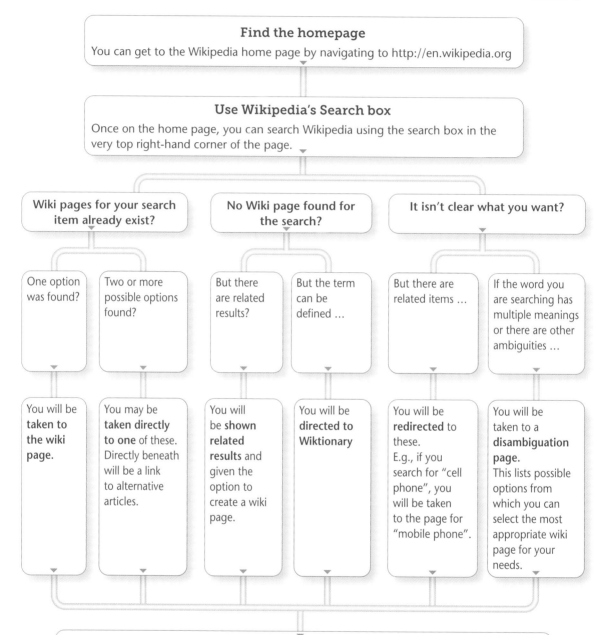

Find the homepage

You can get to the Wikipedia home page by navigating to http://en.wikipedia.org

Use Wikipedia's Search box

Once on the home page, you can search Wikipedia using the search box in the very top right-hand corner of the page.

Wiki pages for your search item already exist?	No Wiki page found for the search?	It isn't clear what you want?

Wiki pages for your search item already exist?

One option was found?

Two or more possible options found?

You will be **taken to the wiki page.**

You may be **taken directly to one** of these. Directly beneath will be a link to alternative articles.

No Wiki page found for the search?

But there are related results?

But the term can be defined ...

You will be **shown related results** and given the option to create a wiki page.

You will be **directed to Wiktionary**

It isn't clear what you want?

But there are related items ...

If the word you are searching has multiple meanings or there are other ambiguities ...

You will be **redirected to** these. E.g., if you search for "cell phone", you will be taken to the page for "mobile phone".

You will be taken to a **disambiguation page.** This lists possible options from which you can select the most appropriate wiki page for your needs.

Follow up the citation – so you can read and reference the original source

- Use the references provided on the Wikipedia article to find the original sources.
- Call these up and read them yourself.
- If the material is relevant to your assignment, draw this from the original source, cite that in your work, and provide a reference to that source in your list of references. Avoid using Wikipedia as your source of information.

Understanding the Wikipedia layout

All Wikipedia's pages have a similar layout, which makes it easy to identify and navigate. In the top left-hand corner of the page is the Wikipedia branding and beneath this are links to the home page, contents, featured content and help. The article is within the main body of the page.

Article | Talk | **1** | Read | Edit | View hIstory | Search 🔍

Brain **2**

This article is about ▬▬▬▬▬▬▬▬▬▬▬▬▬▬

▬▬▬▬▬▬▬▬▬▬ **3**

Contents
1 Anatomy **4**
1.1 ▬▬▬▬▬
1.2 ▬▬▬▬
1.3 ▬▬▬▬

Anatomy

▬▬▬▬▬▬▬▬▬▬▬▬▬ **5**

See also **6**

References **7**
1 ▬▬▬▬▬▬▬
2 ▬▬▬▬▬

External links **8**

Rate this page **9**

Categories: Brain | Organs **10**

This page was last modified (date) (time)

1 Top bar Along the top of the article are tabs, which enable you to view the 'article' and 'article discussion'. You can also choose to 'read', 'edit' or 'view history' of an article. The default tabs visible are 'article' and 'read'.

2 Title The title of the wiki article (or other type of wiki page) is clearly shown in large font.

3 Introduction Most wiki articles begin with an introduction, which may be a few paragraphs long.

4 Contents Most wiki articles have a contents box which consists of a list of hyperlinks to sections in the article.

5 Main body The main body contains the contents of the article and may have a number of sub-sections, indicated by sub-headings. Contents may include text, hyperlinks to other wiki pages, citations, images, diagrams and tables.

6 See also At the end of the article there may be a list of hyperlinks to topics related to the wiki article.

Notes Some wiki articles have a section of notes, which provide hyperlinks or supplementary information.

7 References Most wiki articles have a list of references to scholarly articles. References will be linked to citations in the main body of the text.

8 External links Some wiki articles include hyperlinks to web pages outside Wikipedia, for further information.

9 Rate this page You can use this to check how other people rate the page.

10 Categories At the bottom of wiki articles is a box showing the categories of knowledge that the article relates to. You can use this to cross search or understand the context of the article you are viewing.

Finding good quality material on Wikipedia

How do I find good articles in Wikipedia?

Wikipedia uses a rating system to help users to identify high quality articles. Although this is not undertaken from the perspective of academic study, the categories system can help you to:

- identify the items most likely to be reliable;
- eliminate items as not appropriate for your assignments.

Wikipedia category system

Good quality articles are categorised as follows by Wikipedia's editors.

Featured article

These are Wikipedia's best articles and are recognisable by a small bronze star in the top right-hand corner. These articles are complete, accurate, neutral and stylish. There are over 3000 featured articles on Wikipedia.

Good article

These are articles which have been judged as well written, factually accurate, verifiable, broad and neutral. Good articles are indicated by a green cross in the top right-hand corner. There are over 12,000 good articles on Wikipedia.

Rated categories

There are other categories of article on Wikipedia, including A-rated and B-rated articles, but these are not used universally.

Stubs

'Stubs' are articles that are not a complete description of a topic and are indicated as such on Wikipedia.

Tips for identifying good Wikipedia articles

- Look for 'featured article' or 'good article' symbols on articles, as described above.
- Look for Wikipedia warnings (cleanup tags) about the quality of the article.
- Look at the number and quality of citations and references accompanying articles. If these come from reputable sources such as academic journals or government papers, then these are likely to be useful for academic study.
- Look at the page ratings for an article.
- Look at the style of the article, for example the use of sub-headings, images and table of contents.
- Look at the discussion tab for evidence of disagreement between editors about the contents of an article.

The risks of using Wikipedia

1. Wikipedia is largely written by amateurs.
2. Its articles are not necessarily reviewed by experts in the subject.
3. It can be edited by anyone with a username – even you.
4. Its articles evolve until a consensus is reached amongst contributors. This means that, at best, it is only as good as the level of expertise of those contributing to date; the consensus may not be the position that the academic community would take on the subject.
5. It refers mainly to other sources, which means that the information is second hand. As with any second-hand information, this increases the risk of errors arising through misinterpretation, miscopying, or applying information incorrectly to a different context.

While these issues may seem quite serious and off-putting, Wikipedia does work well as a community of regulated encyclopaedias. This is due to the efforts and diligence of a large number of volunteer editors working continually to improve the quality of the articles.

Using Wikipedia as a source of information

It is perfectly acceptable to use Wikipedia as part of your toolkit for sourcing information, as long as this is done in a manner appropriate to study in higher education. You may find that academic staff do not accept direct references to Wikipedia. There are a number of reasons for this, the most common being the following.

Training in the discipline

Your lecturers are training you to develop skills appropriate to research and use of knowledge within your subject discipline. Encyclopaedias refer to information gathered from elsewhere – they are not primary research in their own right. That means that they are not generally used by academic researchers except as occasional background reference.

As Wikipedia is an encyclopaedia, it would not be expected that you would use it as your main source of information – any more than you would any other encyclopaedia.

Over-reliance on a single source

Some students tend to use almost nothing but Wikipedia as their source of information rather than demonstrating that they can search for, evaluate and select information for themselves.

Accuracy and scope

The risks identified with using Wikipedia for higher education are referred to on p. 106. There are concerns about the scope and accuracy of Wikipedia articles for use at this level, as the five items on p. 108 below illustrate.

☺ Activity: Using Wikipedia as a source

Read through the summaries of research articles about Wikipedia (p. 108) and then consider the following questions:

→ What would be your own concerns in using Wikipedia after reading these articles?

→ Are there other articles that you can find online that provide a different perspective for Wikipedia articles in your own subject discipline?

Wikipedia – and referencing

As an encyclopaedia, Wikipedia does not contain original research. As such, it is a useful source for:

- background information;
- helping you to locate useful sources of information that you can then follow up for yourself.

This means that, as a student, your prime use of Wikipedia articles should be to lead you back to the original research or original source of information.

Referencing material after using Wikipedia

As you should be using Wikipedia only to take you back to the original source, it follows that:

- in your assignments, you should not normally make any references to Wikipedia itself;
- you should have followed up the relevant reference in the Wikipedia article, reading the original source for yourself;
- you should provide a citation within your work to the original source and provide the full reference for that in your list of references at the end of your work.

The accuracy of Wikipedia for student work

Accuracy of Wikipedia 1: *Nature*

A study by the internationally recognised scientific journal *Nature* found that articles in Wikipedia 'come close to [Encyclopaedia] *Britannica* in terms of the accuracy of its science entries' (*Nature* 438, 900–901, 2005). This view was later contested by *Britannica*. Importantly, both sources were found to contain minor errors, emphasising the importance of double checking factual information.

Accuracy of Wikipedia 2: *First Monday*

A small study in the online journal *First Monday* written by Chesney (2006) from the Nottingham University Business School used responses from a moderate sample of 55 research staff to comment on the accuracy of Wikipedia. The results suggested that experts generally found Wikipedia articles to be accurate and credible, although errors were found in 13% of articles.

Accuracy of Wikipedia 3: *Annals of Pharmacology*

An article by Clauson et al. (2008) in the *Annals of Pharmacotherapy* compared information in Wikipedia with that in a traditionally edited database, looking at information on eight categories of drug from the perspectives of scope, completeness and accuracy. Clauson found that Wikipedia answered only 40% of questions on drug information compared to 82.5% on the Medscape Drug Reference database. Answers in Wikipedia were 76% complete compared to 95.5% complete on Medscape. However, no factual errors were found in Wikipedia, whereas there were some in Medscape. Clauson did note that answers improved on Wikipedia over time, as entries were updated. Clauson concluded that 'Wikipedia may be a useful point of engagement for consumers, but is not authoritative and should only be a supplemental source of drug information.'

Accuracy of Wikipedia 4: *historical articles*

Rector (2008) compared nine Wikipedia articles with those in other sources such as the *Dictionary of American History* and *American National Biography Online*. She found inaccuracies in eight of the entries, two of which were considered to be 'major flaws'. Overall, Wikipedia was found to be only 80% accurate compared to 95% for the other sources.

Accuracy of Wikipedia 5: *age of an edit?*

There have been a number of suggestions of ways that users could identify the quality of a Wikipedia article by using other measurements besides peer review. One method proposed was using the survival time of each edit of an article. It was assumed that older segments would have been edited more and therefore would be more accurate.

Luyt et al. (2007) investigated this proposal but did not find this to be the case. They found there were a high proportion of errors in the first edits and that these tended to remain. They concluded that the survival rate of edits of earlier segments of an article are not a good indicator of accuracy.

Student assignment: edit a live wiki page

Teaching staff may set students assignments to create or edit wiki pages on Wikipedia. A typical assignment, and how you might tackle it, is outlined below.

🏃 Case study: Assignment to edit a live wiki

Students were allocated to groups of four, each of which was assigned an existing Wikipedia article to edit. All these articles had been judged by the lecturer as being incomplete, lacking breadth, style and/or neutrality.

Students were given basic instruction on how to edit wiki pages and advised to view 'featured articles' on Wikipedia to gain a sense of how their articles could be improved.

How to approach a project like this

1 Read the article

The first step is to establish the accuracy and breadth of the existing article. Begin by reading the article so you know what it says.

2 Investigate the topic

Conduct your own research into the topic by making an extensive literature search using a reference database. Make notes of the topics to be included and collect references of original sources to support your article.

3 Compare your findings

Once you have completed this independent review, compare your findings to those in the existing Wikipedia article.

4 Familiarise yourself with the article

Some Wikipedia articles have many active contributors (Wikipedians) who have invested their time in improving the article. Before you begin to edit it, look at previous edits to the article and read the talk notes. This process will give you an idea of the article's evolution, philosophy and ethos, as well as an insight into the personalities and background of some of the article's main editors. This will help you if you contact them about major edits.

Divide your proposed edits into 'minor' and 'major' changes

Minor edit changes to articles might include:

- inclusion of additional references;
- inclusion of additional, relevant facts;
- minor editorial changes to sentence structure;
- typographical and/or grammatical changes.

Examples of major changes to articles might include:

- large changes to text with alterations of facts;
- additional images, tables or diagrams;
- additional subsections to extend its breadth.

5(a) Make minor edits

When you have prepared a list of minor edits, you can begin to edit the wiki article. First, log in and preview changes. Tag your alterations as minor. Provide notes to accompany them if necessary.

5(b) Making major edits

It is advisable to discuss any major edits on the Talk page for the article. Post a section describing your proposed changes and your reasons and evidence for these. Existing editors of the article will probably comment on your proposals and may help you to improve your ideas. Once you have reached a consensus with the article's existing editors, make the changes on the live article.

6 Invite comment

After you have completed all of your changes to the article, invite comments from the community of editors. You could also submit the article for peer review for consideration as a 'good' or 'featured' article.

Editing the content of a live wiki page

1 Read

- Read the article assigned to you.
- Make sure you know what it says.
- Check the dates of the last edit to see how current (up to date) the article is.
- Look at its references and note the dates of these and where they come from.
- Jot down any initial observations on the strengths and weaknesses of the article.
- Gain a feel for how it might be improved.

2 Investigate

- Find out as much as you can about the topic from sources other than Wikipedia.
- Use a reference database to find out what has already been written on the topic.
- Read several of the most reputable of these.
- Make notes about the key information that you consider the article should include – checking whether these are already fully and accurately covered in the article you were assigned.
- Collect references of original sources to support your article.

3 Compare

Make a systematic comparison of your research with the contents, accuracy and perspectives taken by the article you were assigned. Identify a few areas where you could make a valid contribution to improving the article.

4 Familiarise

Read through existing edits and notes to gain a feel for the article and how it is evolving, and what interests other readers.
- Decide how far you will take those edits into account.
- Identify any inaccuracies in the previous edits.

6 Invite comment

- Once you have made your changes to the article, invite comments from the community of editors.
- Submit the article for rating as a 'good' or 'featured' article.

5(b) Major edits

Decide on a focus for your edit.

- On the Talk page, post a section describing your proposed changes, and your reasons.
- Consider seriously the comments that you receive to see whether they help you to improve your ideas.
- Once you have taken on board the comments and, preferably, reached a consensus with the article's existing editors, make the changes on the live article.

5(a) Minor edits

Make a list of your minor edits.
- Log in.
- Preview changes.
- Tag your alterations as minor.
- Provide notes to accompany them if necessary.

How to edit a wiki page

Create a username

It is possible to edit Wikipedia without creating a user profile on the site. However, you gain more functionality if you register as a user, and it is free to do so.

Practise as an editor

Wikipedia recommends new users to use the following features that it provides for free:

- online tutorials on editing the content;
- 'sandboxes' and user pages to practise on before editing live pages.

Editing a wiki page

Click on the Edit tab at the top right of the page that you wish to edit. The title of the page will change to '*Editing* [page title]'. The text will be visible in a text editor and will look very different from the formatted text on the *Read* page. To add text, just type it in at the appropriate place in the text editor.

Table of contents

Wikipedia will automatically add a 'Table of contents' box to your article when it has at least four headings.

Line breaks

If you add a single line break in the text editor, this does not create a line break into the layout. Instead, either insert an empty line to start a new paragraph or break a line by adding <br/> at the appropriate point in the text.

Adding references

All content on Wikipedia should be verifiable, otherwise it is likely to be removed by an editor. Citations should be provided in the text including a reference which will appear in the reference section at the end of the article. To include a citation and reference on a wiki page, you use the <ref> tag. For more information, see the 'Citing Sources' page on Wikipedia.

Special characters

The following special characters are used frequently to format text on wiki pages and most are contained within toolbars above the text box:

- Italic text: ''____''
- Bold text: '''____'''
- Bold and italic text: '''''____'''''
- Link to another Wikipedia page: [[name of page]]
- External links: [website URL]
- Section headings: ==Section heading==
- For lower-level sub-headings, just add an extra = on each side).
- Bulleted list: use an asterisk (*)
- Numbered list: use a #

For more complex characters, see the Wiki mark-up Help page on Wikipedia.

Adding images

To use images, first upload the image to Wikipedia and assign the appropriate copyright permissions. Once, uploaded, you can insert an image on a wiki page using the following command:[[File:filename.fileextension]].

To add a caption, include the caption in the command: [[File:filename.fileextension|imagecaption]].

For further advice see the 'Picture tutorial' wiki page on Wikipedia.

Saving your edits

Click the 'Show preview' box to see your edits before saving them. Categorise your edits into minor or major changes. Add notes to accompany changes made. These notes will appear on the page history tab.

Creating a wiki page or article

You may be asked, for a student assignment, to write a Wikipedia article.

Step 1: Decide on your article content

The first step is to check that the item you select to write about would be appropriate for inclusion in Wikipedia: as it is an encyclopaedia, only some topics will be relevant. Bear in mind that encyclopaedic articles must be suitably notable, or broadly relevant and important to a general audience. They will need to be factually based rather than written with the critical analysis and argument typical of essay-based assignments.

Step 2: Check your article doesn't already exist

Once you have decided on a subject, search Wikipedia to see whether it contains such an article already. Search using a range of terms in case a similar article is written under a different title. If it does, consider whether you could make a major edit that would update or broaden the content in such a way that would meet the assignment criteria.

Step 3: Choose a good title

Choose a title for your article. A good title:

- will enable people to find it easily;
- clearly fits the subject of the article;
- uses terminology everyone understands;
- is precise;
- is brief and concise;
- is easy to remember.

Follow Wikipedia's own conventions for creating new titles. For example, articles about people, places or things should use everyday names and not specialist, formal or scientific versions. For more information, see the 'Naming conventions' page on Wikipedia.

Step 4: Gather references to sources

All content in encyclopaedia articles in Wikipedia must be verifiable through references to reliable sources. This means that you must include a reference to a trustworthy and scholarly source for every statement of fact that you include.

Generally, the following are reliable sources of information for inclusion as references in Wikipedia:

- books published by major publishing houses;
- peer-reviewed scholarly journals;
- reputable newspapers and magazines;
- government and public papers.

References are only needed for anything that might be considered to be open to 'challenge' or 'likely to be challenged'. For example, you don't need to provide a reference for a statement such as 'London is the capital city of England' as that is an indisputable and easily verified fact. This statement is attributable and could be confirmed by many reliable sources.

Step 5: Write in a neutral tone

Wikipedia articles must only include factual information. This must be presented in a neutral way, in line with the five principles of Wikipedia outlined above (p. 103). This means being even-handed in presenting any differing perspectives and avoiding writing from any given point of view of your own.

Step 6: Write in your own words

In Wikipedia, as for coursework, you must not present anyone else's work without acknowledgement. You can paraphrase your sources or use quotations in Wikipedia as long as you cite the source of these immediately following their use. You must also provide a full reference to the source.

Step 7: Create – then move to 'live' space

As a registered user you have a user space where you can create articles, make changes, seek opinions and finalise material. Once complete, you can move the article to the 'live' Wikipedia site. For more detailed advice, see the 'Your first article' page on Wikipedia.

Collaborative writing assignments using wikis

Another type of wiki-based assignment that you may be set as a student is to produce a collaborative report using a wiki in the institution's VLE/LMS.

Case study: Collaborative writing assignment

Students were assigned to groups of four to write a wiki article within their VLE. They were given a specific title for their encyclopaedia article and were told to produce a wiki article similar in quality, breadth, length and style to any 'featured article' in Wikipedia. Assignments were assessed according to:

- the quality of the final article overall; and
- individual students' contributions, edits and discussion of the article on the Talk page.

The group's experience of wikis

The students were second-year engineering students; they had all used Wikipedia as a source of information but only one of them, Simon, had a user account for Wikipedia. He had made occasional edits to existing wiki pages. The others, Anisha, Lola and Rory, did not know how to edit or construct a wiki page.

Getting started on the project

The group met in the library to discuss how to approach the project. They worked around a single PC to look at a number of 'featured articles' in Wikipedia.

They discussed the format, style and structure of the articles they liked best and those that didn't appeal. They made notes of features that they wanted their own wiki page to contain.

Rory was quite daunted by the project at first:

> "When we were sat looking at the example wikis, they looked so professional and well written that I was worried about whether we could produce something that good and how we would get a decent grade for our assignment."

The group then looked at the wiki in the VLE where they were expected to produce their own wiki page. The site provided some basic instructions about editing the page that had been created for their group but they still felt unsure about how to produce the document.

> "We couldn't decide whether to write the article in Microsoft Word and then copy it in to the wiki or just write it all in the Wiki from scratch."

Organising the group

It soon became apparent that they were all talking over each other, coming up with lots of ideas, not always listening to each other, and not taking any notes of what they had decided.

They decided that it would be good to take a break and think about how they would manage the task.

Creating a team ethos

Anisha told them about a previous project she had taken part in where the team had considered any concerns that members were experiencing and had checked that they all understood the project brief in the same way. The group decided to put 20 minutes aside to do this – they ended up spending a helpful 2 hours instead.

> *"That was probably the most useful thing we did. We had each assumed that we were the only one with any worries, and we were heading in different directions, assuming we all would have the same ideas."*

> *"I was worried it was going to count towards my final grade, and didn't know if the rest of the group was as bothered as me about getting good grades."*

> *"I couldn't see how the lecturers would know who had made which contribution and how grades would be allocated. What if I didn't like someone's edit of my section? Would I lose points for their edit?"*

Identifying ground rules

The group agreed that they all wanted to work towards really good grades. They set out a project plan of:

- things they wanted their wiki to achieve;
- when to meet, and what to do between meetings as well as when they met up;
- how to keep track of individual contributions.

Identifying group roles

The group decided that they would share all roles, but would each take on a chief role to ensure that aspect of the project worked smoothly. They drew up a list of all the tasks that needed to be done and then shared these out as fairly as possible. They decided that the four roles that would help bring everything together were:

- *Chair (Rory),* to keep discussions on track and make sure everyone's voice got heard.
- *Co-ordinator (Anisha),* to jot down their ideas and decisions and then make sure these were followed up.
- *Chief editor (Simon),* to ensure that there was a coherent voice and style once they had finished their sections.
- *Manager (Lola),* to keep track of times and keep everyone on task.

Sharing out the work

The group divided the research equally, so that they could all contribute a section to the wiki. They each took on editorial responsibility for one section, and consulted with the overall editor on how to develop a coherent group approach, style and 'voice'.

Researching for the wiki article

They each spent a week reading around their topic and collecting references. On the whole, they did this separately, but looking out for material for other people's sections and passing that on.

Editing the wiki

Simon was the first to start editing the wiki as he felt most confident writing in the basic text editor.

> *"I just typed stuff in like I would in Word, but I had to look up how to make things bold or italic. Other than that it was quite straightforward."*

The others soon began to contribute their sections to the document and it began to grow in length. They realised that some features such as the table of contents and reference list were automated.

Checking the drafts

The group met again in the library and reviewed their wiki. They noticed that it still read too much as four separate documents. They decided on ways they could each adapt their sections before the chief editor did a final edit. It also lacked sub-headings and didn't contain enough references. They agreed to all go away and work on the whole article, making changes to improve the structure and content.

As they worked and talked about what they were doing, the group soon gained confidence editing the wiki and even began to use the 'Talk' page to discuss possible changes to the document before implementing them.

Consulting on edits

Although everything seemed to be going well, just before the deadline the group ran into some difficulty. Simon in his role as chief editor had spent a few hours making some major changes to the last section of the article, which Rory had originally researched and written. Rory preferred his own edit and was unhappy with the changes. Without speaking to Simon, he used the 'History' tab to undo Simon's changes.

> "I was really unhappy that Simon had altered my work so much – I had spent ages writing that section and I couldn't see how his version was any better."

Simon was then annoyed as he felt that although Rory's edit was good in its own right, it made the overall article too disjointed. He felt that if they kept Rory's edit, the only way of creating a single voice was for everyone else to change their edits. This didn't seem fair as their work was also good already, and it would take too much time.

The group met in the library to discuss and agree the most appropriate way to resolve this. Ultimately, they decided that most of Simon's edit should stand since it worked best for the article overall. However, they agreed that there were some lines in Rory's edit that read well and that, with a minor adaptation that Rory could make, would add to the article overall. Rory was still not completely happy but agreed to this as the best overall solution.

The outcome

The group produced a high quality wiki page which received an outstanding ('first class') grade. Their lecturer commented that they had worked well as a team and had resolved their differences professionally and sensibly.

Anisha wrote to her lecturer about the assignment after the grades were released.

> "I really enjoyed the wiki assignment. It was great to use a tool that is so popular on the Web and once we figured it out, it was easy to edit. I have learnt so much from this assignment – not only about engineering, but wikis and group working as well."

What can you learn from the case study?

The case study above illustrates many important issues about collaborative writing using a wiki.

Reflection: Writing a collaborative wiki

In your reflective log, jot down your thoughts about how you could learn from the experiences of the students undertaking the case study above that you could then apply to a similar assignment.

Tips for collaborative wiki writing

Shared understanding

Make sure that you all interpret the assignment requirements in the same way. If, after discussing this and re-reading the brief, there is any disagreement or confusion, check with your lecturer before launching into the task.

Think as a team

A group project is set in order to develop a different set of skills, such as discussion, sharing ideas, working collectively, bringing out the best in others, arriving at decisions that are best for the final outcome rather than for any one individual. This means thinking more of others' perspectives rather than insisting on your own point of view.

Group planning and roles

Plan your approach to the task as you would any small group project. Share out work and roles equitably. Make sure that all group members are aware of their responsibilities and roles.

Time management

Set clear and achievable deadlines for all group members and stick to them. Remember that success in this assignment is partly down to your ability to work as a team.

Develop the right skills

Make sure that all group members have the appropriate IT skills to edit the wiki before starting the writing stage. Use the free resources to learn and practise first. Try out the tool before you start writing your contribution to the article – experiment with formatting, styles and headings.

Conceptualise a good end product

Look carefully at good examples of existing wiki pages, for example 'featured articles' on Wikipedia.

Coherence

Remember that it is a collaborative writing exercise with the aim of producing a single assignment. You need to ensure there is a consistent 'voice', and coherent approach throughout the document.

In the spirit of wiki writing

Use the wiki tool as it is intended – let your document evolve and improve with continuous changes by group members. Keep in mind the five principles of wiki writing outlined on p. 103 above.

Consult on edits

Even if you decide to appoint a 'chief editor' for the role, work as collaboratively as you can. Discuss all major changes with the group using the 'Talk' feature before making them on the article. It can be upsetting for an individual if all of their work is suddenly removed or altered without any discussion or obvious reason.

Consensus

Make sure all group members are happy with the final article before the assignment deadline.

Checklist for writing and editing wikis

Aspect	Done	Comments and notes for your wiki
1 Read carefully the article to be edited		
2 For a new item, choose a good title		
3 Share out group tasks and assign roles		
4 Research the topic in detail		
5 Gather references to original sources		
6 Read the 'Talk' pages and notes for the wiki		
7 Identify improvements you could make		
8 Identify minor and major edits		
9 Consult with existing editors		
10 Create a clear structure for your edit		
11 Provide images and captions if relevant		
12 Maintain a neutral point of view		
13 Cover the subject from all angles		
14 Avoid any copying or plagiarism		
15 Link to other wiki pages (if possible)		
16 Invite comment		
17 Submit for rating		

How useful are wikis for students?

A number of research studies have investigated the value and effectiveness of wikis as a tool for undergraduate assignments. Three are referred to here.

Study 1: *Reliability and accuracy*

A small-scale research study conducted at Manchester Metropolitan University examined the accuracy of Wikipedia pages related to healthcare studies. They concluded that over half of the references cited on Wikipedia pages related to reputable sources.

Haigh (2011)

This study highlights the relative value of Wikipedia as a source of quality information suitable for academic assignments. From this, you could draw the conclusion that Wikipedia is a useful resource, but you would need to use the information found there with care: almost half the references were *not* reliable sources of information.

You should consider that even if the sources cited are good, the author may have not have used them appropriately. There could be contextual omissions, genuine misinterpretations, or typing errors that alter the meaning of the material significantly. You would need to go back to the original sources that the authors of those pages cite in order check for accuracy.

Study 2: *Ecology students' use of Wikipedia*

This research paper, written by graduate students, describes the process of learning how to update existing Wikipedia articles on ecology. Students first evaluated existing articles. They found the Wikipedia articles to be rather limited in their breadth, depth and relevance, and to be lacking in appropriate references. The graduate students updated pages, following Wikipedia guidelines on article layout and revision.

They concluded that updating Wikipedia was straightforward and useful. It could help students to gained good critical thinking and communication skills. On the downside, students were frustrated by existing article editors who repeatedly undid their changes.

Callis et al. (2009)

This study is helpful as it details, from a student perspective, the real issues encountered when using Wikipedia. These graduates found that:

- some articles do not have the depth and breadth necessary for use for academic study;
- difficulties can arise when you edit articles.

Discussion with editors on the Talk page before editing articles may have reduced the frustrations described.

Study 3: *Improving student writing skills through use of Web 2.0 tools*

This discussion paper argues that increased use of Web 2.0 collaborative writing tools, such as Wikipedia, improve students' research skills. The evolving, collaborative and flexible nature of wikis was found to be especially helpful in this respect. The author also argues that teaching staff should educate students in how to make effective use of Web 2.0 tools for study.

Purdy (2010)

It can be helpful to know that using Wikipedia and other Web 2.0 tools:

- offers a useful parallel to the process of research;
- can help develop a range of academic skills.

Reflection: Using Wikipedia as a student

Consider the following points and decide how they might affect your future use of Wikipedia for study.

- Wikipedia is generally a reliable source of background information.
- Wikipedia content should always be verified by checking original sources.
- Wikipedia is open content and can be edited by anyone.
- Wikipedia articles are not always comprehensive in their coverage of a topic.

Student reflections on using wikis in their studies

Makose: *editing the lab research wiki page*

A final year student, Makose, was asked to maintain a wiki page on the research conducted in her host laboratory during her final-year research project. The wiki was updated by other members of the group, including her academic supervisor, and Makose was responsible for maintaining the structure, accuracy and flow of material within the wiki, which was publically available on the university's website. This activity formed part of the assessment for Makose's final-year project.

"I learned how to edit a wiki in my first year but it was a completely different job when I was responsible for maintaining the lab's wiki site. At first, I was very nervous about deleting important sections but I became quite an expert at moving text around and using all the formatting commands. Towards the end of project, I became quite protective of the wiki and would diligently edit any contributions from lab members, even my academic supervisor's rushed comments on his latest findings."

Phil: *over-reliance on Wikipedia*

A first-year student, Phil, used Wikipedia to help research an essay on the history of the British government. As the articles he used seemed to be very detailed and covered all of the topics he required, Wikipedia was his main source of information. When he got his essay back from his lecturer, he received a low grade for referencing, as he had not used or cited original sources.

"My lecturer gave me some really useful feedback on how to use Wikipedia for researching essays. He told me it was fine as a source of background information, i.e., to become familiar with the topic, but that I should always check the information in academic books or journals. He also told me that I should have referenced the journals and not Wikipedia … I won't make that mistake again!"

Anil: *experiences of a group project*

A second-year student, Anil, was assigned to a group for a mini-project during a field course. The assignment required students to work collaboratively to collect data during the field course and then to write a group wiki. The students had to complete this within a very tight deadline of 2 days at the end of the field course. They were required to collate their research data, analyse the findings and present them in a wiki document along with a literature review and discussion.

"The field course assignment was very demanding. We all had our own data which we had to combine and then analyse and write up using a wiki. We made notes on the wiki during the data collection stage while out in the field – luckily we had good mobile access. When we got back to camp we worked in the computer room and all edited separate sections and then worked on producing a cohesive document. We improved our research and writing skills massively in a short space of time."

Juliana: *exam preparation*

Juliana set up her own class wiki to help her to make sense of, and remember, course material.

"I found it hard to remember the material I had to use for the clinical part of the course. I got about six of us together and we drew together all we needed into a class wiki. We had to research it and talk about it as well as write it which made me feel it was 'our' material. It was much easier to remember it in my clinical exam."

💬 Reflection: Effective use of wikis

Jot down your ideas on how you could use wikis more effectively, drawing on the tips and the experiences of students referred to in this chapter.

Summary

Wikis, especially the better known wikis such as Wikipedia, are used widely as a source of information. It is acceptable to use Wikipedia as part of your initial search for information about a subject. However, in higher education you are expected to follow up the references in the wiki to call up the original sources. You should read these and, if you refer to them in your assignment, provide a reference directly to that source, and not to Wikipedia. Beware of using Wikipedia as a direct source of information in your assignments.

The more interesting use of wikis in higher education is as a vehicle for contributing to the creation and dissemination of knowledge. By creating new articles or editing existing articles, you can hone your skills in researching a topic and writing it up for a real audience. This gives you the chance to gain feedback from others with an interest in the subject such as existing editors.

Writing wikis creates good opportunities for developing a range of skills that are relevant to academic study and which are also applicable to the world of work. These include:

- researching a topic in depth;
- comparing different resources;
- becoming disciplined in writing to a given set of conventions and guidelines;
- drafting and editing documents;
- seeking and taking on board feedback from others;
- applying feedback in order to improve a piece of writing before submitting it as a final piece;
- working collaboratively with others, sharing tasks, making joint decisions, dealing with difficulties in a group and working to arrive at a consensus.

If you are given the choice of producing an assignment as a wiki, and especially doing so as part of a collaborative group project, it is well worth taking up that opportunity so as to develop such a broad range of skills. If chances to do so do not arise naturally during the course of your studies, then see if you can create these for yourself. You can create a wiki with others on your programme to support your understanding and exam preparation.

Chapter 7

Social media

Learning outcomes

This chapter offers you opportunities to:

- identify ways of using social networking tools to enhance your learning;
- build community networks using social networking tools;
- understand how to apply generic study skills when using social media for academic work;
- combine multiple networking tools to support your study and professional development.

Introduction

Social media are a relatively recent addition to the range of teaching and learning methods used in higher education. Although many students use these media in everyday life, they are less likely to apply them to their study. This is a missed opportunity.

In this chapter, you can find out how to use the most popular social networking tools, such as Facebook and Twitter, in order to:

- enhance your online research tools;
- create profiles on social networking sites;
- build effective study communities;
- use social media as a student;
- avoid some of the common mistakes made by students when applying social networking tools to academic study.

Social networks and social networking sites

What is a 'social network'?

A social network is a dynamic set of people-to-people connections. Such social structures are made up of two or more individuals who share something in common and link up around that shared connection. Most of us belong to several interconnected social networks at any one time – and these change constantly.

The common connection could be anything, such as family membership, being on the same sports team, a shared taste in music, a common interest such as graphic novels, shared religious or political beliefs, being on the same programme or in the same workplace, having children at the same school, or taking the same bus to work.

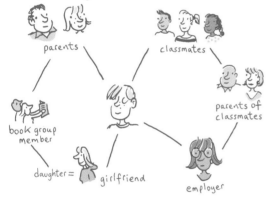

Reflection: Your networks

→ What are the strongest social networks that you form part of currently?

→ What social networks are you part of as a student?

→ How do these social networks add to your life?

What are social networking sites?

Social networking sites are online services that enable people to link up in order to communicate and socialise online. Access and information can be restricted to chosen individuals and groups or can be shared widely with the public. Social networking is becoming synonymous with online networking.

Typical features of social networking sites

- They enable you to interact over the Internet.
- You can use them to share information, images and multimedia.
- They usually encourage you to create a personal profile so that users can get to know you.
- You can usually decide who can see your profile and its content.
- You can search for others with similar interests.
- You can make new friends.

What are the main social networking sites?

It is thought that there are over 200 social networking sites in use around the world, with some sites being more popular in specific countries or continents.

In terms of general social networking sites, Facebook is the most famous globally, followed by Twitter, Google+, MySpace, LinkedIn and Bebo. Some social networking sites are for specific functions: for example, Flickr specialises in images while Flixster focuses on movies.

What equipment would I need?

The only equipment you need to use social networking sites is a computer device connected to the Internet and a valid email address. This could be a personal computer (PC), laptop or a mobile device such as a smartphone.

Can I use social networks at my college/uni?

This varies depending on the institution. Some colleges and universities encourage their use for study and administration; others prevent access while on campus so as to reduce distractions to study. Check your own college/university policy.

Activity: Explore new sites

Ask your friends which social networking sites they use and why. You may find some you don't know about that have features useful for your studies.

Features of key social networking sites

Below are some examples of popular social networking sites and their main features. Consider how their features might be useful for your studies. Which sites look the more useful to you?

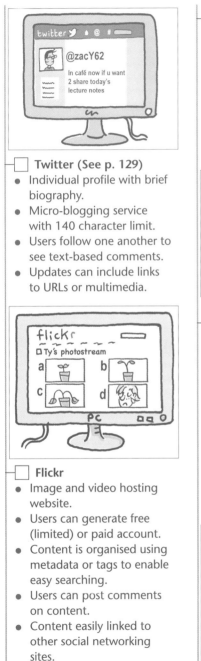

Twitter (See p. 129)
- Individual profile with brief biography.
- Micro-blogging service with 140 character limit.
- Users follow one another to see text-based comments.
- Updates can include links to URLs or multimedia.

Flickr
- Image and video hosting website.
- Users can generate free (limited) or paid account.
- Content is organised using metadata or tags to enable easy searching.
- Users can post comments on content.
- Content easily linked to other social networking sites.

Google+
- New personalised service from Google.
- Allows users to create profiles and select friends.
- Allows sharing of multimedia content within defined groups.
- Users follow one another to see content.

Facebook (see p. 124)
- Very large number of users worldwide.
- Individual profile for personal details.
- Users select friends for sharing content.
- Content includes status updates, comments, images, multimedia, chat, applications.
- Users can create groups or pages for communities.

MySpace
- Individual profile giving full personal details (can be limited).
- Social entertainment site.
- Content includes sound and video files, comments, applications.
- Users add content to their profile.
- Users can generate groups or communities.

LinkedIn (See p. 134)
- Business relationship network.
- Users have professional profiles.
- Users can connect with one another to build a contacts network.
- Users can upload content, e.g., curriculum vitae.
- Useful information to support employability and entrepreneurship.

Understanding Facebook

Who uses Facebook?

Facebook started out as a student networking site and now has over 600 million registered users worldwide, drawn from all walks of life. As well as individuals, many companies, organisations and groups use Facebook for advertising and marketing purposes.

How do I get a Facebook account?

You will need to supply a valid email address. To register a Facebook account, visit www.facebook.com and follow the instructions to create a new account.

Should I make my profile public?

Facebook is a public site which can be accessed by anyone with an account – which means that millions of people could see your information if you do not take care with your privacy settings.

- Check the details of these carefully and often.
- Decide which information you want to be private, and which publicly available.
- New users are advised to keep most information private and share their profile only with people they know.

How do I build up a social community?

Facebook will help you to find your friends on their site by importing contacts from your contact list, searching email addresses or surnames.

- You can search for a Facebook user by typing their name into the search box.
- As you build a community of friends, Facebook offers suggestions of 'People you may know'.

What is a friend request?

When you request to be Facebook friends with another user, that person has to 'Confirm' or 'Ignore' your request. You will also be asked to do this if another user asks to be friends with you.

How do I share content with my friends?

- Facebook has a wide range of features. For beginners, the list below shows some ways you can interact with friends.
- **Status update:** You write something about yourself (such as what you are doing); these comments go on your 'wall'.
- **Comments:** You can comment on another user's status updates or on their wall.
- **Like:** You can give a 'thumbs up' to content that you particularly like when posted by another user.
- **Upload content:** You can upload images and videos or share links.
- **Email:** You can send direct messages to your friends' email addresses.
- **Timeline:** You can share your favourite memories, events and stories with your Facebook friends.
- **Applications:** You can install Facebook applications such as games and then play against other users.
- **Groups:** You can join, create or Like groups of users with similar interests.
- **Events:** You can advertise upcoming events to friends.
- **Chat:** You can use Facebook for instant messaging with your friends.
- **To support your study:** You can use these tools to keep on top of your academic work by:
  - building online study groups;
  - asking questions;
  - interacting with your lecturers.

☺ Activity: Facebook at college

Log in to Facebook. Find your university or college's page and Like it.

→ Search for something you are interested in (e.g., a future career) and join a relevant group.
→ Set up (or join) a group for your course/degree programme or department.

Using Facebook to support academic study

What students say about using Facebook for academic studies

"Facebook helped me to build a bigger academic community, both with students on campus and in other universities."

"We organised a big student conference using Facebook – it was really well attended and people posted useful comments about our research in the group discussion area."

"My lecturer didn't like us using mobile (cell) phones in his lectures but when I said I was asking a friend a question about the lecture through Facebook, he started to encourage us to use social media for studying."

Do's

Do remember who gets to see what you write. If you have a public profile your words will be publically accessible: they may be found through search engines. Remember that your comments are permanently recorded and may be used by prospective employers when you apply for a job.

Do contribute to group discussions regularly – such discussions work best when all members share and update content.

Do make copies of important conversations, links or content and store them locally on your computer. Remember that content stored online may not be available permanently.

Do share useful information about your studies with your Facebook friends; getting into the habit of sharing will encourage your friends to do the same.

Do think of others' feelings before you comment: avoid making any comments in group areas that may be offensive or hurtful to other students.

Do be discreet and respect confidentiality: it is easy to forget that your comments are seen by all of your friends and that you may get someone else into trouble by what you write.

Do think about timing: organise events at times when the majority of group members are likely to be able to attend.

Do check your Internet access. Access to Facebook needs a computer or mobile device connected to the Internet. Don't rely on it if you can't get on the Web or have no wi-fi signal.

Do separate your social and academic time – it is easy to become caught up in the social aspects and to run out of time for working on your academic work and assessed assignments.

Do respect lecturer wishes on use of Facebook in class. If you are permitted or encouraged to use Facebook, do restrict your use to educational purposes. Avoid its use in class for social activities.

Do check your institution's policy on use of social media on campus.

Do use responsibly

Use constructively for feedback. Avoid making comments about your lectures, tutors or any other staff. There have been cases where students have suffered disciplinary action for comments made about staff on Facebook.

Take care advertising events on Facebook. If you are organising a meeting make sure the venue will hold all of the people that could possibly attend. Be sure you know how many people the invitation will go to.

Privacy, security and netiquette

These are especially important when using social media. If you haven't checked these already, see the appropriate sections in Chapter 1.

Using Facebook for peer support

Using Facebook for peer support

As part of your programme, you will be required to spend time in self-directed study. Much of this will be used as preparation for taught sessions or working on assignments, and will consist of research, reading, thinking, organising your materials and writing your assignments, whether at home or in a library.

It can be hard to keep yourself motivated and focused when studying on your own in this way. Social networking tools can be used to keep you connected to other students for mutual support, whether informally or as part of an online peer support group.

Sharing your experience

If you are grappling with a difficult concept or problem, it may help to take a few minutes to share it with friends. You won't be alone. It is likely that others on your course or in your online study group will be struggling with similar issues.

- It can help to read that other Facebook friends go through the similar experiences.
- You may receive comments from Friends offering encouragement and advice.
- Many students find it helpful simply writing down their experience, even if they do not then post it for others to read. It can clarify your thinking and help you arrive at a solution.
- When you read other people's experiences, you can often see solutions that they cannot see themselves. Sharing these can help everyone to consider those solutions for their own contexts.

What students say about using Facebook for support

"I am always on Facebook so it is easy to ask friends for help when I don't understand something."

"I have hundreds of Facebook friends – someone always knows what I need to know, and I get instant responses."

"Once, a friend from another university replied through Facebook and got me to think about the problem in a completely different way."

Tips for using Facebook for support

- Put separate time aside for (1) your own private study, (2) supporting other people and (3) using Facebook for social networking. This helps ensure your study time doesn't get eaten up by support and Facebook activity.
- For every 5 minutes you spend on Facebook that is not purely 'study', add 5 minutes to your study time. This will help to ensure that your study time does not get used up in socialising and general messages.
- Avoid using Facebook as a distraction if you can't settle down to study; instead, ask friends to encourage you to get down to work.

Asking questions

You are more likely to receive useable answers that support your study if you pose your questions in ways that encourage others to make a response.

- Ask straightforward questions. Keep your question brief so that your friends are more likely to read it.
- Ask specific questions so that it is clear what kind of answer you need.
- Don't ask friends for copies of their working out or their answers.

Example

I think I get this – but do I? What I think happens is: if X changes in this way, then this always means that Y will happen … is that right?

This question is short and generally to the point so is more likely to create discussion amongst your friends in the form of comments to your post. A consensus or shared understanding may result from the discussion.

Making Facebook work for group projects

Facebook in group projects and assignments

It is likely that, at some time as a student, you will be asked to work in a group with other students to complete a specific task or assignment. This is true of campus-based programmes but is often the case on distance learning or work-based programmes too.

The assignment might be anything from producing a poster to conducting a lab-based, field-based or work-based research project. A project of this kind will require teamwork and good communication between group members. Facebook can help you to keep in touch and up to date with the project and to maintain a record of your discussions and decisions.

Using Facebook for group work

- **Set up a private group** on Facebook including all group members.
- **Set ground rules** about how you will use the online group.
- **Include everyone:** make sure all group members are familiar with how to use the group tool.
- **Contribute to the group** regularly by posting updates, commenting on other group members' updates and uploading relevant content.
- **Organise group meetings** using the Events tool.
- **Use the poll/question tools** to gauge group members' opinions as the project progresses.
- **Use the group tools for online discussions** in between face-to-face meetings.

It may be useful to know that conversations on Facebook (other than instant messaging) are stored for future use. If you have an academic discussion with friends though a status update and comments, you will be able to refer back to this at any point.

What students say about using Facebook for group assignments

"Our lecturers suggested using Facebook for a group research project – it was brilliant! We all saw Facebook completely differently after discovering it was a really good project management tool!"

"Setting up a group for our business group project was easy – we used Facebook to schedule meetings and to post updates."

"We did a field project on plants in marshlands – we uploaded photos from our mobile phones to our Facebook group and identified each others' plants."

Here is the photo of our group's model for Architecture 101 - still a work in progress.

Here is our group's model so far. A few teething problems with the glue. Of course, still very much a work in progress.

Facebook: wider considerations for study

Library sites within Facebook

Some universities have library sites within Facebook which encourage students to ask research-related and referencing questions through the tool. A study by librarians at a US university found that students were very keen to use Facebook for this purpose. (Mack et al., 2007)

If your institution's library offers this service through Facebook, it could help to improve your studies.

Organisations' use of Facebook

Facebook pages are commonly used by companies or organisations to inform users about products, services or updates. If you Like their page, you will see their posts on your News Feed. This gives you a way to keep up to date with important information relating to your studies, research or future career.

Does Facebook help you to study better?

It may improve your grades

Many students use Facebook socially and can be seen looking at it in the library at university or college. It can form a major part of students' social lives. A recent study in China and Hong Kong showed that students mainly use Facebook for social and educational purposes (many of which are described in this chapter).

The authors produced a theory about how students' social use of Facebook could evolve into educational uses that may help improve academic success (Tian et al., 2011).

Excessive switching may reduce your grades

A recent study of US higher education students showed that excessive use of Facebook can reduce the time spent studying and lead to lower grades. This study hypothesised that students who constantly switch between social networking sites and their assignments may make more mistakes in their work (Kirschner and Karpinski, 2010).

You can avoid this by separating your academic and social time. When you are studying, avoid checking Facebook repeatedly for social updates.

Reflection: Using Facebook

(a) In what ways could you make use of Facebook to enhance your studies?

(b) Does your current use of Facebook have any negative effect on your studies, such as through excessive switching? If so, how could you change your use so that you gain the best use of the tool?

Micro-blogging and Twitter

Chapter 5 looked at using blogging for academic purposes. Blogs can be quite long and detailed. Sometimes, you may want to communicate in ways that are short and punchy yet informative. If so, you may find that micro-blogging is a more useful approach for you.

What is micro-blogging?

Micro-blogging is an abbreviated form of blogging – publishing your opinion or thoughts online for others to read. The only difference is that micro-blogs are very short.

History of micro-blogging

Micro-blogging is believed to have been conceived in 2005 when bloggers starting referring to shorter blog entries as *tumblelogs*. By 2007, a number of micro-blogging sites had been created, the most popular of which is known as Twitter.

Forms of micro-blogging

Micro-blogging exists in a number of forms. In addition to sites such as Twitter, which only publish micro-blogs, other online sites have incorporated micro-blogging functionality. For example, Facebook, LinkedIn and MySpace all allow micro-blogging, in the form of Status Updates.

Accessing micro-blogs

Tools such as Twitter are successful because you can access them on mobile/cell phones and smartphones as well as through your PC. Users can read and post to Twitter via applications on the device or using SMS.

Twitter is a micro-blogging tool useful for building an academic community and keeping up to date with social and educational interests. (137 characters.) The Twitter site is http://twitter.com

Tweets

- Messages on Twitter are referred to as tweets.
- Tweets are text-based posts of up to 140 characters.
- As they are short, you can scan them easily for relevance.
- They can include links to websites, blogs, images or multimedia resources.

At first you may be frustrated by the lack of characters available to get your message across. However, with practice you should adapt to the medium.

Tweet skills = academic skills?

Good tweeting can help develop skills relevant to academic study, such as:

- summarising your key messages;
- combining brevity and clarity;
- writing succinctly and precisely;
- avoiding waffle;
- selecting only the most important information, cutting out material you find interesting but that is not essential;
- ensuring your message comes across to your audience despite being succinct.

Twitter on mobile devices

If you use Twitter on a smartphone, you can:

- upload photos or videos with your tweets;
- include a Geotag, which pinpoints your exact location;
- use tools to shrink URLs so that they fit within the 140 character tweet limit.

Getting started with Twitter

Opening an account on Twitter

To start micro-blogging on Twitter or any other site, first you need to create an account. Twitter is free and simple to use. When setting up your Twitter account you will need to provide the following information:

- **Full name:** This appears on your public profile.
- **Username:** This will be your online name in Twitter. When you publish your tweets, they will appear next to this username. You should think carefully about your username, particularly if you may be using it for academic purposes.
- **Email address:** This will be used to authenticate your account and to send you updates etc.

Privacy settings

Decide who will be able to read your tweets. The default setting is that your tweets are public, but you can elect to only allow your 'followers' to read them.

'Following' and 'followers'

Because of the very high volume of tweets posted on Twitter even in one minute, you couldn't read all messages available. To help you filter the content you see, Twitter lets you 'follow' people of your choice. If those individuals have public tweets, you will be able to 'follow' them immediately. If not, they will be alerted that you wish to follow them and can accept or decline your request. This principle works for your tweets as well.

Building a community

Tweets are not intended for private use. Users generally aim to build a community of followers – there is not much point in you publishing regular tweets if they are private and you have no followers. If you post public tweets then this may not matter. You can use hashtags to give keywords to your tweets to attract followers.

'Mentioning' Twitter users in your tweets

In Twitter, your username can be referenced by others as @username. This means you can include other users in your tweets, by including their username. This is known as a *mention*, and you can see how many times you get mentioned using Twitter or a mobile device app.

Using tagging in Twitter

Tweets can be grouped into conversations or topics by adding a #, for example #politics. You might include this in a public tweet if you wanted the world to know about a political comment made by the Prime Minister.

You can use Twitter to search for hashtags, and you can see constantly what topics are 'trending' at any given moment in time.

Re-tweeting

If you see a tweet which you particularly like or you think is particularly important to you or your community, you can re-tweet it. This means that your followers will see the tweet.

Lists

In Twitter, you can create lists of people or organisations you want to keep track of, without seeing their updates in your main news feed. This might be useful for particular projects or aspects of your life, such as job hunting.

Linking Twitter to other social networking sites

You can use various tools such as Hootsuite to update all your social networking sites simultaneously. For example, if you wish to inform your Twitter community and your Facebook friends of a particularly important event, you can post updates to both sites simultaneously.

Using Twitter for academic purposes

Following organisations relevant to study

Many organisations have public Twitter accounts; you can follow them and receive their tweets. These can be useful for keeping up to date with developments in your field, hearing breaking news and seeing links to important articles and documents.

- **Universities**: tweets relevant to you as a student, such as changes to lecture times.
- **Journals**: so you can see what is being published in your subject.
- **Charities**: may provide details of their work, research, and vacancies for student jobs.
- **Government departments**: tweet updates on policy changes and statutory guidance.
- **Commercial companies**: provide tweets relevant to business studies, product design or applied science programmes.

Following your lecturers

Your lecturers may use Twitter to post information about your course or about their own research or fieldwork if they consider this relevant to your study.

Searching Twitter for 'people' information

You can use the search facility on Twitter as a research tool to find new information posted by organisations or people. This can be useful for gaining updates for assignments in areas where policy and practice changes relatively quickly, such as education, health, business and politics.

Using Twitter 'trends' for event information

You can use the 'trending' facility to search for popular events, discussions or conversations. Twitter produces trends based on the use of words or hashtags in tweets. For example, if many people tweet about a significant event, it is likely to trend on Twitter. If you click on a trending topic you will be able to see all of the public tweets where the keyword or hashtag are mentioned. This facility can be useful if you are conducting research or completing an assignment on an event such as a world trade meeting, political summit or art exhibition.

Getting instant help from other students

Twitter provides an instant mechanism for asking questions, discussing learning activities and reflecting on your progress. You may be able to use it to ask each other questions during lectures, providing your lecturer is happy for you to use mobile devices during their sessions. This can provide a quick way of resolving study problems. See Chapter 8.

Using Twitter in student projects

If you are undertaking a group project with other students, Twitter can be a helpful tool for keeping you in touch with each other's progress. You could:

- *either*: all follow each other and post tweets about the project amongst other tweets;
- *or*: you could use a hashtag (e.g., #fieldproj). All group members would include the hashtag at the end of all project-related tweets and could then search for the hashtag to see all project tweets, replying, mentioning and re-tweeting as necessary.

Can Twitter help you as a student?

There have been research studies conducted on the use of Twitter by university students as part of their studies. As Twitter is quite a new tool it is too early to judge conclusively, but it certainly seems to help students feel part of a learning community and can improve student engagement (Junco et al., 2011; Virendra, 2011).

Students' use of Twitter: Sarah

Sarah: first-year undergraduate student

Sarah is a student in biomedical sciences. She hadn't used Twitter before she started at university but was asked to set up an account as part of a module (course) she was studying. Her lecturer wanted students to use Twitter to build up a learning community and to keep up to date with news about the course and the subject area.

In the first few weeks of using Twitter, Sarah followed only the course leader who posted tweets about the course and tips about how to use Twitter. However, as she got used to using the Twitter app on her smartphone, she became more adventurous.

Sarah started to follow other students from her programme who were also on Twitter. She found them by looking at her course leader's list of followers. She recognised some of the names of her friends and clicked Follow. Some had public profiles and she could see their tweets straight away. Others had private profiles (indicated by a padlock) and she had to wait for them to accept her request.

As Sarah's confidence grew, so did her Twitter account. Within 2 months of using Twitter, she followed over 100 users and had around 70 followers. She started to Tweet every day and checked her Twitter account every couple of hours. Here is a list of some of the users Sarah followed on Twitter.

> @bbcbreaking – breaking news from the BBC
> @skills4study – study advice from Palgrave MacMillan
> @BBCR1
> @ ScienceNewsOrg – for information on molecules, 'Genes and Cells', and 'Body and Brain'
> @guardianscience
> @NUS

How Sarah uses Twitter for study

- Asking friends about course-related questions.
- Checking she has understood definitions of technical terms.
- Reading tweets on science topics.
- Following organisations relevant to her studies to keep up to date.

Building a learning community

Sarah finds it encouraging and motivating to receive tweets from other students while she is studying – it makes her feel part of a community. Some of the tweets are informative, and others just help her to avoid a sense of isolation when studying independently.

Examples of tweets Sarah receives

> "@paul_gd I am studying in the main library. Do you want to meet?"
>
> "@y3b99 Great lecture eh? I searched for #science on twitter and found loads of useful links."
>
> "I just found a really good article in the current issue of @newscientist."
>
> "Having a bit of a science love in. Studying while a documentary about DNA is on. Love it."

Sharing ideas for things to read

For one assignment, the students were asked to conduct their own search for relevant material and recommend one item for others to read. They had to sum up in a tweet why this was a good item to choose. Sarah now finds this a useful way of making a quick evaluative overview of materials that she reads. Since that assignment, she and others on her programme often send each other quick messages about items they think others will find interesting.

Sarah's comments

> "I was a bit unsure about using Twitter at first – it seemed to be full of rubbish. But when I got used to it and started following the right people it provided a constant flow of handy information. I find it particularly good for working with friends on my course."

Students' use of Twitter: Imran

Imran: final-year student

Imran, who is on a food sciences programme, had a Twitter account before he started at university and used it mainly for social purposes. Since then, he has gradually built his Twitter profile to nearly 300 followers, mainly friends and family, Facebook friends and people he has met at university. He follows over 700 users.

As Imran is reaching the end of his undergraduate degree, he now has two priorities: firstly, to complete his final-year dissertation (research project), and secondly, to get a good job. His use of Twitter has changed in the last few months. He uses it much less for general social comments and much more to support his studies and search for a job.

Support from his peers

Imran's use of Twitter for communicating with others focuses currently on:

- providing supportive comments to others working on their dissertations;
- asking specific questions about completing the dissertation, such as how others are coping with writing the abstract, which he finds difficult;
- checking specific technical details about food processing with those working on similar projects in food science;
- complaining when he gets tired or bored: his friends are good at telling him when to have a break and when he needs to get down to work.

Imran's comments

"A lot of us work best at night when there are no distractions. That part is good but then after a few hours, you can feel your enthusiasm wane. I like it when I get a tweet that reassures me that others are out there and working just as hard. It gives me a boost."

Imran's academic uses for Twitter

As well as using the library catalogue and more common search tools such as Google Scholar, Imran uses Twitter as an additional resource to search for articles and news relevant to his final-year dissertation. He uses the search facility to search for relevant keywords and hashtags. He then clicks links and reads relevant tweets.

Imran's career-related uses of Twitter

Imran had spent time with the Careers Service investigating the wider range of jobs that would be open to him as a graduate, rather than those specifically related to food sciences. He identified a range of generic careers sites and reads tweets that appear on these.

He has already applied for dozens of jobs and is waiting to see which ones offer him an interview. In the meantime, he is reading tweets from organisations to which he has sent in an application. He follows links and makes notes about any updates from the companies. This has already proved useful to him in his first interviews: his excellent background knowledge of one company indicated to them that he was serious about his application and interested in the company. As a result, he has been successful in going through to the second round of interviews.

Imran's comments

"I am a Twitter fan! Once, I went for an interview and they asked me what I knew about the company … Because I follow that company on Twitter I had seen all their recent press releases and blew them away with my knowledge."

Career-focused sites

Below is a selection of the career-focused users Imran follows on Twitter. He created lists to follow the main employers he was interested in working for, so that if he got an interview with them he would have useful information ready to draw upon:

@monstercareers   @prospectsjobs
@guardiancareers   @milkroundonline
@prospects   @milkround_jobs

LinkedIn: build your professional community

LinkedIn

LinkedIn is a professional networking tool. In the early stages of your studies, this may not seem very relevant to you. However, as you move towards the end of your degree or programme of study and start to think about applying for jobs, you may find it to be very beneficial to you.

How does LinkedIn work?

When you register with LinkedIn at www.LinkedIn.com you will be asked for personal details for your profile: these include your name, profession and location. You can then start building connections with other users.

Connections in LinkedIn

Professional communities are all about connections between people. LinkedIn helps you join these communities by building connections. You can build connections with individuals, through groups or by following companies.

Groups

LinkedIn will suggest groups for you to join based on your profile information. For example, if you say you are studying neuroscience, you will be asked if you want to join groups such as the Society for Neuroscience.

Companies

You can search for companies on LinkedIn. Once you find a company you are interested in, you can choose to Follow that company to receive regular updates. You can also see the following information about the company:

- New hires – people recently employed at the company.
- Employees – all employers of that company who are on LinkedIn.
- Job opportunities – postings of jobs available at the company.
- Employee statistics – lots of useful data about employee education, experience, roles etc.
- Employee movement – details of new employees and which companies they come from.

Social networking features

LinkedIn has a variety of features similar to sites such as Facebook and Twitter. You can:

- post updates;
- send messages to other users;
- join groups;
- add connections.

☺ Activity: Using LinkedIn

LinkedIn has many features for building professional contacts. Consider if you could use it for any of the following activities:

- [ ] organising voluntary work during term time;
- [ ] gaining familiarity with businesses and companies relevant to your career interests to give you a better idea of where you might wish to work later;
- [ ] building up your knowledge of relevant companies so that you are well informed when you go for interview;
- [ ] using employment-related information to support an assignment in careers education or personal planning;
- [ ] arranging summer work to enhance your CV;
- [ ] searching for job opportunities;
- [ ] building a list of professional contacts;
- [ ] searching for internship opportunities;
- [ ] researching a particular employer in preparation for a job interview;
- [ ] researching companies for enterprise projects;
- [ ] keeping up to date with professional interests;
- [ ] using its Get Answers facilities to help launch your own enterprise.

LinkedIn: features of interest to students

Knowledge exchange

Employers, entrepreneurs and would-be professionals of all kinds use LinkedIn to share ideas and advice. Contributions are extremely broad ranging.

Range

Browsing LinkedIn, you gain an appreciation of the varied ways that businesses approach their work and the issues and activities with which they engage. In particular, you can see how business is concerned not just with the core concerns that you might expect, but also broader areas such as:

- cultural awareness and festivals to celebrate this;
- use of language;
- thinking skills;
- happiness;
- renewable energies;
- social networking in business;
- how one part of the business world is seen by others.

These are covered in such areas as:

- Blog
- Get Answers
- News
- New Features
- Archives (by month)

> ### ☺ Activity: Look at LinkedIn
>
> → Connect to LinkedIn.
> → Check what is being covered by its blog as a current issue.
> → Browse the archives for items covered in the last few months.
> → The archive for August 2011 provides tips on non-traditional careers.

Speaker series

LinkedIn provides videos of speakers on topics of relevance to entrepreneurs. You may find these worth a look if you are interested in setting up a business yourself or studying a business-related subject. Two examples of featured speakers are given below.

Thomas Friedman

In October 2011 LinkedIn featured video footage of Pulitzer Prize winner Thomas Friedman talking about his new book *That Used to Be Us*, and his insights on transforming the US economy. An article reviewing the talk was also provided. Posts related to the item made recommendations of similar books that members might enjoy if they liked Friedman's. Friedman, T (2011) 'That Used to be Us'. LinkedIn 28/10/11. Available at http://www.linkedin.com/groups/that-used-be-us-Info-1016247.S.77939283 (Accessed 1 April 2012)

Leila Jana and Samasource

In the same month, there was an article about Leila Janah, the founder of Samasource, and footage of her talk as part of the LinkedIn Speaker series. Her talk focused on how Samasource uses crowd-sourcing to provide opportunities for thousands of people in developing countries to take part in the global economy. Samsource breaks large-scale data projects into many smaller ones that can be achieved over the Internet. Thompson, D (2011) 'Speaker series: Changing the world through Crowdsourcing'. LinkedIn 20/10/11. Available at http://blog.linkedin.com/2011/10/20/linkedin-samasource (Accessed 1 April 2012)

> ### Articles and linked articles
>
> #### The socialising of business
>
> See how businesses such as IBM are changing the ways they link with potential customers by using social media. (16 Sept. 2011)
>
> #### Thinking creatively
>
> A link is provided to an article by Tony Schwartz in the *Harvard Business Review* on how he has used publications about creative thinking in his own work as Chief Executive Officer of The Energy Project. (18 Nov. 2011)

LinkedIn: for entrepreneurial students

Get Answers

One significant aspect of LinkedIn is the Get Answers section. Experts from business, industry and the general public offer their advice to those posting questions. These provide interesting insights into how business professionals think, communicate and interact. That is of general use for building up your awareness of the business world, which helps when applying for jobs, going on work placement or for writing client briefs for assignments.

Entrepreneurship and enterprise projects

Inevitably, the questions and answers include many from those developing and launching new businesses, especially small businesses that wouldn't be able to afford to pay for such a range of expertise.

Some of these questions and answers may be helpful if you are setting up a student start-up or undertaking an enterprise-based project.

Examples of the types of questions posed

"What are the biggest mistakes that you find small business leaders make when using social media?"

"Can a start-up use methods, processes, code snippets and other IP published in an academic paper?"

"How do you write a business proposal?"

"Can anyone suggest a cloud-based ERP system for a start-up organisation?"

Building links with other enterprises

Company status updates This facility enables companies to communicate with their LinkedIn followers. The site provides some initial guidance on how to get started in building a relationship with other businesses that may be able to help your own enterprise in some way.

If you are setting up your own business as a student, it could be helpful to connect via LinkedIn to other businesses for such activities as:

- sourcing materials;
- sharing research costs;
- finding out about expertise that would be available for you to call upon;
- helping you to recruit staff;
- developing supplier networks;
- sharing services to reduce costs;
- finding IT solutions;
- balancing life and work;
- building relationships with those in similar or complementary businesses;
- gaining advice on legal issues.

International dimension

LinkedIn, in November 2011, was used by 135 million professionals and would-be entrepreneurs from across the world: 6 million of these were in the UK and 35 million across Europe; 14 million of its members were students.

This means that browsing the information on LinkedIn gives you a sense of some of the issues that are relevant to business and to students internationally. This is helpful in:

- providing a general background on matters that are of current relevance to business internationally rather than only in Britain;
- becoming more familiar with business on a global basis, and possibly seeing opportunities for yourself within that;
- being able to see how far issues topical in Britain are also raised globally.

Case study: a student's use of social networking tools

Here is a case study of a student who uses social networking to help with study for his undergraduate degree.

John is a final-year undergraduate studying engineering at a large university in the UK. He will be finishing his degree soon and is currently looking for a job. John uses three main sites, Facebook, Twitter and LinkedIn, to keep in contact with his friends and remain up to date with professional organisations.

Facebook

John's friends on Facebook

John has over 120 friends on Facebook. Apart from family and friends from home, he is also connected through Facebook to:

- friends on his course;
- a group set up by his course organiser to encourage discussion and collaboration between students on the course;
- an engineering student interest club he joined at the university;
- a learned society of engineering.

How John uses Facebook as a student

He uses Facebook for:

- social updating with friends at university and home;
- sounding out with other students how they are tackling problems set for their course;
- asking for help from people on his course when he gets stuck with his study;
- breaking up his study time for chats with two course mates, to help keep each other motivated;
- updates from the society of engineering about developments in the field and available jobs.

"I like to use Facebook to contact class mates about problems I am having with my work, particularly late at night when the library is closed and my lecturer has gone home – I get instant help from lots of people."

Twitter

Who John follows on Twitter

John follows 350 people on Twitter. Most of these are professional organisations, groups, engineering journals, companies or news outlets.

How John makes use of Twitter

Using Twitter helps John to feel part of a global community of engineers with similar interests:

- keeping up to date with engineering news;
- finding out about the latest developments in his area of study;
- finding out about jobs;
- undertaking his own online marketing by posting informative tweets about engineering.

"Twitter is a great tool for keeping up to date – there are literally thousands of tweets about engineering every day and I can quickly scan them to see what is relevant to me."

LinkedIn

As John is currently looking for a job, he spends a lot of time online looking at vacancies. He has a professional profile on LinkedIn and has around 60 connections with potential contacts in engineering companies and organisations. His LinkedIn profile includes his curriculum vitae and can be viewed by prospective employers.

"I have found LinkedIn really useful for building up professional contacts – I had no idea there were so many job opportunities in engineering until I registered with LinkedIn."

Referencing social networking sites

When would you reference these sites?

You would rarely use addresses from social networking sites for academic assignments because these are not from authoritative sources – that is, they are not peer reviewed.

The following list provides some examples of when you might legitimately make use of information from a social networking site within an assignment – and so need to make a reference to your source.

- **Quoting a public figure** – such as a politician, economist, artist, writer or sportsperson when his or her comment is suitable as a primary source for your assignment.

- **Citing subject experts** – when someone known to be an authority for your subject discipline has made comments on a social networking site and you consider these relevant to your assignment.

- **Doing an assignment about new media and communications** – if you are studying a subject discipline where media resources are themselves the focus of research or critical analyses; this may be a subject such as media studies, social studies or politics.

- **Using information about companies** – if you find information or quotations on LinkedIn relevant to a business or industry you are covering for an assignment.

- **Using photographs** – using a photograph of a building or art work from a collection on Flickr in order to illustrate your argument for assignment in architecture, fine art or history of art.

Principles for referencing the sites

- For each source, list the details of the item and when and where you last saw it online.
- List details exactly as outlined below and in the order provided.
- Ensure all details are accurate – including the use of italics, brackets and other punctuation.
- Provide the main web address (only registered and accepted members will be able to see items).
- Provide the name of the site in italics.

Referencing items in Facebook

1 Name of the author (surname and initials)
2 Year that the site was last updated
3 'Title of the page'
4 *Facebook* (or social networking site)
5 Date of the posted message (day and month)
6 *Available at* http://www.facebook and the rest of the URL address:
7 (Accessed: full date last viewed or downloaded)

Example: Facebook

Oxfam launched the Grow campaign in 2012 to change global food production systems.

Oxfam (2012) 'Join the Grow Campaign'. Available at http://www.facebook.com/oxfamGB/app_172837349434129 (Accessed 25 March 2012)

Referencing items in Twitter

1 Name of the author (surname and initials)
2 Year that the site was last updated
3 'Title of the page'
4 *Twitter* (or social networking site)
5 Date of the posted message (day and month)
6 *Available at* http://www.twitter and the rest of the URL address:
7 (Accessed: full date last viewed or downloaded)

Example: Twitter

Science magazine (2012) 'NASA Video: Getting to know the Goldilocks planet'. 31/03/12. Available at bit.ly/H8WRRU (Accessed 31 March 2012)

Referencing items in LinkedIn

1 Name of the author (surname and initials)
2 Year that the site was last updated
3 'Title of the page'
4 *LinkedIn* (or social networking site)
5 Date of the posted message (day and month)
6 *Available at* http://www.linkedin and the rest of the URL address:
7 (Accessed: full date last viewed or downloaded)

Example: LinkedIn

Elwin, B. (2012) 'Thailand takes first steps on long road to inclusive mainstream education'. LinkedIn, 30/03/12 Available at http://www.linkedin.com/groupAnswers?viewQuestionAndAnswers=&discussionID=104601844&gid=18383467goback=%2Egde_183846_member_98255114&trk=NUS_DISC_Q-ttle (Accessed 30 March 2012)

Referencing photographs in Flickr

1 Name of the photographer
2 Year photograph was published (if relevant)
3 Photograph title
4 *Flickr* [Online] (or name of other online collection (in italics)
5 Available at: http://www.flickr.com/photos/ and the rest of the URL address:
6 (Accessed: full date last viewed or downloaded)

Example: Flickr

Wayne, S. H. (2008) Usain Bolt wins another gold in the 4 x 400m relay in 2008 Beijing Olympics [Online]. Available at http://www.flickr.com/photos/wayne_t/2787901480/ (Accessed 30 March 2012)

Summary

Although many students enjoy social networking tools for their everyday life, they do not always consider fully how they might make use of these to support their academic study. When students do apply these tools, their feedback can be very positive.

The variety of ways that social networking tools can be applied to study depends to some extent on:

- how far a college or university makes use of social networking tools, such as providing library or departmental pages on Facebook or a similar networking tool;
- how far external organisations relevant to the student's subject discipline make use of the same social networking tools;
- whether the teaching staff permit use of social networking during taught sessions;
- what kinds of formal and informal peer support networks are organised through the programme.

Students can benefit by engaging in social networking with other students, whether those in their department, those with similar social interests at their HEI, or those with similar subject or social interests at other universities. It can help to overcome some aspects of isolation that students may experience when they are away from home for the first time, or if they study from home rather than on campus.

From an academic perspective, social networking can help students to take more responsibility for their learning, looking to each other for answers rather than always looking to a lecturer for these. This has the added advantage that, if a number of students on the same programme of study are using the same social networking tool, they can:

- gain instant feedback on study issues rather than having to wait for a lecturer response;
- build a learning community that supports them as a student;
- develop the experience of acting as a mutually supportive team for solving problems, much as would now be expected in professional life.

Chapter 8

Classroom and communication technologies

Learning outcomes

This chapter provides you with opportunities to:

- gain a feel for some of the class-based technologies that you may come across on your programme and understand broadly why they are used and what is expected;
- understand how to use these technologies in ways that help you to develop your own learning;
- identify technologies that you could use in order to support collaborative work with other students;
- consider how you might make use of mobile devices and apps to enhance your study.

Introduction

Class-based technologies and communications tools are used increasingly within higher education as means of engaging students further in the process of learning. These technologies can help study in such areas as:

- making class-based learning more interesting through involving all the students in the class rather than, as may happen in other circumstances, only a handful of students offering answers when asked, or contributing to discussions;
- enabling lecturers to see how far the whole class really understands the material;
- enabling students to learn from and better support each other, in and out of class;
- enabling students to take part in group or paired learning activities even when away from the formal classroom;
- supporting individual students who may be at some distance from the classroom.

This chapter focuses on five interrelated aspects of such technology:

- voting handsets;
- lecture capture and chat;
- video conferencing;
- collaborative learning tools;
- mobile devices.

It outlines some of the tools that you might encounter in class, and provides guidance on how you might make the best use of these if provided. It also looks at tools that support communication and collaborative working for academic study, some in class, some at a distance, and some in both settings.

Exploring the terrain

A range of class-based and other communication tools can be combined on and off campus to provide an enriched learning experience.

In class - - - - - - - - - - - - - - - - - - - **In class and at distance** - - - - - - - - - - - - - - - - - - **At a distance**

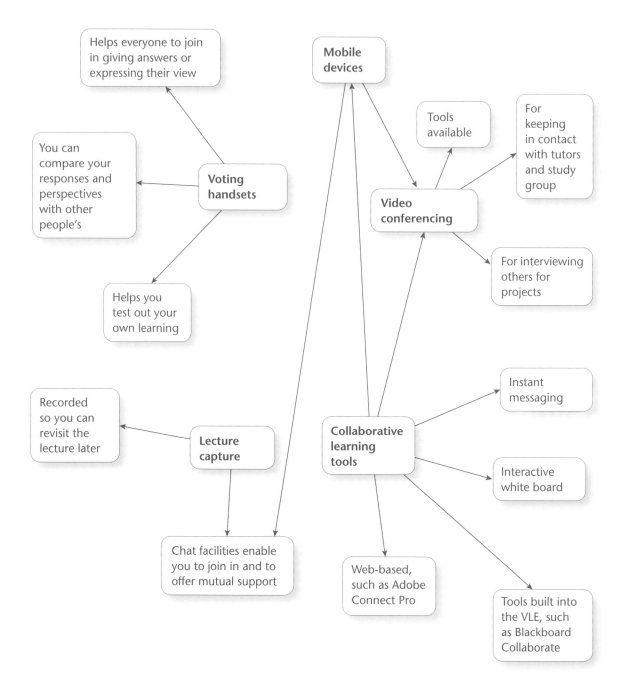

Helps everyone to join in giving answers or expressing their view

Mobile devices

Tools available

For keeping in contact with tutors and study group

You can compare your responses and perspectives with other people's

Voting handsets

Video conferencing

Helps you test out your own learning

For interviewing others for projects

Instant messaging

Recorded so you can revisit the lecture later

Lecture capture

Collaborative learning tools

Interactive white board

Chat facilities enable you to join in and to offer mutual support

Web-based, such as Adobe Connect Pro

Tools built into the VLE, such as Blackboard Collaborate

Student voting handsets

What are student voting handsets?

These allow you to press a button on a hand-held device in response to a question posed on a screen used for the lecture or class.

The handsets work in much the same way as audience voting handsets used in TV programmes such as *Who Wants to Be a Millionaire?* Depending on the question, students make a *Yes/No* response or select from 4–6 choices that they can see on the screen. Responses are collated and displayed on the screen, and can be discussed by the class.

Voting can also be undertaken on students' mobile phones or smartphones instead of dedicated voting handsets. This is likely to be more widespread in the future.

Are responses anonymous?

Handsets issued for a single class

In such instances, you would usually collect a handset given out on a random basis as you entered the room. This would mean that your responses would be anonymous, so only you would know how you responded to each question.

Handsets linked to student ID

If each student is allocated an individual handset for a set of lectures, it is likely that these will be numbered and a record kept of which one you have been given. In general, this means that, although your individual responses can't be seen by the class, lecturers would be able to link your responses back to you. They would also be able to keep a record of each student's responses and track their answers or performance over one or more sessions.

Why are handsets used?

Lecturers may use student voting handsets for one or more of the following reasons:

- **As an icebreaker,** to identify what students in the class have in common.
- **To canvas opinion,** to identify viewpoints and perspectives held in the class.
- **To make class more interesting,** by involving everyone.
- **To check students' understanding** of the lecture so far, and to identify areas that might be proving difficult or confusing.
- **To generate discussion** of the results of the whole class's responses.
- **For problem solving,** working towards a solution together as a group.
- **To monitor changes of opinion,** identifying whether students' understanding or viewpoints alter following certain kinds of information or discussion.
- **To check understanding of essential information,** such as safety procedures. You could be asked to confirm your understanding by pressing a button on your response handset.
- **For class-based tests:** you would need to answer questions relatively quickly and may not be able to change answers once submitted.
- **To teach the understanding of data:** the collated responses from the class can be presented as data charts on the screen, which can be used to help understand what such data can and can't reveal.
- **To help exam preparation,** engaging students in working with the material in interesting ways that test and reinforce their understanding and recall.
- **To gather student feedback** about the quality of teaching for that class or for the whole course.
- **For course democracy,** enabling students to vote on issues relevant to them.
- **Any combination of the above.**

Making use of voting handset opportunities

Take an active part

If you have been given a voting handset to use in class, the experience is much more enjoyable if you join in. Be aware that lecturers can tell whether everyone has responded, and may be able to identify who didn't.

Make constructive choices

There may be a temptation to select choices on a random basis when you are asked certain kinds of questions, especially if you feel that you don't really know the answers. In such cases:

- Making your 'best guess' can still be useful: you may find you have better residual understanding and knowledge than you thought.
- Thinking through the issue in order to make a good guess will, in itself, help you to formulate the issues better in your own mind. This may help you in future assignments, exams or at work.
- Engaging fully in making a response, even if just a good guess, will help you to gain a sense of how effective guessing is for you as a strategy. This could serve you well in future situations or tests in knowing how far to trust your guesswork.
- You are likely to find the lecture or class discussion far more interesting if you have a genuine response of your own to compare with those of other people.

Compare your views and responses

If you are provided with the chance to see the whole class response on the presentation screen:

- Consider how your own responses compare with those of other people in the class.
- Take note of how others voted for each question, such as whether everyone who got the answer wrong selected the same incorrect answer. This helps you to put your own responses into context.
- Note other perspectives that people in your group hold on the issues; consider why that might be the case.

Test out your own learning

When handsets are used in class for activities that check for understanding or for exam preparation, make full use of the opportunity to gain insights into what you really know and can remember. Having to make voting responses at speed can show up areas of unexpected strength and weakness.

- **Test your memory:** check your accuracy and speed of recall, depending on how well you responded.
- **Note any incorrect answers** that you made; this will help you to identify where you need to find out more about the subject or do more work on that kind of problem. Making an incorrect answer can help you identify areas where your understanding may be weaker than you thought, indicating to you areas to work on further before your assignment or exam.
- **Keep a record** of the questions and answers you got wrong.
- **Note the right answers,** or follow up with the lecturer to gain these later.
- **Check that you understand** the correct answer and why your own response was incorrect.
- **Go back over that aspect of the course,** using your notes, reading more about it or discussing it with others in your class, until you are sure that you fully grasp the material.
- **Ask for help** if you find you still don't understand why you were getting questions wrong.
- **Note your track record** Your course lecturers may hold your responses to class tests and quizzes in a database or within the VLE/LMS. If so, check whether you can look at your record of responses in order to gain an overview of how well you performed.

Lecture capture

What is 'lecture capture'?

Your lecturers may choose to use one of a range of tools that enable them to record aspects of the lecture, so that you can use it again later. Depending on the tools they use, the lecture capture might be:

- a simple audio recording of the lecture;
- a recording that is synchronised with presentation materials such as slides;
- an integrated set of resources that includes such features as audio, video, slides and other presentation materials, chat and electronic whiteboards;
- some or all of the above, integrated into the VLE/LMS.

How will I know if lecture capture is in use?

It is likely that you would be in informed in advance or at the start of the lecture. You might also notice the lecturer wearing an additional microphone and there may be a video camera. The presentation screen may look different if specific software is being used to record the lecture.

How can I benefit from lecture capture?

Depending on the type of lecture capture used, you can do some or all of the following:

- interact with teachers and peers during class;
- listen, or watch, the lecture again later as many times as you like as part of your private study;
- go over any difficult parts of the lecture to help you understand the material;
- review parts of the lecture in a study group to stimulate discussion of the issues raised;
- use some or all of the lecture as an aid for exam preparation.

Accessing recorded lectures

Recordings would normally be made available to you through your VLE/LMS or a link to an external site. Content may be provided in Flash format or as a website, so you would need to check that your computer or mobile device can view the content.

Using recorded lectures effectively

Audio or video recordings

These are, in effect, podcasts or vodcasts. See Chapter 4 for guidance in using these for study.

Audio, video, presentation materials and narration

If you are provided with such a comprehensive set of resources to accompany a lecture or class, then:

- Plan in time soon after that lecture to go through these thoroughly.
- Read through notes that accompany the lecture as soon as possible afterwards, as this will help to clarify and reinforce the lecture content.
- Consider how you can make best use of each separate resource. Identify which are best to use while the lecture is fresh in your mind.
- Consider which parts of the lecture or the accompanying resources look most useful for assignments that are coming up for that course.
- Make your own notes about the content of these resources, integrating them with your own notes of that lecture.

What students say about lecture capture

"Recorded lectures were an invaluable aid for my exam preparation – I just wish I had allocated more time to use them effectively."

"I found it particularly useful to be able to see the lecture slides while listening to the lecturer speak; I used these resources a lot."

Lecture capture: chat

In some types of lecture capture (e.g., Adobe Connect Pro or Blackboard Collaborate), there are inbuilt facilities that enable students to post short instant messages or questions during the lecture, using a laptop computer or mobile device, which will appear on the presentation screen. These messages might be scrolled below the screen or displayed in a panel at the side. The lecturer may then use these to stimulate debate, monitor understanding and check issues arising for the class.

Chat (or instant messaging) tools offer a number of opportunities for in-class interaction. These can include:

- providing information to other students, such as details of books, articles, websites or materials relevant to the programme;
- commenting on the session, class or teaching materials;
- asking questions of other students.

> Can you explain that again?

> Is that always the case?

> Can you give us an example?

💬 Reflection: Chat tools in lectures

→ What kinds of questions would you find it helpful to raise if this facility were provided?

→ What kinds of questions or comments by other students would annoy you? How would you deal with these if the situation arose?

Dos and don'ts of using chat tools in class

If you are provided with the opportunity to use an on-screen chat function during a lecture session or class:

Do

- Take part.
- Use the chat tools to make a valid contribution – (not just because they are there).
- Always consider what questions or comments are generally useful for those in the room.
- Ensure all your questions and comments are relevant.
- Keep contributions brief and to the point.
- Be constructive and kind in your responses to the lecturer or other students – even if you disagree with their point of view or their style of presentation.
- Leave space for the lecturer to complete the lecture – avoid 'hogging the floor'.
- Leave space for other students to contribute when they are ready. Avoid jumping in as soon as there is a space.
- Remain focused on the main messages of the lecture.

Don't

- Don't abuse the opportunity.
- Don't waste other students' time. Students who want to focus on the lecture will be annoyed by distracting and irrelevant chat comments.
- Don't ask questions just to be noticed by the lecturer or other students.
- Don't try to outdo or outsmart other students or the lecturer.
- Don't take up all the chat time available.
- Don't let yourself be distracted by the chat if it goes off the point.

Preparing to use collaborative learning tools

What are collaborative learning tools?

These tools are designed to allow you to interact online with your lecturer or tutor and other students. They may be:

- located within your VLE, as in Blackboard Collaborate; or
- accessed via a website on the Internet, as in Adobe Connect Pro.

The specific features available vary according to the product used by your university or college, but as a student you would normally be able to access all features free of charge.

What features do they offer?

Collaborative learning tools generally offer:

- **Interactive whiteboard facilities** for developing ideas, notes, diagrams or drawings together as a group.
- **Presentations or discussion** of learning resources, such as your lecturer's PowerPoint slides. You could also access webinars provided by external companies or organisations.
- **Audioand/or video stream** so you could listen to, and possibly see, lecturers and students. Your lecturer might invite you to an online tutorial to discuss a particular topic or find about a forthcoming assignment.
- **Instant messaging or chat facilities (with audio)** so that you can ask questions of the lecturer or students.

Where would I find these tools?

Your lecturer or tutor will normally inform you if you are going to be using such a tool in your learning and will provide you with instructions about how to access it. Access will normally require a login to identify you as a student on the course.

Why are collaborative learning tools used?

These tools are used for communicating with students over the Internet, instead of face to face. Traditionally, they were used with students on distance learning programmes where there was little face-to-face teaching. Now, they are often used to supplement class-based teaching.

Preparing for a collaborative class

Before the class begins, prepare for the session. The following checklist may help your preparation.

Internet access and computer setup

- [ ] The Internet connection is working.
- [ ] The microphone is plugged in and working.
- [ ] The webcam is plugged in and working.
- [ ] My login information is available.
- [ ] I remember how to use the tools in an online class.

Learning preparation

- [ ] I have completed my background reading for the class.
- [ ] I have prepared a short list of questions about things I want to have clarified from the reading, the last taught session, or about our assignments.
- [ ] I have completed the preparatory work set by the lecturer or the group.

Environment

- [ ] I have a quiet place to study for the duration of the class.
- [ ] I am not expecting any disturbances such as phone calls or visitors for the duration of the class.
- [ ] I have all the materials I need to hand.
- [ ] I am focused and ready to learn and participate.

Using collaborative learning tools in class

Working collaboratively

People react differently to collaborative learning. It can be extremely stimulating to bring ideas together, and see ideas develop from embryo into fully fledged plans, drawings or other group outputs.

Once you have learnt the basic mechanics of using collaborative tools, these can provide an exciting electronic or class-based atmosphere for generating thought and discussion. The speed at which ideas can sometimes develop when many people are contributing through the same tool can be surprising as well as productive.

On the other hand, not everybody feels as comfortable working with the technology and it can feel:

- chaotic, if everyone is trying to contribute at once;
- rather flat, if nobody joins in;
- frustrating, if one or two people dominate.

Play your part

- Be open to participating.
- As with other kinds of group work, be mindful of your own contributions. Take note of how often you contribute compared to others.
- If you are a keen participator, leave space for others to join in.
- If you don't tend to contribute, be more proactive in coming up with ideas and sharing these through the tools. If you find that you don't have much to say, do more preparation before class so that you are well informed and can draw on your reading and list of questions.
- Look for opportunities to bring in other people so that everyone gets a chance to contribute.
- Respond to comments and ideas from others in the group rather than interacting only with the lecturer (unless that is the protocol).

Making the most of an online class

When the class begins and you log in, your lecturer will explain how to use the tools available and how you can join in during the class.

The following checklist may help you make the most of the class:

Using collaborative learning tools

Learning from others

- [ ] Focus on what the lecturer and other participants are saying, writing or drawing.
- [ ] Make selective written notes about what the lecturer or other participants say, to help you remember important points later.
- [ ] Jot down any questions that arise while listening to the lecturer; ask these when there is a break for questions or post them as instant messages if that option is used in your class.

Interacting with others

- [ ] If you have the choice, decide whether you prefer to ask your questions aloud or by using instant messaging.
- [ ] Make sure you know how to use collaborative tools for writing notes or drawing collaboratively.

Practicalities

- [ ] Make sure you know how to use your microphone/webcam for when you want to participate.
- [ ] Check whether you are posting public or private instant messages.
- [ ] Avoid becoming distracted by the features provided through the collaborative tools; focus on those which have been identified for use during that class.

Observe the courtesies

- [ ] Find out the protocol for asking questions and contributing when these tools are used, as this may be different than in a traditional class.
- [ ] Avoid disrupting the class for other learners.
- [ ] Be a good team member: participate without feeling that you have to express all your ideas at the expense of other people having a chance to take part.

Case study: collaborative tutorial

Online collaborative tutorial

Luke was enrolled on a communication studies degree course. This included a series of online group collaborative tutorials with his lecturer and five other students. Before the first tutorial, Luke was provided with information about:

- how to log in to the collaborative learning space;
- how to use the features available;
- work to complete in advance of the class.

For the tutorial, the group was asked to read a number of press releases in advance. They were asked to jot down outline responses to several questions provided by the lecturer; students would be asked to talk through their answers and compare their views with those of others in the group, so as to stimulate discussion about the best ways of presenting the issues. Following on from that, the students would use the interactive tools in order to prepare, as a group, a model press release.

Luke was apprehensive before the first online collaborative tutorial. It was scheduled at a time when he would be at home in his student flat and he was worried about his Internet connection being reliable on his laptop. He was also a bit worried about using the webcam and microphone on his laptop as these hadn't worked well the last time he had tried to use them for a social purpose.

At the allotted time, Luke logged into the online collaborative tutorial. From the list of participants, he could see that his classmates and lecturer were already logged in. He followed the instructions to check his microphone was working but was unable to get his webcam to display his image.

During the tutorial, Luke did contribute to the discussion and tutorial activity using instant messaging and speaking via his microphone, but he felt he missed out by not having a working webcam.

When the group worked together to produce a collaborative document, the students were all able to contribute to an online document simultaneously while discussing the changes using the voice tools and the instant messaging tool. They also used the whiteboard to sketch out a plan of the document during the planning phase.

Luke's comments

"I enjoyed the online tutorial – it was actually quite productive. It felt just as good as working on an assignment sat around a table in the library. We managed to draw up a list of all the best and worst features of the press articles that we read – though I hadn't read them all so some of it went over my head. It didn't help that I couldn't see what the others were pointing to in the articles. We did get as far as drawing up some initial bullet points as an outline for our press release but we didn't get it finished. Also it was only the first tutorial so we may get better.

My webcam wasn't working … I couldn't see the others, I felt a bit left out. They couldn't see my body language so if I paused to think when I was speaking, somebody else always cut in. They could see the other speakers so I think they were more patient letting them think through what they wanted to say when they were speaking. After a while, I became a bit frustrated so I didn't contribute as much myself. One thing I really liked was that we had a permanent record of the conversation and the resources, which was a bonus."

☺ Activity: Preparing for collaborative sessions

Consider Luke's experience of an online collaborative tutorial.

→ What would you recommend that he did differently before and during his next online tutorial?

→ How would you prepare for such a tutorial yourself?

Video conferencing tools

What are video conferencing tools?

These tools are designed to allow you to communicate with another person (or group of people) using the Internet. The most commonly known example, currently, is Skype™.

Video conferencing tools are increasingly complex and share many features with online collaborative learning tools (see pp. 146–9 above).

What equipment do I need?

You need:

- access to a computer or mobile device with the video conferencing software installed (or available via the Internet);
- a reliable high quality Internet connection;
- an integral, or external, webcam attached to your computer or mobile device;
- an integral, or external, microphone connected to your computer or mobile device.

Install Skype on your computer, smartphone or mobile device. You can download the PC software from www.skype.com, where you will find full instructions for other downloads.

Using Skype while away from campus

- Check in advance that you will be able to gain access to the Internet (either via wi-fi or a data package) in that location.
- Check that you have an Internet-enabled device while on placement.
- If you are taking your own device, install the necessary software and check it is working before you leave home.
- Remember to take with you your login details so that you can access your Skype profile.

What is voice over Internet protocol (VoIP)?

VoIP allows you to transmit audio and video information via video conferencing tools across the Internet. There are many VoIP providers and services that allow you to make and receive calls over the Internet. This section focuses on Skype as a VoIP tool which has many features that you can use in your studies.

Helpful features of Skype for academic study

- **Internet calls (audio and video)** You can make audio/video calls to other Skype users' computers (or mobile devices) for free.
- **Calls** You can make calls to telephones from Skype, although for a charge.
- **Profile** You can display a public (or private) profile including your personal information.
- **Contacts** You can set up a contact list of your Skype friends, family, peers and lecturers.
- **Instant messaging** You can send SMS or instant message-style messages to your Skype contacts.
- **Links with social networks** You can link Skype with social networks such as Facebook.
- **Mobile device support** You can use Skype on a range of smartphones and tablet devices.
- **Conference calls** You can conduct conference calls (including video at a cost) with multiple Skype users.
- **Screen sharing** You can share your screen with Skype users (at a charge) during a call.

Using video conferencing as a student

How would I use this in my studies?

How you use video conferencing will depend on your programme, the projects that you are involved in, and the personal preferences of you, your lecturers and those in your class. You might use it for online conversations, discussions or meetings in the following ways:

- **with your tutors or lecturers**, such as for tutorials, coaching or support;
- **with other students**, for formal or informal peer support, socialising, discussing assignments;
- **with study group or project group members**, such as to update each other on your individual contributions to the assignment or to call upon each other for ideas and support;
- **with participants in research projects** that you may undertake for your programme;
- **with your university contact**, if your programme of study is based mainly in the workplace or is a distance learning course;
- **with a workplace supervisor**, to keep in contact when on campus or otherwise away from the workplace for study-related activity.

Keeping in contact while on placement

Many students do a work or industrial placement as part of their degree or course, which means spending time away from the campus, and may include travelling to a foreign country. During these placements, students remain in contact with a lecturer or academic supervisor at their university or college, often via email. Video conferencing tools provide an opportunity to engage in a conversation that can feel more meaningful, and enable you to feel more in touch.

Interviewing participants for your research project

Most students will be involved with one or more research projects over the course of their degree programme. For some, this will involve collecting data from other people, either in the form of questionnaires or through interviews.

If your project requires you to conduct interviews with people located at a distance from your institution, it may be most efficient and cost-effective to arrange interviews via Skype.

Using Skype for conducting interviews

- **Check the ethical and legal considerations** For example, you may need to obtain special permissions for interviewing children and there would need to be solid procedures for ensuring that the interviews were age-appropriate, and that the material would not be used on the Internet in unintended and unethical ways.

- **Check for feasibility** Check that your interviewee is able to access Skype. Depending on the kind of project that you are undertaking, the participants involved, and the nature of the involvement of employers or other organisations, it may be possible for participants to use Skype facilities offered at work or by others.

- **Support your interviewee** Check that your interviewee is comfortable using such technology. Explain clearly what will happen and what they need to do. If they are not happy speaking online, look for an alternative method of interviewing them or a different interviewee.

- **Manage your environment** Ensure that you won't be disturbed during the interview and the background visible in the screen is appropriate for the interview.

- **Check the technology** Ensure your Internet connection is reliable. Check that your interviewee can hear and see you clearly before starting.

Case study: video conferencing for research project interviews

The project

Malika was a final-year psychology student conducting a research project on the diet and fitness regimes of top athletes. Her project required her to conduct interviews with eight to ten athletes competing at county level.

Malika quickly realised that she couldn't afford to travel to speak to participants across the country. At first, she decided to use Skype for interviews with four participants who lived over 30 miles from her university. However, her lecturer said that she needed to control the interview conditions as a variable; this means that she had to be consistent in using either a Skype or a face-to-face interview. She opted to conduct all ten interviews through video conferencing.

> *"I chose Skype over phone interviews because I wanted to see participants' body language in order to make judgements about the emotional content of their responses."*

The process

Malika first checked whether everyone could use Skype. To her dismay, several didn't know what it was and felt rather reluctant, to begin with. A few were anxious that they would go blank if put on the spot answering questions when talking into a camera. Malika talked through what would be involved and helped potential interviewees to think through how they might access Skype through work or people they knew. For one person she negotiated an interview through a local sports club. All of this took a lot of time.

> *"I hadn't realised how anxious and self-conscious participants would be about using the technology. I would know that for future projects."*

Once she knew Skype was a real possibility, Malika finalised the details by email and phone, making sure everyone knew the time of their interview, and how to work Skype. She also reminded them by email the day before their interview. She sent guidance, in advance, of the kinds of topics she would cover so that interviewees felt confident that they would have something to say.

> *"I had been warned to make sure that my own connection was good. I hadn't thought through that there would be many aspects of participants' own technology that could go wrong. Three participants had very poor connections, and I couldn't really use the visual information in the same ways as for other participants. I couldn't use the material so had to find at least one new participant at short notice so as to have the minimum of eight interviewees."*

Her conclusions on using this approach

Malika's overall judgement was that it had been useful to use video conferencing:

- It was more affordable for her.
- It helped that she could see participants.
- She learnt more about the process of video conferencing which she could draw upon for future projects.

Malika's comments

> *"It was a definite bonus to be able to see people while interviewing them rather than conducting interviews by phone. For this research, it was fine that I could just see people's faces. I did notice, though, that it was hard to read other aspects of body language as I couldn't always see participants' hands or more than head and shoulders. That might be relevant for future projects.*
>
> *I would certainly use it again, but only if a project required a relatively small number of interviews or if I didn't need to control the interview format for variables. I would plan in more time for preparation, especially if I was working with people who are not used to video conferencing."*

Case study: video conferencing for support on placement

Gareth was a pharmacology student undertaking a year-long industrial placement at a pharmaceutical company in Singapore. Gareth heard monthly from the lecturer at his institution in the UK who was his contact while on placement.

Before leaving for Singapore, Gareth requested a brief video conference with his future line manager in Singapore so that they could introduce each other. This led to a series of short Skype conversations where Gareth was able to clarify details about the work arrangements and speak to future work colleagues. He asked about the kinds of things he should bring for the year ahead and was able to gain a feel for life in Singapore and at the company.

"Although I had much of this information already in the documentation provided, it felt different being able to talk it through, ask questions about things I didn't fully understand, and be able to see who I was talking to. It was helpful just to see what they were wearing – I realised that I would need different clothes for the working environment than I had imagined. I felt I made a good connection with people there, so I felt less anxious about travelling so far away."

Although Gareth enjoyed the experience of living and working abroad, there were some aspects of the placement that he found problematic. He spoke to his lecturer on Skype a number of times during the placement to help clarify his thinking. He also missed his family and found it invaluable to see them from time to time through using the technology.

Gareth also used Skype to talk to a careers adviser at his university about what preparation he needed to undertake prior to applying for jobs when he returned. After university, Gareth went on to a career in the pharmaceutical industry.

"I did feel a bit homesick and it helped to see a face from home or my university. It was great to speak to my family and especially to be able to see for myself that my Dad was OK – I had been worried about him. Being in touch with my family and my lecturer made the critical difference for me in completing my placement successfully. The video and sound quality were surprisingly good given the distance."

Reflection: Using video conferencing

From your reading of Malika's and Gareth's experiences of video conferencing:

→ What insights have you gained about when and how this technology might be of benefit to you – and when it would not?

→ What tips and insights have you picked up about how to prepare in advance when using this technology as part of your studies?

Dad, I think you need to step back …

Mobile devices

Many of the activities and technologies discussed in this book can be performed and used on a mobile device. If you are wondering whether to purchase a smartphone, tablet or other portable media device, or already have one, consider the following.

Selecting a mobile device for study

- Can you view content on the Internet easily when using it?
- Can you use it to access your VLE/LMS, either through the Internet or a specific app?
- Can you purchase and use apps on it? There are educational apps available in app stores that could enhance your study.
- Can you access e-books through it? There are textbooks available in electronic forms, often with interactive content. Would you find it easy to read these from its screen?
- Are you intending to use it to write assignments? If so, would you be able to type on it for long periods of time?
- Can you attach a portable keyboard to it, if you prefer that option?
- Can you make notes and/or record audio on your device? If so, that could be an advantage in lectures and for capturing ideas for an assignment when on the move.
- Realistically, would you carry it onto campus or use it for study in these ways?
- What are the total costs, including that for apps, downloads and ongoing connection charges?

Pros and cons

Advantages of smartphones for learning

Smartphones are adapting quickly to offer a broader range of ways of accessing and interacting with academic learning materials. Depending on the model, these are just some of the ways you could use a smartphone to support your academic study:

- access your VLE/LMS and the range of resources and tools provided there;
- access your HEI's mobile learning app or website;
- keep up to date with course emails;
- stay organised with a calendar available through the phone;
- download apps such as study aids and encyclopaedias (see pp. 158–9);
- read online content via websites configured for mobile access, or via apps;
- record lectures using an audio recording tool;
- take photographs or videos of relevant objects or activities for inclusion in assignments or use in group discussions;
- take brief notes;
- use social networking tools such as Facebook or Twitter for group learning (see Chapter 7);
- contribute to on-screen instant messaging chats in lectures (see p. 146);
- access podcasts of lectures from iTunesU or other sites (see Chapter 4);
- take part in online quizzes;
- participate in SMS voting;
- participate in online video conferencing.

Disadvantages of smartphones for learning

It is not easy or advisable to use a smartphone for more than limited typing or reading. You would need to use additional alternative equipment for activities such as:

- writing lengthy and complex assignments;
- reading journal articles, online books or lengthy course materials;
- those tasks that require you to switch regularly between applications.

Mobile devices: tablets and e-readers

Tablet devices

These are relatively expensive so it is important to weigh the total costs, especially connection charges. Most devices fall into one of four main categories, according to the operating system that they use:

- Apple (iOS operating system);
- Android (Android operating system);
- BlackBerry (BlackBerry Tablet operating system);
- Windows (Microsoft operating system).

Well-known examples are:

- Apple iPad (Apple);
- Samsung Galaxy Tab (Android);
- BlackBerry PlayBook (BlackBerry);
- ExoPC slate (Windows).

Using a tablet device for study

A tablet can be a convenient alternative to a laptop. They are relatively light to carry and, providing you have Internet access, offer easy access to online services and tools. The quality of your Internet connection is key.

Word processing and printing

You may need to download a word-processing app to your device and update your operating system to do so. You can then export your document (i.e., send it to another computer or to a printer with a wireless connection) in order to work with it on a different computer or to print it.

Ways of using a tablet device for study

- Access resources from your VLE/LMS in class or off campus.
- Keep up to date with course emails.
- Use the calendar provided.
- Record lectures using an audio tool.
- Write notes during lectures or class.
- Add to your notes after a lecture.
- Download apps for learning.
- Write assignments.
- Access interactive e-books.
- Look up definitions, terms and concepts on the Internet or apps.
- Write assignments if you download the appropriate word-processing tools.
- Access multimedia content such as podcasts and educational videos.
- Search databases for journals.
- Use social networking tools such as Facebook or Twitter for group learning.
- Participate in online video conferencing.
- Store references.
- Read copies of papers and references.

Using an e-reader for learning

e-Readers are tablet-shaped devices designed for reading digital books or other digital content. They have screens that are made to assist reading under different kinds of light conditions. The key advantage of these is that you gain access to a great many books when you are away from a library. Before investing in one of these for study, check that the books needed for your course are available in suitable format.

e-Book apps

iBooks Online bookstore (free and paid books); also stores PDFs.
Inkling Interactive textbooks for many subject areas.
Kindle Online bookstore from Amazon.

Using mobile devices for study

Considerations for using a mobile device

- **Security** Consider the environments in which you transport and use mobile devices.
- **Weight** Although relatively light, mobile devices are still a considerable weight to carry around all day. Check if secure lockers are available.
- **Multiple sets of hardware** It is likely that you will need to have access to other hardware such as a PC for updating the operating system and to a printer. Think about whether your mobile device is best for reading, writing or audiovisual tasks.
- **Simultaneous updating** There are apps such as Dropbox that allow you to work on documents on your PC and mobile device simultaneously, so that they are automatically updated. If you lose the connection, Dropbox would update the file automatically once you reconnect.
- **Instant information** It can be helpful to use your mobile device to make quick searches in class such as to find a definition or translation.
- **Distraction** It is easy to become distracted from study by various tools available on the device. Have a plan for managing this.

Using searching and reference tools on mobile devices

- **Your library catalogue** may be available in a mobile version, such as through an app or a mobile-compatible website.
- **Bibliographic databases** sometimes have a mobile-compatible website so you can use them on a mobile device. If not, then use a PC.
- **Online search engines** are all mobile compatible; some such as Google and Yahoo have apps to make searching even easier.
- **Reference management tools** can sometimes be used on a mobile device. For example, Mendeley is available as an app and you can synchronise your references between the Web, your desktop version and your mobile devices. This allows you to maintain and search a single reference database, which would be more efficient.

What students say about mobile devices

Below are quotes from students who have used a tablet PC for a few months as part of their course:

"It completely changed the way I study – everything is at my fingertips."

"I take it everywhere."

"I used my iPad for all my data collection during my final-year project … It was my laboratory notebook."

"I use my mobile device to record all of my lectures. I listen to them in the library while making notes."

Viewing sound, images and video

Mobile devices are well configured to listen to audio and view images and video. You can easily:

- listen to podcasts;
- browse online images;
- watch videos.

Capturing information

Mobile devices are excellent for:

- recording audio (e.g., lectures);
- recording video (e.g., for video assignments);
- taking photos (e.g., from field studies);
- recording GPS information (e.g., for sports studies).

Reading news feeds on a mobile device

Mobile devices are ideal for viewing news feeds delivered by RSS. There are many apps that allow you access to news feeds and deliver the content in a very accessible and digestible format.

You can use apps to keep up to date with RSS content on your mobile device:

- RSS readers
- Podcaster
- Twitter
- Google apps

Apps to support your studies

Accessing study information using apps

Smartphones and tablet devices allow you to download apps. Many of these are free and useful for study. There may also be apps specific to your subject discipline. The following are examples of Apple apps for iPhones and iPads.

Dropbox
Free online storage which can synchronise across multiple devices.

Google Docs
Free online storage which can be accessed from multiple devices.

Storing your files

If you are using online storage facilities, remember to make regular backups. Many universities recommend that you only use their file systems for storing university work.

Mendeley
Reference management tool.

Papers
Journal article search and storage tool.

Reference management apps

These make it easier to store and use details of your books, articles and other sources, for use in the reference section of your assignments.

Soundnote
Soundnote
To record audio and make notes which are synchronised to the audio: for recording lectures.

MaxJournal
Diary tool for recording reflections on your study or work experience.

Coursenotes
Note-making tool.

Dictionary
Comprehensive dictionary with thesaurus.

iTunesU
Academic podcasts

Study aids

Apps for Android devices

Android users can access some of the apps described on p. 157 through the Android Market: https://market.android.com/apps. For example, Dropbox and Dictionary are available on both Apple and Android devices. However, some apps are currently only available on Apple devices. Here, we suggest some Android alternatives.

 **Audionote:** For writing notes and recording audio. This app has similar functionality to Soundnote (an iOS app).

 Evernote: For writing notes and capturing assets. This is available on Android and Apple devices.

 Springpad: A popular note-writing app.

 Referey: While Mendeley is not available on Android, Referey allows you to access your Mendeley database and references on an Android device. You can also access your Mendeley database via the Internet.

Lifemate Diary: This is a multimedia diary tool on Android that allows you to record your life in words, photos, videos and sounds.

At the time of writing the Papers app was not available on Android. For more information about this app, see: www.mekentosj.com/papers/

e-Books

Many e-books, including student textbooks, are also available through the Android Market, as are e-book apps such as Kindle and Google Books.

Apps for BlackBerry devices

BlackBerry users can search for apps via the BlackBerry App World on their device or at: http://appworld.blackberry.com/. With the release of the BlackBerry Playbook, there is sure to be a rise in useful apps for BlackBerry users.

Apps such as Dropbox, Google tools, Facebook and Twitter are available on BlackBerry but few of the study apps (or equivalents) described on p. 157 were available at the time of writing.

Popular apps for BlackBerry, relevant for students, include:

 **Evernote:** For writing notes and storing digital assets.

 **Student Buddy:** For organising assignments, classes and deadlines.

e-Books

Overdrive media console: Allows you to check out digital copies of books and audiobooks from your library (if registered).

Mobi-books, Free Books, Book Reader for EPUB and Kindle books: These provide access to many e-books and textbooks.

Mobile devices in practical study settings

Mobile devices in academic environments

The award-winning Assessment and Learning in Practice Settings (ALPS) academic project examined the role of mobile devices in health and social care professions.

Students used mobile devices successfully for reflective and assessment purposes. They were asked to record their competencies and skills on mobile devices and were assessed while out on practice in healthcare settings.

Staff were able to provide students with appropriate learning resources via a mobile device and to receive regular feedback on students' progress and competencies. Students could include feedback from peers and clients, captured through their mobile devices. If required, they could use their mobile devices to complete an e-portfolio as a record of their professional development activities.

The ALPS team have begun to develop mobile apps for students to use to develop their communication and reflective skills.

ALPS maps in iTunes

ALPS maps is available as an app through iTunes and provides a number of maps in key areas. These include:

- communication;
- ethical awareness;
- patient safety skills;
- teamworking.

Students can use this to develop and show evidence of their professional competencies.

For more information, see www.alps-cetl.ac.uk.

Mobile devices in practical settings

Students at some universities and colleges are now given tablet devices to use in practical settings such as workshops and laboratories, usually for a particular activity and for a limited time. Students can use these to look up information, learn how to use equipment, collect data and analyse results. Often the device will be pre-configured with appropriate content, apps and links before the students start using it, so as ensure that it best supports activity in class.

Experience from these settings is still being gathered, but early indications suggest that students highly value the opportunity afforded by this use of technology. Evidence to date suggests that students find it easy and enjoyable to use and that it gives them confidence to engage more deeply in the learning activity; this helps their learning.

Example: neuroanatomy class

In one recent trial at the University of Leeds, students were provided with a tablet device in a neuroanatomy practical class where they were learning about structures within the brain. The devices were configured with a number of apps to help with 3D visualisation of brain structures, and students used the apps extensively during the class. Students found the devices highly beneficial for enhancing their understanding of the material covered during the class, and one student commented:

> "The 3D brain app on the tablet device really helped me to understand how different regions of the brain are related to one another in ways that models and pictures weren't able to do."

Summary

The technologies covered in this chapter are deployed by academic staff primarily as a means of engaging students more actively in the process of learning. This is partly to make class-based and other activities more interesting by varying the format of lessons. It is also for stimulating thinking and debate, and to encourage students to join in so that they have better understanding and recall. The technologies provide different ways for students to ask questions, consider the issues and contribute to the creation of new knowledge.

While technologies such as voting handsets are used in class, others, such as video conferencing and some collaborative learning tools, are used at the other end of the spectrum to support study when all participants are not in the same place. These might be used to keep in contact and provide help for students whose study is primarily work based, or who are temporarily away from campus on field trips or placements. They may be used simply to save students from making additional journeys onto campus when that might be inconvenient or costly.

Many of the technologies outlined above can be used irrespective of location although, for optimum use, most are dependent on the quality of the Internet connection. Some make use of technologies already popular with students, such as mobile phones, smartphones, tablets and Skype. The advantage of this is that the technologies are either already familiar to students or, if new to them, can be used for other areas of student life such as socialising and keeping in touch with friends and family.

To use these tools effectively for study, it is important to remain aware of the nature of academic study and its conventions. In general, traditional ways of interpreting and using information for study are not abandoned when new technologies are used.

The technologies themselves are also adapting to better fit the kinds of purposes for which students might wish to use them and in a variety of contexts and locations. As the diagram on p. 142 illustrates, the technologies often assume that you will already be familiar with a range of other hardware, software, search methodologies and tools. Mobile devices such as tablets and smartphones provide the means to call upon and combine a range of technologies, tools and means of communication all through a single tool, to support different aspects of study.

Chapter 9

Drawing it together

By this stage in the book, you have covered:

- many kinds of technology;
- many ways of using those technologies;
- study skills relevant to using those technologies for academic purposes.

The changing scene

The range of ways that technologies are adapted to support academic study is growing all the time. There isn't a standard set of technologies that would be used by all teaching staff. This book has looked at:

- those technologies that are most likely to be used by some or all of your lecturers, including more established technologies such as virtual learning environments (VLE) and more recent arrivals such as voting handsets, lecture capture, blogging and collaborative tools;
- and technologies such as Facebook, Twitter and video conferencing tools that you might use already for other purposes. If you enjoy these already, you may wish to harness their use for your study.

Already, new technologies will have appeared, or be about to appear, that will add further richness to this area.

Using technological diversity

The book has included some areas that are more controversial, such as:

- the use of popular social networking tools;
- student-to-student communication through chat;
- the integration of smartphones and other mobile devices into your learning;
- the use of wikis and, if used appropriately, Wikipedia.

These can all add to your enjoyment, interest and convenience in studying your subject. They can open up new sources of information and ways of thinking. However, they do need to be used in ways that are mindful of the conventions and values of your subject discipline. They also need to be used with due attention to such matters as netiquette and personal safety.

Using technologies on your programme

Lecturer approaches

Every programme of study takes a distinct approach to the use of these technologies, from no use at all in some cases to very particular combinations of technology and face-to-face teaching in others.

Your lecturers will each have distinct views about how useful such technologies are in the context of academic study and whether they are suited to the subject matter and teaching style used in their field. They may also use particular technologies to suit the type of class or the learning activity.

You may find that they use new technologies a great deal – or not at all. It is likely that they will be individual in the ways that they:

- select and combine technologies to suit the programme;
- make use of any given technology.

Your choices

It follows that there isn't one 'right way' for you to use such technologies either. It is likely that there will be a great deal of scope for you to combine these course-based technologies with your own in order to suit your own preferred ways of studying.

Case studies: mixing it up

Below are three case studies that illustrate how students can work with the technologies in distinct ways.

Case study: combining the technologies (1)

Scenario: Osmane

An announcement in the VLE/LMS informed Osmane that three local employers had been invited to speak at his next lecture about projects that they were running for students interested in entering those industries. It mentioned that this lecture would be recorded and would offer chat.

Using online information

Osmane arrived early on campus. He went to the café and used his tablet to search for details about the companies and type questions he might want to ask the presenters. He joined their groups on LinkedIn to see more about them.

Downloading slides from the lecture

When he arrived at the lecture room, Osmane saw two pieces of information displayed on the screen. The first provided details of websites from which he could download the presentations. He downloaded these straight away and was pleased to see that he could insert his own notes in two of them for his private use.

Online chat using Twitter

The presentation screen also gave the address of a Twitter account for students to use for comments and questions during the lecture. Osmane's friends logged into this from their laptops but he decided to use his smartphone to log in to the chat.

Once the presentations started, students' questions started to appear down the side of the presentation screen. The speaker didn't refer to these at first. Students sent multiple tweets, answering each other's questions and referring each other to sites in the VLE/LMS or to other sources that answered their questions.

Osmane's classmate, Billy, tweeted that he had missed a reference mentioned by the employer. Osmane had noted this, so showed Billy on his own tablet screen. Several students had tweeted responses; from these, Osmane noticed that he had made an error in his own notes and so he corrected that.

Presentations available on the VLE/LMS

Osmane's other friend, Rosy, preferred just to listen and take notes on paper. She downloaded the presentations from the VLE/LMS later.

Question and answer

Osmane wanted more information about how the company selected students to work on the projects, so he tweeted a question to find out. This clearly interested other students as several related questions came up on the screen. After a while, the speaker summarised the comments that had been tweeted and responded to the questions. She gave details of a website that provided the details Osmane wanted.

Group discussion and debate

The final presentation included technical information and some data that the class found surprising. This stimulated a burst of tweets on screen that the speaker also opened up for discussion in the room. After the lecture, Osmane and his study group picked up on one of the issues on their class discussion board.

Osmane found that some of the students' posts on the discussion board showed they had confused points made by the first two speakers. He posted a comment of his own to clarify that the points made by each speaker applied only to their own businesses, and not generally to the industry.

Using a podcast of the recording

Later that day, Osmane logged in to the VLE/LMS and downloaded the recording of the third speaker as a podcast. He listened to this on his way home. He found the explanation of the technical detail very helpful so stored it to listen to it again when studying for his exams.

Case study: combining the technologies (2)

Scenario: Rebekah

Rebekah was a first-year philosophy student enrolled on an elective module (course) in biology called 'Biology of the Mind'. Her experience of this large, lecture-based module was very different from the teaching and learning in philosophy, which was based on small group tutorials.

A blend of teaching approaches

The lecturers on the 'Biology of the Mind' module all used voting handsets in their lectures to check students' knowledge and understanding. This was completely new to Rebekah but she really enjoyed getting individual feedback in each lecture about which parts of the lecture she had understood. She noted down questions that she had got wrong so she could look up the answers.

All of the lectures were also made available as audio recordings in the VLE/LMS. At first Rebekah wasn't aware of this. She tried hard to write down everything that the lecturers said, until another student told her about the podcasts. In subsequent lectures, she spent more time listening and trying to understand the concepts, making more focused notes and jotting down questions, knowing that she could pick up on other details later. After each lecture, she used the audio recording, her initial notes and the recommended reading to write a more detailed set of notes about each topic covered.

One of the lecturers on the module used social media – Twitter and Facebook – to post links to research papers, websites and YouTube material every week. Rebekah had never used Twitter, so she chose to Like the module page in Facebook. She used these resources to add extra detail to her lecture notes. She found some of the YouTube videos helped her to understand difficult concepts.

Interacting with other students

Rebekah found it a bit lonely being the only philosophy student on a biology module with over 300 other students. She missed the opportunity to discuss problems in weekly tutorials as they did on her philosophy programme. Instead, she had to adapt to using online resources to discuss topics with other students and the lecturers.

The module manager provided a discussion board for students to ask questions about the lectures and Rebekah checked this at least once a week. She found that other students were asking questions about things she didn't understand and she found the answers and discussion really useful. She posted a few questions on the board during the course, and even replied to another student's question, with a link to an online resource she had found useful.

The neuroscience students enrolled on the module had formed a group in Facebook. Rebekah requested to join the group and was accepted by the group administrator. When she reviewed the previous posts, she saw that students had been discussing topics about the 'Biology of the Mind' module. She became an active member of this group as the discussions helped her understand the module and she also made new friends through it.

Consolidating knowledge and studying

Rebekah had three exams to prepare for, including one for the 'Biology of the Mind' module. She started preparing in the last few weeks of term, reviewing the online resources in the VLE/LMS. She found a whole collection of online practice assessments in the 'Biology of the Mind' module. Rebekah used these questions to check her understanding of topics she had studied, noted areas where she scored badly, and used those insights to give focus to her preparation.

At the end of the module, Rebekah attended a study session in which the lecturer asked students a number of questions using the voting handsets and then discussed the answers. She found this session helpful for checking how effective her exam preparation had been, and for noting where she still needed to add to her knowledge.

Scenario: Jake

Jake was a third-year medical student intercalating in microbiology. This meant he took a year out of medicine to complete a BSc degree; he entered the microbiology degree programme in the third (final) year. Jake faced a number of study challenges because the programmes of medicine and microbiology used different teaching. He found that his prior experience with technology helped him with this challenge.

Keeping abreast of research

On the microbiology degree, Jake was faced with lectures that discussed current research papers and assumed a great deal of prior knowledge from the earlier year of the programme that he had not taken. He attended a library session on how to use his tablet device to search for, store and manage research articles from journals. He used his own device to read, annotate and then make notes about research papers that his lecturers referred to. Jake found it useful that he could search for new papers on his mobile device during lectures. He also liked using Mendeley as a reference management tool as it gave him information and comments about the papers he was reading, and links to related journal articles.

As an avid Twitter user, Jake made good use of this to view tables of contents from journals and links to papers on social media tools. He posted links to relevant papers that he thought other people would be interested in. He began to follow microbiology learned societies and organisations to find out about developments in the field.

Professional development

As a trainee doctor, Jake was used to developing and recording his professional development skills. Within microbiology, he was also required to record his competencies, both within the laboratory and as part of his academic development. Before his laboratory classes, Jake was required to complete online health and safety training exercises within the VLE/LMS and record the results in his e-portfolio. He also had to reflect on his professional development within his blog in preparation for meeting his personal tutor (academic adviser). He had been recording his academic progress since the beginning of his studies so this provided a useful background for his initial discussions with his lecturers in microbiology.

Group project: teamwork with technology

Jake was assigned to a group of three students for his final-year project. He met them along with his academic supervisor before the project started and they agreed to use technology to help them keep in touch, plan the project, record progress and share information. The group discussed how best to use the technology available to them and agreed to use the following resources:

1 Private Facebook group for sharing and discussing ongoing progress and planning meetings.
2 Google Docs for sharing documents, data and presentation materials.
3 Dropbox for sharing raw data files incompatible with Google Docs.
4 Mendeley for storing and sharing references relevant to the project.
5 A Wiki tool in the VLE/LMS for writing the final collaborative project report.

One of the assignments for the project was to produce a video demonstrating the methods used to collect data. The group recorded the video using a handheld video camera provided by their academic supervisor. They edited and posted it within YouTube and provided the link to the video in their project write-up. Their video accumulated over 100 views and 50 Likes within 3 months of posting. Their academic supervisor was so impressed with the video that she encouraged them to submit it for publication in *the Journal of Visualized Experiments* (www.jove.com).

Using technology to resolve study difficulties

☺ Activity: Your recommendations

What kinds of advice would you give to the following students about how they could study more effectively given the resources they say are available to them?

Compare your advice with the suggested responses on p. 181.

Albertina

"I have a job because I need to work and I find that nearly all my time gets eaten up by that and my course. When I get home after work, I study for at least 3 hours every night, but I don't know if I have done enough to pass. I am very worried that I will fail my exams, especially because everyone expects me to do well. To test myself, I write out my own exam questions and answer these. I get them right so that helps build my confidence but then I wonder if I am just setting myself questions that are too easy.

I think the other students know more than me but it might be my imagination – I don't really have time to get out and mix much. I have no idea really what they are like or if they struggle like I do. It can feel quite lonely studying on my own so much."

Kiran

"I have my smartphone on – always. Even in lectures or the lab, I'm checking to see what is going on with my mates – tweeting, messaging, messing about with the apps, seeing what is new on YouTube, there's always something. I'm a very sociable person, I guess, and curious. That's probably why I like to be connected in.

My grades aren't too hot at the moment. Do I get a bit distracted? Maybe. Is help available? Don't know – pass. Do we have a VLE/LMS? I think we do, yeah. But I'm not going to cart a laptop around so if there is stuff on there, I guess you'll say I'm missing out on it."

Justine

"Today is kind of typical. I commute to uni so that was an hour on the bus. I find the journey boring but I pass the time reading the free newspaper, texting my friends about what I did last night and listening to music on my MP3.

First up at uni today was a lecture on anatomy. It's not exactly my best subject so I type down notes at 50 miles an hour as he – the lecturer – rattles it out. In anatomy, the lecture is quite fast moving. We all have trouble trying to catch everything he says and typing it down at the same time. I try to catch it word for word so I can look it up later, but half the time, I don't even know what the words are.

I spend ages after the lecture trying to match what I have written with what is in the books and sometimes I can't see any connection between the two at all. Maybe background notes are up on the VLE/LMS before the lecture – I haven't looked."

Thomas

"We live a long way from the college and I can't get onto campus very often. The students I have met so far all hang out a lot together so when I do get in, I am not really part of the group. There must be others like me who feel a bit cut off. It would be nice occasionally just to be able to communicate with somebody on the course about what we are studying."

Self-evaluation: how well do I use the technologies available to me?

Use the column on the right to consider your responses to each of the following questions.

Consideration	Response
1 How do I use technology now to support my studies?	
2 How is that different than a year ago?	
3 Which combinations of technology do I find most helpful?	
4 Which technologies, or combinations of technologies, do I prefer? Which do I find the least helpful?	
5 How efficient am I now in the way I use technology – and the time I spend using technology?	
6 What else could I do in order to make better use of technology to support my studies?	

Self-evaluation: achievements to date and future priorities

Overall achievement	Areas of relative strength	Areas I want to develop further
Studying with new technologies (Chapter 1)		
☐ Excellent ☐ Good ☐ OK ☐ Weak ☐ Very weak	☐ I understand what it means to be part of an online community ☐ I make contributions as a member of an online academic community ☐ I have knowledge of building an online community ☐ I have good experience of building an online community ☐ I use good netiquette ☐ I take care of my online presence ☐ I pay attention to online security ☐ I show respect for, and due acknowledgement of, others' work ☐ I am sensitive to other people's differing usage of, and attitudes towards, IT	
Virtual learning environments (Chapter 2)		
☐ Excellent ☐ Good ☐ OK ☐ Weak ☐ Very weak	☐ I am aware of the full range of resources made available to me via our VLE/LMS ☐ I have had a go at using all of these ☐ I use the VLE/LMS on a frequent basis ☐ I check frequently for new material provided by lecturers/ trainers ☐ I make full use of resources on the VLE/LMS to support my independent study	

Overall achievement	Areas of relative strength	Areas I want to develop further
Managing online information for academic study (Chapter 3)		
☐ Excellent ☐ Good ☐ OK ☐ Weak ☐ Very weak	☐ I understand the different stages of managing information for academic study ☐ I understand how these different stages are linked ☐ I know how to evaluate whether a resource is of suitable academic quality ☐ I know how to conduct appropriate searches to find easily the material I need ☐ I am aware of the bibliographic databases that are most useful for my study ☐ I am aware of the digital repositories that are most useful for my study ☐ I make use of relevant automated searches ☐ I make use of reference management tools ☐ I know how to store and share bookmarks ☐ I know how to use news readers to receive updates ☐ I am aware of the Google tools available to me that could help my study	
Podcasts (Chapter 4)		
☐ Excellent ☐ Good ☐ OK ☐ Weak ☐ Very weak	☐ I know how to find and subscribe to podcasts ☐ I know how to evaluate podcasts for suitable academic quality ☐ I am aware of different ways I could use podcasts to support my study ☐ I use podcasts to supplement (rather than replace) taught sessions ☐ I apply good organisational skills when using podcasts, to use them effectively ☐ I make useful notes when using podcasts ☐ I apply critical thinking skills to my use of podcasts ☐ If I use a podcast as a source in my work, I cite and reference it properly ☐ I am able to make my own podcasts to help my understanding and exam preparation ☐ I am able to apply good design principles to producing a podcast	

Overall achievement	Areas of relative strength	Areas I want to develop further
Blogs (Chapter 5)		
☐ Excellent ☐ Good ☐ OK ☐ Weak ☐ Very weak	☐ I know how to find useful blogs ☐ I have a good sense of the range of ways that blogs could support me as a student ☐ I know how to create a blog ☐ I have a good sense of the features that lead to a well-designed blog ☐ I bring good audience awareness to the creation of my blog ☐ I know how to publicise and share my blog ☐ I make supportive and constructive comments on other people's blogs ☐ I know how to use blogs to support academic reflection ☐ I know how to produce a blog as part of an academic assignment ☐ I know how to use blogs to support project work ☐ I know how to make use of other people's blogs, if required, for academic work ☐ I apply critical thinking skills to my use of blogs ☐ If I use a blog as a source in my work, I cite and reference it properly	
Wikis (Chapter 6)		
☐ Excellent ☐ Good ☐ OK ☐ Weak ☐ Very weak	☐ I understand and can apply the five principles, or 'pillars' of Wikipedia ☐ If I use Wikipedia, I know how to identify academically suitable material there ☐ If I use Wikipedia to find sources, I also make use of a range of other avenues to find material ☐ If I use Wikipedia, I go to the original sources it cites and read and reference those ☐ I am aware that I need to check sources for accuracy ☐ I know how to edit a live wiki page ☐ I know how to create a wiki article ☐ I know how to write a wiki collaboratively as part of a group project	

Overall achievement	Areas of relative strength	Areas I want to develop further
Social media (Chapter 7)		
☐ Excellent ☐ Good ☐ OK ☐ Weak ☐ Very weak	☐ I know how to build a social community ☐ I make use of social media for peer support ☐ I know how to make use of social media for group projects ☐ I am aware of how I could make use of micro-blogging for academic purposes ☐ I know how to use social networking tools to support my professional development	
Classroom and communication technologies (Chapter 8)		
☐ Excellent ☐ Good ☐ OK ☐ Weak ☐ Very weak	☐ If given voting handset opportunities, I know how to make effective use of these ☐ I know how to make helpful contributions to lecture chat ☐ I am confident about using video conferencing ☐ I am aware of the collaborative learning tools that are available to me ☐ I participate when opportunities are provided to use collaborative tools ☐ I am aware of how mobile devices could be used to support my study ☐ I am aware of the apps that are available for my own devices (if relevant) and make use of these for my study	
Combining technologies for study		
☐ Excellent ☐ Good ☐ OK ☐ Weak ☐ Very weak	☐ I experiment with different ways of combining technologies ☐ I adapt the combinations of technology I use depending on the context ☐ I am aware of the most efficient ways of combining technologies for my study	

Technologies not covered in this book

You may come across other technologies during your course that are not in this book. If so, you may find it helpful to copy and use the following checklist to check how useful each item would be.

Issue Tick/check all of the areas that you want to consider further. Then investigate these and record your comments opposite.	Comments
1 ☐ **Effective and enjoyable study** Would this technology make a positive difference to the way I study? If so, how?	
2 ☐ **Combining technologies** Will use of this technology add to (or just duplicate) the range of things I can do with my existing technology? How can I best combine these?	
3 ☐ **Professional development** Will this technology help my professional development? If so, how?	
4 ☐ **Availability and access** Is the tool available on campus or will I need to configure my home computer to access it?	
5 ☐ **Skills (my own)** Do I have the skills needed to make good use of this technology? If not, which skills do I need to develop and what support is available?	
6 ☐ **Skills (the group's)** Is the technology intended to facilitate group work? If so, are all group members able to use it? Will they want to? How can we get the whole group up to speed?	
7 ☐ **Course assessment** Is there any assessment based around this technology or tool? If so, how would my use of the technology be assessed?	
8 ☐ **Purchase** If this is something I can choose to purchase, is it worth the time and expense? If not, what alternatives are open to me?	

The technologies covered in the book are likely to change quickly – some may have advanced significantly by the time you come to read this, and others may already have been replaced by new technologies. That may be frustrating, but it is part of the excitement and interest in making use of these resources.

This book should have given you a broad overview of the technology, added to your previous knowledge at least to some extent, and reassured you about the use of technology for your assignments. Ideally, it will have encouraged you to come up with your own ideas for applying technology in new ways to support your study. You may find ways, not covered here, of applying these technologies. Be willing to share these with others and add to the enjoyment of studying collaboratively as part of an online learning community.

We hope you enjoyed this book and that it added, even in a small way, to improving your experience as a student.

Glossary

application/app Software program installed on a personal computer or mobile device.

asynchronous Activities (such as online conversations, debates, editing or online) where individuals join in at whatever time suits them rather than all at the same sitting.

audio file Computer file containing audio (sound) information.

bibliographic database Collection of entries about published research articles (such as journal and newspaper articles, conference proceedings, books, patents), searched using keywords and containing links to the full text of these articles.

blog (full name 'weblog') Website containing information updated with individual entries which usually appear in reverse chronological order.

blogger A person who writes a blog (or weblog).

blogosphere A term used to refer to all blogs (or weblogs) on the Internet and the links between them.

bookmark A digital record of the location of a website saved locally for easy future access; also called Favourites.

Boolean operators Search terms (such as AND, OR, NOT) used to construct complex online searches.

chat Text-based messages between individuals using instant messaging tools, social networking tools or chat functionality within online collaborative tools. Chat may be private between two individuals or broadcast to many individuals.

chat room See *discussion board*.

citation Author and date details of a reference (e.g., Jones, 1994), provided in the text of a document to acknowledge the source of an idea or knowledge. The full details are then provided in a reference list at the end of the document.

collaborative learning tool Software or website that allows multiple individuals to enter an online virtual space to view and interact with the same resources simultaneously; often used for online teaching where a teacher may speak to students and present learning resources electronically, allowing students to speak, write notes and ask questions.

collaborative writing The process of multiple individuals simultaneously editing a shared document.

comment A text-based message posted on a website in response to another message or material.

copyright Legal rights assigned to a creator of content or knowledge.

course Can mean either a unit of teaching (also called module) or a whole programme of study.

curriculum vitae (CV) Known as a résumé in North America. Document used when applying for jobs, providing details about employment, qualifications, skills, experience and interests.

digital repository A digital resource providing access to information or research in a variety of formats.

discussion board A tool that allows multiple individuals to share information and communicate online (often asynchronously), organised by themes or topics. Also called message board or chat room.

download To save a copy of a file (e.g., document) from a website or server to a personal computer or mobile device.

e-book A digital version of a book.

editor An individual who edits (changes) documents to improve the language, flow of material etc.

electronic whiteboard A tool that allows multiple individuals to view (and draw on) a virtual whiteboard. Often used within collaborative learning tools or virtual learning environments.

episode In the context of podcasts, a single audio file which is part of a series.

e-reader Hand-held computer device tailored for reading digital books.

favourites See bookmarks.

flame, flaming Disagreement or argument between Internet users.

Flash Platform for delivering multimedia (e.g., audio, video, animation) interactive content within web pages.

formative assessment A test or quiz that does not count towards a module/course mark and which helps the learner to develop their knowledge and understanding.

full text In the context of journal articles, getting access to the full article and not just the abstract.

global positioning system (GPS) Satellite navigation system that provides location information on mobile devices.

Google Docs Set of tools freely available from Google for producing and sharing documents and presentations online.

group assignment Coursework or project that requires a group of students to work together.

hashtag In the context of the social media tool Twitter, use of the symbol # (hash) and a keyword to search for themes or topics.

host In the context of the Internet, an Internet service provider.

instant messaging See chat.

Internet Access to the content and networks provided by computers around the world.

iTunes Online software provided by Apple for the downloading of music, podcasts, apps, videos and other content.

iTunesU Dedicated area of iTunes for academic material, including podcasts.

journal In academia, this means a scholarly publication containing original research, reviews and letters, normally reviewed by experts before publication.

keywords Words used to describe themes or topics.

laptop A portable personal computer; also called notebook.

learning management system (LMS) Known as a virtual learning environment (VLE) in Great Britain. Online site, normally password protected, which contains learning resources and tools useful for learning.

lecture A teaching event where a subject expert (referred to as the lecturer) speaks to, and interacts with, an audience.

lecture capture Tools used to record the sound and/or video in lectures.

lecturer An expert who can speak authoritatively to a group of students about a given topic. In UK universities, 'lecturer' is a rank for a member of academic staff.

message board See *discussion board*.

micro-blogging Short text-based messages often containing URL links, used within social networking tools such as Twitter.

mobile device Broad term encompassing all hand-held computing devices, normally with touch-screen functionality. May refer to devices that have telephony services (e.g., smartphone) or not (e.g., tablet devices).

mobile phone A hand-held device that can make and receive telephone calls. Normally refers to devices with few other functions, as opposed to smartphones.

moderator In the context of discussion boards or lecture capture, means an individual who has administrative rights and oversees content.

module A unit of teaching on an individual topic within a programme of study. May also be called a course.

netiquette (short for Internet etiquette) Describes the conventions, rules and responsibilities for online behaviour, particularly within blogs and discussion boards.

network (short for computer network) A collection of interconnected computers.

news feed (or web feed) Provides a user with updated text-based (or multimedia) content automatically to a dedicated area. Commonly used for news, podcasts, video, blogs.

online test or quiz Questions that can be assessed by computer and automatically marked, e.g., multiple choice questions.

peer In the context of peer support, another student studying at the same level.

peer review For scholarly work (e.g., journal articles, books etc.) this means getting feedback and opinion from one or more academics who are experts in the area, before publication.

personal computer A computer that is normally desk-based with a separate monitor.

ping In the context of blogs, this means informing other computer servers that content on the blog has been updated.

placement A period of study or work at a particular institution or business, for a given time, whilst still registered as a student.

plagiarism The act of copying the work or ideas of other people without proper acknowledgement or reference.

podcast A series of audio files published on the Internet in a file format that can be accessed by podcasting software or tools.

podcaster A person who produces podcasts.

podcatching software Tools or software on the Internet or your computer/mobile device that provide access to podcasts and allow users to listen to podcast episodes and/or subscribe to podcasts.

portable media device A hand-held device for listening to audio and/or video content.

post In the context of blogs or discussion boards, this means publishing a content item (text based or multimedia).

professional development Ongoing acquisition of skills and training throughout studies or work.

programme Normally refers to all of the units of study that have to be completed in order to qualify for a higher education award.

rating The ability of users to provide quantitative feedback on online content they have viewed. Can be numerical (e.g., 1–5) or stars which are then averaged for other users to see.

really simple syndication (RSS) System for creating news (or web) feeds. See also *news feed*.

reference Full details of an academic source used in an assignment or scholarly document. Normally appears at the end of a document in a list, containing author, year, title, source and volume/page details. Linked to citations embedded within documents.

reference management tool Software tool of application for managing multiple academic scholarly documents (usually in the form of journal articles). Can normally store documents and provide automated reference lists.

résumé Known as a CV or curriculum vitae in Great Britain. Document used when applying for jobs, providing details about employment, qualification, skills, experience and interests.

search engine Tool available on the Internet for searching for web pages, images, content etc.

server A computer that provides information to users or computers, normally across a computer network.

short message service (SMS) Text messages normally sent between mobile telephones or smartphones.

smartphone A hand-held device capable of making and receiving telephone calls but with other computing facilities, normally including access to the Internet and installation of software applications (apps).

social bookmarking tool Online services that allow users to store, share and access Favourites (bookmarks) for websites. Some tools also allow user ratings and comments.

social media Tools to allow users to create personal profiles, build networks of users and interact online via a variety of media (e.g., text-based update, links, photos, videos).

social networking Using social media tools to interact with other users online.

spam Unwanted messages sent indiscriminately via email, blogs, discussion boards or social media.

sponsored link In the context of search engines, these are links to web pages/services that appear at the top or side of the search results page. Often used by advertisers.

subject gateway service In the context of finding scholarly information on the Internet, these are validated lists of links relevant to students, researchers and academics in a specific discipline.

subscribe In the context of podcasts or vodcasts, this means to commit to receiving future episodes or content on your computer or mobile device.

synchronisation The process of connecting your mobile device to your computer or service provider to upload/download material.

tablet computer A form of mobile device with a large touch screen that has a wide range of functionality.

tags Keywords added to content to signify themes or topics.

technology Use of tools or machines to perform tasks.

text editor Feature built into web pages or tools that allows users to enter and format text.

thread In the context of discussion boards, this means a series of messages (posts) about a particular topic or theme.

trackback In the context of blogs, this means informing a blog that another user has linked to it.

trend (trending) In the context of social media tool Twitter, this means a continually updated list of the most common words or hashtags being tweeted.

troll, trolling Posting unnecessary or irrelevant message on discussion boards.

tutor In academia, this normally means an academic member of staff who interacts with students in small groups, or individually.

tweet A text-based message of less than 140 characters. Also called a micro-blog.

URL (uniform or universal resource locator) For web content, this is the address (or reference) for accessing material on the Internet.

video conferencing Tools that allow multiple users to interact with one another through the medium of video.

video file Computer file containing video information.

virtual learning environment (VLE) Known as a learning management system (LMS) in North America. Online site, normally password protected, which contains learning resources and tools useful for learning.

vodcast A series of video files published on the Internet.

voice over Internet protocol Tools for making and receiving telephone calls using the Internet.

voting handset Hand-held device connected wirelessly with a receiver that allows users to respond to on-screen questions.

WAV file A common type of sound file that can be played and edited by many software tools and media devices.

web-based Content or material on the Internet.

webcam Device for recording and sending video information.

webinars Online seminars or discussions that you register for and attend using your computer or mobile device. They are usually free and are very convenient since you do not need to travel to a physical seminar.

web feed See *news feed*.

weblog Full name for blog. See *blog*.

website Set of related web pages on the Internet accessed from a URL's home page.

wi-fi Mechanism allowing mobile devices to connect wirelessly to the Internet.

wiki Online document that can be edited by multiple users.

Wikipedian Individual who edits Wikipedia.

wireless Mechanism for sending digital information between devices without the use of wires/cables.

wizard Step-by-step instructions to complete a setup or installation process.

work placement See *placement*.

Useful resources

Chapter 1: Studying with new technologies

Resource	Good for ...
http://www.skills4study.com	Free website from Palgrave Macmillan covering a range of study skills
http://www.bbc.co.uk/webwise/	Webwise, from the BBC. A beginner's guide to using the Internet
http://www.google.com/goodtoknow	Google's simple guide to staying safe on the Internet
http://www.copyrightservice.co.uk/copyright/	The UK copyright service website containing lots of useful information about copyright
http://www.ofqual.gov.uk/plagiarism-students	A guide for students on using sources
http://www.open.ac.uk/skillsforstudy/	Free online basic study skills resources from the Open University

Chapter 2: Virtual learning environments

Resource	Good for ...
http://www.studentdiscussion.co.uk	Using a discussion board and getting advice about university
http://behind.blackboard.com/s/student	Support for students using the Blackboard VLE
http://docs.moodle.org/22/en/Student_FAQ	Support for students using the Moodle VLE

Chapter 3: Managing online information for academic study

Resource	Good for ...
http://www.webofknowledge.com	Broad bibliographic database useful for searching for academic publications
http://www.pubmed.com	Bibliographic database for medical, biomedical and life science disciplines
http://www.pubmedcentral.com	Free full text service for biomedical and life science journal articles
http://scholar.google.com	Broad bibliographic search engine

Resource	Good for ...
http://arXiv.org	Open access repository for physics, mathematics, computer sciences, statistics and non-linear sciences articles
http://www.jstor.org	Digital repository for journal articles for many disciplines
http://www.intute.ac.uk	Subject gateway service providing access to many useful resources (formally closed in 2011, but still contains resources)
http://zetoc.mimas.ac.uk	Broad research search service
http://www.youtube.com/t/creators_corner	YouTube guide for making high quality video
http://www.mendeley.com	Reference management tool
http://www.delicious.com	Social bookmarking tool
http://www.citeulike.org	Online journal tagging tool
http://www.zotero.org	Reference management tool

Chapter 4: Podcasts

Resource	Good for ...
http://www.apple.com/education/itunes-u/	Apple's educational podcast site, iTunesU
http://www.apple.com/itunes/podcasts	Apple guide to finding, playing and sharing podcasts on iTunes
http://audacity.sourceforge.net	Free audio editing software
http://www.podcast.com	Online podcast collection
http://www.ted.com	Educational videos from leading experts
http://www.dimio.altervista.org/eng/	To download open source text-to-speech programme, DSpeech
http://www.texthelp.com	Commercial text-to-speech software. Read and Write Gold. A free trial is available

Chapter 5: Blogs

Resource	Good for ...
http://www.blogger.com	Creating free blog site
http://wordpress.com	Creating free blog site
http://www.blog.co.uk	Creating free blog site
http://www.google.com/blogsearch	Dedicated search engine for blogs
http://mashable.com	Top-ranking blog on technology

Chapter 6: Wikis

Resource	Good for ...
http://en.wikipedia.org/wiki/Schools_and_universities_project	Advice on using Wikipedia to produce collaborative writing assignments.
http://educationalwikis.wikispaces.com	List of student-produced wiki resources
http://www.thestudentroom.co.uk/wiki/TSR_wiki	A collection of student-written wikis
http://www.scholarpedia.org/article/mainpage	Peer-reviewed wiki covering a broad range of disciplines

Chapter 7: Social media

Resource	Good for ...
http://www.facebook.com	Access to Facebook, social networking tool
http://www.twitter.com	Access to Twitter, micro-blogging social networking tool
http://www.linkedin.com	Access to LinkedIn professional networking tool
http://www.flickr.com	Photo management and sharing tool
http://www.bebo.com	Access to Bebo, social networking tool
http://www.myspace.com	Access to MySpace, social networking tool
https://plus.google.com/	Access to Google+, social networking tool
http://hootsuite.com	Managing multiple social networks simultaneously

Chapter 8: Classroom and communication technologies

Resource	Good for ...
https://play.google.com/store/apps	Finding content for Android devices
http://www.apple.com/uk/itunes	Finding content for Apple devices
http://uk.blackberry.com/services/appworld	Finding content for BlackBerry devices
http://www.imedicalapps.com/	Mobile medical apps reviews and commentary by medical professionals
http://www.skype.com	Video conferencing tool

References and further reading

Callis, K. L., Christ L. R., Resasco J., Armitage D. W., Ash J. D. et al. (2009) Improving Wikipedia: educational opportunity and professional responsibility. *Trends in Ecology & Evolution* 24, 177–9.

Chesney, T. (2006) An empirical examination of Wikipedia's credibility. *First Monday*, 11:11. Available online: http://firstmonday.org/issues/issue11_11/chesney/index.html (accessed 14 Feb. 2012).

Clauson, K. A., Polen, H. H., Boulos, M. N. and Dzenowagis, J. H. (2008) Scope, completeness, and accuracy of drug information in Wikipedia. *Annals of Pharmacotherapy* 42, 1814–21.

Cottrell, S. M. (2008) *The Study Skills Handbook* (3rd edn). Basingstoke: Palgrave Macmillan.

Cottrell, S. M. (2010) *Skills for Success* (2nd edn). Basingstoke: Palgrave Macmillan.

Cottrell, S. M. (2011) *Critical Thinking Skills* (2nd edn). Basingstoke: Palgrave Macmillan.

Cottrell, S. M. (2012) *The Exam Skills Handbook* (2nd edn). Basingstoke: Palgrave Macmillan.

Giles, J. (2005) Internet encyclopaedias go head to head. *Nature* 438, 900–901.

Haigh, C. A. (2011) Wikipedia as an evidence source for nursing and healthcare students. *Nurse Education Today* 31, 135–9.

Junco, R., Heiberger, G. and Loken, E. (2011) The effect of Twitter on college student engagement and grades. *Journal of Computer Assisted Learning* 27, 119–32.

Kirschner, P. A. and Karpinski, A. C. (2010) Facebook® and academic performance. *Computers in Human Behavior* 26(6), 1237–45.

Luyt, B., Aaron, T. C. H., Thian, L. H. and Hong, C. K. (2007) Improving Wikipedia's accuracy: is edit age a solution? *Journal of the American Society for Information Science and Technology* 59, 318–30.

Mack, D., Behler, A., Roberts, B. and Rimland, E. (2007) Reaching students with Facebook: data and best practices. *Electronic Journal of Academic and Special Librarianship*, 8. Available online: http://southernlibrarianship.icaap.org/content/v08n02/mack_d01.html (accessed 14 Feb. 2012).

McKinney, D., Dycka, J. L. and Lubera, E. S. (2009) iTunes University and the classroom: can podcasts replace professors? *Computers & Education* 52, 617–23.

Morris, N. P. (2010) Podcasts and mobile assessment enhance student learning experience and academic performance. *Bioscience Education* 16, 1–7.

Pears, R. and Shields, G. (2010) *Cite Them Right* (8th edn). Basingstoke: Palgrave Macmillan.

Purdy, J. P. (2010) The changing space of research: Web 2.0 and the integration of research and writing environments. *Computers and Composition* 27, 48–58.

Rector, L. H. (2008) Comparison of Wikipedia and other encyclopedias for accuracy, breadth, and depth in historical articles. *Reference Services Review* 36, 7–22.

Tian, S. W., Yu, A. Y., Vogel, D. and Kwok, R. C. W. (2011) The impact of online social networking on learning: a social integration perspective. *International Journal of Networking and Virtual Organisations* 8, 264–80.

Virendra, M. (2011) Critical care training: using Twitter as a teaching tool. *British Journal of Nursing* 20, 1292–6.

Feedback on activities

Constructive comments (p. 89)

1 **Constructive**. As well as receiving a positive response, the blogger can see from the comment exactly what was appreciated. The post adds a further tip, building on those provided by the blogger, to the benefit of future readers.

2 **Constructive**. The blogger would feel they had made a real impact through their blog if they received a comment saying that they had inspired others to action.

3 **Destructive.** The content of the comment may be factually true, but would probably leave the blogger feeling that their feelings were devalued.

4 **Destructive.** Although there is useful practical information within the comment, this is presented in a negative way. This usually means that it is harder for the recipient to absorb and act upon the advice given.

5 **Constructive.** The comment would probably have the effect of leaving the blogger feeling that they were not alone either – that they were part of a supportive community.

Using technology to resolve study difficulties (p. 165)

Albertina

Albertina comes across as too isolated as a student. As a result, she misses out on the support and motivation that can come from being part of a group. It also means that she is not in a position to make reasonable comparisons of her own knowledge compared to that of other students. Albertina could use social networking tools to link to other students. There might be other students in a similar situation who would welcome it if she set up an online support group. There may be discussion boards for her course that she could use to gain a

better sense of the concerns of other students or, again, she might be able to start one. Albertina designs her own self-tests; she could check to see whether there are copies of previous tests for her course and/or online tests available to her through the VLE. If so, this might save her time which she could then put into getting to know other students. Joining with others in writing a course wiki would help study and help overcome isolation, whilst giving her a sense of what other students did and did not know. She could also link in with other students through Skype – especially other students whose days are as busy as hers.

Kiran

Kiran mentions that his grades are not very good and that he tends to become distracted when studying. As he loves using technology, he could consider using it more to support his studies as well as his social life. He is a curious person, so if he directs this well when using technology, it could be a real bonus for his study. He would be well advised to find out what is on the VLE/LMS and, if there are essential or useful materials there, to plan more systematically how he will make use of these. If he doesn't want to carry a laptop around, he might find a tablet easier to use; otherwise, he needs to plan in times in the day when he can sit at a screen to keep his study up to date. Using planning tools available through his smartphone might help him to bring more focus to his study.

Justine

Justine writes that she has a poor sense of what is available on her VLE, that she struggles in lectures and that she finds her travel time boring. She could use her travel time more productively by undertaking a range of study tasks, from browsing the VLE and course discussion boards, to undertaking self-testing, listening to podcasts, browsing for new publications and journal articles, maintaining a reflective learning blog, updating her CV, and looking up employer information to improve her career chances on graduation. Justine mentions that she tries to type down every word the lecturer says. For some people, this use of motor memory can help recall. If that is true of Justine, then she could use her travel time to edit down her notes. However, she may find it more useful to see if there are background notes or reading materials provided by the lecturer that she could read before the lecture. If so, these would give her a better sense of what she does and does not need to note during a lecture. It would also be worth her checking whether podcasts of the lecture are available, as she could listen again to those areas that were hard to catch.

Thomas

Like Albertina, Thomas is rather isolated. He doesn't feel he is part of the group. Many students can feel, at times, as though other students are part of a group or groups from which they are excluded. If Thomas feels isolated, the chances are that there will be others in the same position. Thomas could use social networking tools to discuss study, setting these up for himself. He could use a blog to see if that attracts comments, or suggest setting up an online study group. Conferencing tools can help students studying at a distance from each other to get to know each other so that they feel more comfortable discussing their studies.

Index

academic focus, xiii
accessibility, 18
accuracy
  podcasts, 64
  websites, 46
  Wikipedia, 106, 108
  YouTube, 57
Android devices, 158
Apple devices, 157
apps, 157–8, 173
assessment
  in a virtual learning
    environment, 30
Assessment and Learning in
  Practice Settings (ALPS), 159
assignment
  blogs, 90
  collaborative, 37–9
  editing a wiki, 109
  podcasts, 65
  submitting online, 32
  using discussion boards, 37–9
  using Facebook, 127
  video, 59
audience
  considerations when producing
    podcasts, 73, 74
  contributions on podcasts, 65
  for blogs, 83, 86, 87, 94, 98
  for iTunesU content, 65
  sensitivity, 6
Audionote, 158

bibliographic database, 45, 173
  examples, 50, 51
  limiting your search, 50
  mobile device, 156
BlackBerry devices, 158
blog, 77–100, 173
  as assignments, 90

comments, 88, 89
creating, 82–3
critical thinking, 98–9
definition, 78
design, 84–5
equipment needed, 78
reflective activity, 86
self-evaluation, 80, 94
sharing, 87
structure, 78
tools, 83
using on placements, 96
bookmarks, 52, 173
books, searching for, 44
Boolean operators, 46, 50, 173
British Newspapers, digital
  repository, 51

Callis et al. (2009), 118
career planning
  LinkedIn, 134, 137
  Twitter, 133
  using blogs, 93
  video conferencing, 153
case studies
  blogs for a student project, 95
  collaborative report, 55
  collaborative tutorial, 149
  collaborative writing using a
    wiki, 113–16
  combining the technologies,
    162–4
  discussion board, 37–9
  editing a wiki, 109
  group presentations, 54
  literature searching, 56
  social networking tools, 137
  using a virtual learning
    environment, 33
  video conferencing, 152

video conferencing on
  placement, 153
work placement blog, 96
channels, YouTube, 57
chat, 124, 126, 146, 173
cheating, 16
Chesney (2006), 108
citations, 16, 173
  blogs, 97
  case study, 56
  podcasts, 70
  social networking sites, 138–9
  Wikipedia, 104
CiteULike, 52
classroom technologies, 142
Clauson et al. (2008), 108
collaborative learning, 21, 31, 33
  Google Docs, 53
  group report, 55
  tools, 147, 173
  wikis, 101
collaborative writing, 113–16
comment, 173
  blogs, 88, 89
  discussion board, 36
  Wikipedia, 109
communication tools, 147, 150
computer
  equipment, 19
  literacy, xiii
  skills, 23
confidentiality, 15
  blogs, 99
copyright, 15, 173
Cottrell, S., xiii, 22
course notes, 157
critical thinking, 21
  blogs, 91, 98–9
  discussion boards, 37
  podcasts, 69

deadline, 32
Delicious, social bookmarking
    service, 52
designing
    podcasts, 73–5
    videos, 59
devices, 23
    for making video, 59
    for playing audio, 62
Dictionary, 157
digital library, 51
digital repository, 51, 173
    accessing, 51
    searching, 51
    storing bookmarks, 52
    using information from, 51
disability, 18
disambiguation, Wikipedia, 104
discussion board, 36, 173
    features, 36
    frequently asked questions
        (FAQs), 36
    moderator, 36
    thread, 37–9
discussion, online, 29
documents, sharing, 53
downloading, legal issues, 15
Dropbox, 55, 156, 157, 158, 164

e-books, 155, 158, 173
editing wikis, 110–11
electronic feedback, 35
electronic table of contents
    (eTOC), 52
employer, 11
encyclopaedia, 103
Endnote, 52
enterprise projects, 136
entrepreneuralism, 136
episode, podcast, 62, 173
equipment
    for blogging, 78
    for making videos, 59
    for podcasting, 62
    social networking, 122
    video conferencing tools, 150
e-reader, ix, 174
    using for study, 155
Evernote, 158
examinations
    podcasts, 71
    feedback, 35

Facebook

features, 124
friends, 124
ground rules, 125
group projects, 127
instant messaging, 124, 126
public profile, 124
reflective activity, 124, 128
social uses, 126, 128
favourites, storing and sharing
    links, 52
feedback
    in a virtual learning
        environment, 30
    using, 34–5
followers, Twitter, 130

Giles, T. (2005), 108
Google Docs, 53, 157, 174
Google Scholar, 46
Google tools, 53
grades, effect of Facebook, 128
group work
    case study, 33
    collaborative learning tools, 147
    Facebook, 127
    Google Docs, 53
    tips for using online tools, 148
    tips for using wikis, 116
    wiki writing, 113–16
groups
    Facebook, 127
    LinkedIn, 134

Haigh, C. (2011), 118
Harvard referencing, 70
hashtag, 130, 131, 133, 174
host, for blogs, 83, 174
how to use the book, xiv

identity theft, 12
independent study, 28, 126
information
    about programmes, 28, 32
    online, 41–60
    organisation in the VLE, 26
information technology, 18
    computer literacy, xiii
    confidence with, 2
    equipment, 19–20
    self-evaluation, 19–20
    skills, 23
instant messaging, 124, 126
    ground rules, 146
    lecture capture, 146

Internet, 174
    advanced searches, 47
    evaluating websites, 46
    pros and cons, 46
    searching, 46, 48–50
interviews, video conferencing
    tools, 151
iTunes, 63, 174
iTunesU, 63, 65, 174

journals
    content on Twitter, 131
    contents via social media, 52
    electronic table of contents, 52
    finding, 44
    full text, 50
    peer reviewed, 44
    reference management tools,
        52
JSTOR, 51
Junco et al. (2011), 131

Kindle books, 158
Kirschner, P. and Karpinski, A.
    (2010), 128

learning management system see
    virtual learning environment
    (VLE), 25, 174
learning outcomes, 17
learning resources, 30, 31
    blogs, 97
    podcasts, 66
    YouTube, 57
lecture capture, 145, 174
    chat, 146
    reflective activity, 146
lecturer
    approaches to technology, 17,
        161
    blogs, 97
    contacting, 8
    podcasts, 64
    reservations about technology,
        17
    tracking VLE usage, 28
    Twitter, 131
    use of technology, 4
    using student voting handsets,
        143
    using voting handsets, 143
    views about Wikipedia, 17, 101
lectures
    podcasts, 66

recorded, 145
video, 145
legal issues, 15
library catalogue, 45
in Facebook, 128
mobile device, 156
LifeMate Diary, 158
LinkedIn, 134–7
enterprise projects, 136
entrepreneurialism, 136
profile, 134
listening skills
podcasts, 68
YouTube, 58
literature searching
case study, 56
keywords, 47
managing references, 52
mobile device, 156
saving and automating
searches, 52
strategies, 49
tools, 45
using bibliographic databases,
50
using digital repositories, 51
Luyt et al. (2007), 108

Mack et al. (2007), 128
managing your time, podcasts,
67
MaxJournal, 157
McKinney, D. (2009), 72
Mendeley, 52, 156–7, 164
metadata, 51, 52, 59, 85, 87,
123, 175
micro-blogging see also Twitter
definition, 129, 174
types, 129
Mobi-books, 158
mobile devices, 154, 174
practical classes, 159
pros and cons, 154
Twitter, 129
types, 154
video conferencing, 150
mobile telephone, for study, 154
moderators, discussion board, 36,
174
Morris, N. (2010), 72

netiquette, 5–8, 10, 12, 161, 174
Facebook, 125
self-evaluation, 9

new technologies, 161, 171
New York Public Library, 51
news readers, Google, 53
notes
Audionote, 157
Evernote, 157
podcasts, 68
Soundnote, 157

online assessment, 32
online learning community, 5
Facebook, 126
Twitter, 130, 132
online practice tests, reflection,
34
online quizzes, 34, 174
online searches
managing information, 43
self-evaluation, 42
Overdrive media console, 158

Papers app, 157
peer review, 44, 174
peer-reviewed journal, 44
peer support
Facebook, 126
Twitter, 131
ping, in blog, 88
placements, 151 see also work
placement
blogs, case study, 96
video conferencing, 151
plagiarism, 15–16, 35, 117, 175
podcast
definition, 62, 63, 175
episode, 62
equipment, 62
evaluating quality, 64–5
for assignments, 65
lectures, 66
making, 71,73
reflective activity, 64
subscribing, 63
types, 62–3
portable media device, 62, 63,
154, 175
post, discussion board, 36
presentations, group work, 54
privacy, 11, 13, 15
privacy, self-evaluation, 13–14
privacy, Twitter, 130
professional development, using
blogs, 93
programme of study

information, 28, 32
information via blogs, 77
projects
using blogs, 92, 95
video conferencing, 151
public profile, 11–12
Purdy (2010), 118

quizzes, voting handsets, 144

Really Simple Syndication, 53, 75,
156, 175
Rector (2008), 108
reference management tools, 52,
157, 175
CiteULike, 52
Endnote, 52
Mendeley, 52
mobile device, 156
Reference manager, 52
Zotero, 52
references, Wikipedia, 105, 107
referencing, 16, 175
blogs, 97
Harvard style, 70
podcast, 70
social networking sites, 138–9
Referey, 158
reflection, 14
blogs, 91
reflective activity
assessment in VLE, 30
blogs, 86
collaboration, 31
collaborative tutorial, 149
collaborative writing using a
wiki, 116
comments, 89
conducting better searches, 50
critical thinking with blogs, 98
discussion in VLE, 29
Facebook, 124, 128
Google tools, 55
interaction in VLE, 29
learning resources, 30, 31–2
lecture capture: chat, 146
online quizzes, 34
podcasts, 64
social networks, 122
using technologies to resolve
study difficulties, 165
using Wikipedia, 107, 118
video conferencing, 153
RSS news

Google Reader, 53
mobile devices, 156

search engine, 45, 175
  advanced searches, 47
  automating searches, 52
  bibliographic databases, 50
  Boolean operators, 47
  Google, 53
  Google Scholar, 47
  impact of search strategy, 48
  keywords, 47
  refining searches, 47
  saving search, 52
  search strategy, 49
  Wikipedia, 104
Secret Diary app, 158
self-directed study, 126
self-evaluation
  academic skills, 22
  achievements and priorities,
    167–70
  blogs, 80
  blogs for academic study, 94
  collaborative learning tools, 147
  equipment, 19
  identifying your priorities, 2–3
  IT skills, 23
  managing online information,
    42
  netiquette, 9–10
  privacy and security, 13–14
  using technologies effectively,
    166
  wikis, 117
sharing
  blogs, 87
  bookmarks, 52
  documents, 31, 53
  experiences with peers, 126
  resources, 53
Skype, 150
smartphone, 155
social bookmarking, 52, 175
social community, 5
social network
  definition 122
social networking site
  blogs, 87
  equipment, 122
  features, 122, 123
  LinkedIn, 134
  reflective activity, 122
  Twitter, 129

Soundnote app, 157
spam, blogs, 88
Springpad app, 158
student voting handsets, 143
study skills, podcasts, 67
studying
  identifying academic skills, 22
  skills for, xiii, 21
subject gateway services, 45, 175
subscribing
  blog, 88
  news, 53
  podcast, 63

tablet device, 155, 175
  types, 155
  using for study, 155
tagging, Twitter, 130
tags, 51, 52, 59, 85, 87, 123, 175
technology, using effectively, 17
TED, 63
thread, discussion board, 37, 175
Tian et al. (2011), 128
trackback, blog, 88, 175
trends, Twitter, 131, 176
Twitter, 129

Universal Digital Library, 51
universities, use of Facebook, 128
URL, 23, 46, 85, 176
user ratings
  podcasts, 65
  YouTube, 57
username
  Facebook, 124
  Twitter, 130
  virtual learning environment, 26
  YouTube, 58

video, 57
  making for assignments, 59
  quality, YouTube, 57
  study skills, 58
video conferencing tools, 150,
  176
  case study, 152
  definition, 150
  equipment, 150
Virendra, M. (2011), 131
virtual classroom
  case study, 33
virtual learning environment (VLE)
  accessing, 26
  collaboration, 31

  discussion, 29
  discussion board, 36–7
  interaction, 29
  organisation, 26
  reflective activity, 29, 30, 31,
    32, 34
  to support learning, 27–8
  types, 26
  for submitting assignments, 32
vodcast, 62, 70, 176
voting handsets, 143

weblog see blog, 77
website, 46, 176
  advanced searches, 47
  evaluating, 46
  searching, 46
  sponsored links, 46
  storing bookmarks, 52
websites, URLs, 46
wiki, 101–40, 161, 176
  definition, 102, 176
  self-evaluation, 117
  types, 102
Wikipedia, 17, 102
  collaborative writing
    assignment, 113–16
  creating page, 112
  editing, 110–11
  layout, 105
  principles, 103
  quality, 106
  referencing, 107
  reflective activity, 107, 118
Wikiversity, 102
Wiktionary, 102
work placement
  using blogs, 96
  using discussion boards, 36
  video conferencing, 151

YouTube, 57–9
  making videos for assignments,
    59
  tools, 58
  uploading video, 59

Zotero, 52